# Between Beats

# Between Beats

*The Jazz Tradition and Black
Vernacular Dance*

Christi Jay Wells

OXFORD
UNIVERSITY PRESS

# OXFORD
### UNIVERSITY PRESS

Oxford University Press is a department of the University of Oxford. It furthers
the University's objective of excellence in research, scholarship, and education
by publishing worldwide. Oxford is a registered trade mark of Oxford University
Press in the UK and certain other countries.

Published in the United States of America by Oxford University Press
198 Madison Avenue, New York, NY 10016, United States of America.

© Oxford University Press 2021

Library of Congress Cataloging-in-Publication Data
Names: Wells, Christi Jay, author.
Title: Between beats : the jazz tradition and black vernacular dance /
Christi Jay Wells.
Description: New York : Oxford University Press, 2021. |
Includes bibliographical references and index.
Identifiers: LCCN 2020038889 (print) | LCCN 2020038890 (ebook) |
ISBN 9780197559277 (hardback) | ISBN 9780197559284 (paperback) |
ISBN 9780197559307 (epub)
Subjects: LCSH: Jazz—Social aspects—United States—History—20th century. |
Jazz dance. | Music and dance—United States—History—20th century.
Classification: LCC ML3918.J39 W45 2021 (print) |
LCC ML3918.J39 (ebook) | DDC 781.65097309/04—dc23
LC record available at https://lccn.loc.gov/2020038889
LC ebook record available at https://lccn.loc.gov/2020038890

DOI: 10.1093/oso/9780197559277.001.0001

3 5 7 9 8 6 4 2

Paperback printed by Marquis, Canada
Hardback printed by Bridgeport National Bindery, Inc., United States of America

*To Cecile Sherman Cooper, The Lady Miss Dawn Hampton,*
*and Professor Marcus White.*

Ikh bin nokh lernen, viir
Feel *the music*
*Get the light, girl . . . get your light*

# Contents

# Acknowledgments

I didn't think the prospect of writing acknowledgments would freak me out so much, but here we are, and I'm trying to find a clever way in without brushing too close to an "it takes a village" cliché. I guess ultimately it's always a riff on that motive, so let's do the thing.

I shouldn't be surprised this would feel daunting given the intersection of two things about me. First, I am always terribly anxious about excluding rather than including. Second, my life is all about relationships and mutual support, and this book would never have existed without the generosity of the communities in which I move and the people who both support me and trust me to support them. These acknowledgments will be an attempt, doomed to failure, at naming some of those people and in thanking everyone I would want to thank. So I'll start with this: whether or not you see your names on these pages, if you even consider for a moment that you are someone who has made an impact on me or on this work, you are, and you have. Thank you so, so much for that.

Elizabeth Heller has been here through this whole process and was here long before this book was even a seed of an idea. She is my partner in life and in raising three fantastic dogs, and she has supported me in doing this work in more ways than I can name or count. She both pushes me to be fully myself and challenges me to be better. The critical conversation we just had as I'm writing this about the problem of "good wife archetypes" in book acknowledgments speaks to our collaborative discourse on big things and small. Liza, you've encouraged me to be more adventurous and more practical in life and to be enthusiastic about my own work and kind to myself in producing it. Thank you.

My family has done so much to shape my worldview and encourage my creativity and curiosity over the years. I want to first thank my mother, Jacki Cooper Gordon, both for the sort of enthusiastic support a mother often gives but also for being a role model in her own academic and community pursuits and for the many, many hours of work over the years she has put into helping me grow as a writer; having a professional editor for a mom is a luxury I will never take for granted. My father, John Wells, has never been anything but enthusiastic about my pursuits in scholarship and in the arts, and I thank him for his counsel and encouragement when the impostor syndrome hits hardest and for sharing my love of and passion for jazz. My sister Rebecca Muñoz and my cousin Abbie Cooper are two of the coolest, kindest, smartest women I know, and I thank both of them for both keeping me grounded and lifting me up when I've needed the confidence to stay adventurous.

This book also does not happen without the caring support of my mentors and peers at the University of North Carolina at Chapel Hill both during my time as a graduate student and through the years since. David F. García, my doctoral advisor, has been critical to my development as a scholar. He taught me an approach to honoring the intersections and relationships between rigor, boldness, nuance, and honesty that continues to guide my work to this day. On a more fine-grained level, chapter 5 of this book has its roots in a seminar paper I wrote for him on rhythm tap dancing during my first semester of graduate school, and the historiographic focus of that seminar (on the history of ethnomusicology) has informed my thinking ever since. Over many vulnerable conversations during my time as a student, he generously shared with me his own in-process ideas as he was conceiving of and researching what became the phenomenal book *Listening for Africa* even as he was guiding me through my own projects; these conversations were formative for me and have had a strong impact on this book. He's also modeled what it means to be a caring, supportive advisor who is genuinely concerned not only with his students' intellectual growth but also their material well-being, and it's an approach I do my best to pay forward to my own students. In a similar vein, Mark Katz did so much to help me develop my passion for archives and archival research. He has been an unflinchingly caring and supportive mentor and now peer and collaborator. That my comments about him are somewhat brief is but an homage to his own writing. Also crucial to my growth and development at UNC in large ways and small were Perry Hall, Reginald Hildebrand, Annegret Fauser, Tim Carter, Fatimah LC Jackson, Eunice Sahle, Louise Toppin, Cherie Rivers Ndaliko, Brigid Cohen, Victoria Behrens, and Andrea Bohlman. Thanks also to my peers at UNC Chapel Hill for the many conversations and continuing friendships that continue to shape my scholarly community and model an ethic of mutual support, and in particular Naomi Graber, Matthew Franke, Joshua Busman, Brian Jones, Leah Elliot, Douglas Shadle, Kristen Turner, Megan Eagen, Oren Vinogradov, Molly Barnes, Stephen Sacks, Gina Bombola, and Christa Bentley.

In addition to the mentorship I received at UNC, Sherrie Tucker has truly gone above and beyond in her generous support of me and of my work. From the first time we met and I was "fangirling," she has treated me as a peer and an equal, making clear in particular that my embodied practice as a dancer was valuable and necessary to share with the field. Her unflinching and enthusiastic support and generous sharing of her time and energy have been instrumental to the professional and intellectual paths I have taken. She is far from alone in this, however, as I have had many other mentors in the field of jazz studies who, in addition to being great scholars whose work is cited all over this book, have been tremendously supportive of my work and my career for many years. They include Tammy Kernodle, Guthrie P. Ramsey Jr., Patrick Burke, Scott DeVeaux, Ingrid Monson, Jeff Magee, Travis Jackson, Ken Prouty, Karl Hagstrom Miller, Andrew Dell'Antonio, Lisa Barg, Gayle Murchison, Stephan Pennington, and Charles Carson. I don't mean this as a hierarchical separation from "mentors" (either in age or importance), but I do also want to thank the network of peers in my "cohort" in jazz studies and Black music studies whose support has helped to shape my work, rejecting "cutthroat" models of academia in favor of generosity and collective thriving. Particular thanks to Matthew Morrison, Kwami Coleman, Vilde Aaslid, Sarah Gerk, Dale Chapman, Nate Sloan, Kelsey Klotz, Alisha Jones, Mark Laver, Fumi Okiji, Michael Heller, Aaron Johnson, Cookie Woolner, Darren Mueller, Stephanie Doktor, Sarah Provost, and Steven Lewis.

I also sincerely appreciate the support and aid I have received from wonderful scholars in the field of dance studies, many of whom I had the pleasure of connecting with at a Stanford University retreat sponsored by Mellon-funded Dance Studies in/and the Humanities project, where I was able to flesh out and explore many early ideas for this book. My thanks to Susan Manning, Rebecca Schneider, and Janice Ross for creating this opportunity as well as my co-participants, including Joanna Dee Das, Michael Morris, and Sarah Wilbur; the bonds we created during that week really helped me find a home in dance studies. Thanks also to Susan Foster and Thomas F. DeFrantz for their supportive mentorship throughout that week, and I underscore that DeFrantz's mentorship, generosity, thoughtfulness, and willingness to challenge me in supportive and generative ways over the decade-plus we have known each other have had a tremendous impact on my scholarly growth in general and on this book in particular.

The immeasurable value of my dance communities to this project extends beyond academia, and I want to be clear that this work would not exist without the nearly two decades of support, friendship, education, collaboration, scholarship, and mentoring I have found in the lindy hop and blues dance communities. There's no way I can name all of you, but a good start would be to thank Gaby Cook, Julie Brown, Kenneth Shipp, Damon Stone, Kelsy Stone, Zachary Brass, Sarah Elise Rund, Sally Adams, Anna Price, Ryan O'Shaughnessy, Shivani Gorvender, Yancy Poon, Jon Ng, John Vigil, Michael Gamble, Jaya Dorf, Annie Gaye Erbsen, Ramona Staffeld, Cynthia

Millman, Anaïs Sékiné, Karen Turman, Angela Andrew, Daniel Heedman, Mike Legenthal, Danielle Jacobowitz, Breai Mason-Campbell, Bobby Green, Adam Wilkerson, Krystal Wilkerson, Rachel Redler, Jamica Zion, Marjorie Bartell, John Vigil, Maurice Fields, Rheanna May Murray, Laurel Fischer, Steve Conrad, Karen Vizzard Hopkins, Samara Askew, Youngdon Kwon, Dawa Jung, Joey Shelley, Elizabeth Kilrain, Ruth Evelyn, Carolyn Leitschuh, Miryam Coppersmith, Faye Adnak, Genevieve Senechal, Marjorie Bartell, Jalen Williams, Andy Reid, Bobby Green, Hannah Foote, Samara Askew, Joseph Wiggan, Josette Wiggan-Freund, Gabrielle Kern, Kenneth Shipp, and Hannah Lane. Notably, Hannah Lane also produced this book's index, and I am so appreciative for the thoughtful care she put into it as well as for gassing me up about the book. Her infectious enthusiasm helped me get through finalizing copyedits and proofs at the end of a particularly difficult semester (fall 2020, you can kick rocks.) Also members of this community, Judy Pritchett arranged the interviews I was able to do (along with Jocelyn Hassenfeld) with bebop dancers Sylvan Charles and Barbara Sidbury and also introduced me to Jazz 966, Bill Jenkins introduced me to his father Eddie and set up our interview, and Bobby White was generous with his film library as I was looking for the highest-quality recordings I could find from which to capture some of the images that appear in this book. Thanks also to C. Doris Pinn for connecting me with Michael Howard, whose insights into Jazz 966 and its history proved vital to completing the project. In addition, I want to thank Angie Faine, Detra Harrison, and the whole Jewels-N-Gents Chicago Steppin' Family in Phoenix. At time of writing, I'm staying home due to the COVID-19 pandemic, but I hope to dance with you soon!

The research for this book was supported by the Stillman Drake Faculty Research Fund from Reed College, the Adriene Fried Block Fellowship from the Society for American Music, and a Berger-Carter Jazz Research Fellowship from the Institute of Jazz Studies. Over my many visits to the Institute of Jazz Studies, the staff has always been incredibly helpful and supportive, and I want to thank Vincent Pelote, Adriana Cuervo, Elizabeth Surles, Wayne Winborne, Dan Faulk, Dan Morgenstern, and the late Ed Berger. I offer particular thanks to Tad Hershorn for serving me an unprocessed box that led to my discovering important materials related to *Jazz Ballet No. 1* and giving me one of those big-find, "at the buzzer" romantic archival moments we all long for. The New York Public Library for the Performing Arts has also been a fantastic place to do research, and I thank their staff and in particular Jonathan Hiam and Jessica Mack for their assistance and supportive advice. Licensing rights, digital images, indexing, and reproductions were paid for by a HIDA Research Investment Grant from Arizona State University's Herberger Institute for

Design and the Arts, as was the commissioning of Brandy Smith's fantastic cover art. My thanks to Shauna Allison, Theo Eckhart, and Joelle Costello for their help disbursing these funds. Additional funds were provided by the ASU School of Music, Dance, and Theatre, and I thank director Heather Landes for generously supporting and always believing in my work.

My current institutional home, Arizona State University, has been a supportive incubator for my thinking on this book, and I am grateful for the fantastic people I work with there. With that in mind, I want to thank my colleagues Sabine Feisst, Kay Norton, Peter Schmelz, Dave Fossum, Catherine Saucier, Ted Solis, Ashley Pribyl, Bliss Little, Adriana Martinez Figueroa, Evan Tobias, Jill Sullivan, Marg Schmidt, Sandy Stauffer, Jason Thompson, Mike Kocour, Jeff Libman, Melita Belgrave, Max Bernstein, Liz Lerman, Daniel Bernard Roumain, Rashad Shabazz, Lois Brown, Joya Scott, Alex Temple, Naomi Jackson, David Olarte, and the late Marcus White. My advisees Zachary Wiggins, Jayson Davis, Matthew Yuknas, Raymond Lebert, and the numerous other ASU students I have had the honor to teach have been a joy to work with, and I thank them as well for the years of stimulating and often challenging conversation that have certainly helped shape the ideas in this book. I hope you've all gotten as much from working with me as I have from working with you. Particular thanks to my writing partners Kristina Knowles and Danielle Hidalgo for helping me stay on task and for your friendship and support. I also received tremendous support during my previous position at Reed College, and I thank Mark Burford, Morgan Luker, Virginia Hancock, David Schiff, Robert Brigham, Carla Mann, Minh Tranh, Elliot Leffler, Brooks Thomas, Daniel Borrero, Laura Liebman, and many others for making my first job out of grad school such a special experience. In particular, I want to thank Hannah Mackenzie-Margulies, my student at Reed but also a peer in the lindy hop community, for her enthusiasm and insight both during my time at Reed and afterward. Part of why my time at Reed was so special was its profound resonance with my own undergraduate education at Guilford College, which was deeply formative in many ways, and I thank Tim Lindeman, Maria Rosales, Max Carter, Wendy Looker, Ken Gilmore, George Guo, and Eric Mortensen for their wisdom, mentorship, and encouragement during those formative years.

Working with Oxford University Press on this book has been a genuine joy, and I thank Norm Hirschy for a level of investment in this project that extends beyond what one might expect of an editor. Since this project was just a glimmer of an idea, Norm's enthusiasm for it has always been clear, and I can't thank him enough for his constant emphasis on making sure I wrote this book in my own voice and as my authentic self. I also thank Suzanne Ryan for her years of helpful mentorship extending back fairly early in my life as a graduate student and Mary Francis, now at University of Michigan Press, for taking the time to help me turn a broad idea into a concept for a book project. Travis Stimeling, Kimberly Francis, Grey Armstrong, and Fen Kennedy have been supportive friends and mentors to me for many years. All of them took time to give careful and caring thoughts on chapter drafts for this book, as did Kimberly Teal, Joe Schloss, Guthrie P. Ramsey Jr., Joanna Dee Das, Naomi Jackson, Michael Howard, Odysseus Bailer, Stephanie Crease, and Robert Crease. I thank them all for their time and thoughtful comments, and I extend these thanks also to the three anonymous reviewers whose careful reading and helpful suggestions have improved this work immensely.

Finally, I thank the people who have taken time to sit down with me for oral history interviews—some of whom are no longer with us—for sharing their lives, their thoughts, and their time so generously: Frankie Manning, Eddie Jenkins, Norma Miller, Sylvan Charles, Barbara Sidbury, Michael Howard, and Guthrie P. Ramsey Jr. Thank you for sharing your stories with me; I hope I have practiced good stewardship of them.

Okay, we made it!! Now on to the book!

# A Note about Language

This project makes frequent use of the terms "African American" and "Black" as descriptors of people, communities, artistic practices, and aesthetic paradigms. Historically, the specific terminology used to identify and describe peoples of the African diaspora often carries deeply weighted implications regarding one's disposition toward their dignity, their rights, and their very human subjecthood. As such, decisions of nomenclature are both challenging and critically important in any project that discusses Black people and Black culture, and it is particularly important for white scholars such as myself to approach these choices of language with care and intention, even and especially when there is no clear standard practice or "right" answer. Throughout this text, I have defaulted to the word "Black" both to honor the diversity of African diasporic peoples within the United States—who have had and continue to have varying dispositions toward, and senses of kinship with, the identifier "American"—and also to reflect its collocated usage by Black scholars and artists in a number of specific intellectual and cultural formations: the Black dancing body, the Black public sphere, the Black Arts Movement, etc.[1] Recently, the practice of capitalizing Black has become more widely accepted as a best practice. I capitalize Black throughout, except in instances where I quote other authors who have not capitalized it, in which cases I reproduce the capitalization or lack thereof as it appears in the material quoted.

I do at times use the term "African American" throughout the text for multiple reasons and in specific instances. First, I use the term "Black" nearly exclusively as an adjective throughout and rely on "African American" when using a noun for a person or group of people in order to avoid the usage of Black as either a singular or plural noun to denote a person or group as that usage is broadly understood and experienced as a dehumanizing slur. I also use the term African American when it feels important to highlight either the first or second word of this formation to throw its difference with another identity into relief (as I do frequently in chapter 5 when discussing African

---

[1] Here I refer specifically to Brenda Dixon Gottschild, *The Black Dancing Body: A Geography from Coon to Cool* (New York: Palgrave Macmillan, 2003) and Mark Anthony Neal, *What the Music Said: Black Popular Music and Black Public Culture* (London: Macmillan, 1999).

American art in in relation to both white American and West African culture and practices). I also use the term African American as an adjective in those instances where it seems to make clearer how I intend the reader to parse something. For instance, I tend toward "African American jazz audiences" rather than "Black jazz audiences" as the former seems to more clearly signal that I mean African Americans who are audience members for jazz whereas the latter could be read to signify "audiences of Black jazz" (whatever "Black jazz" might mean as a specific formulation). While one often ends a note like this with "it is not my intention to offend," intentions matter little relative to the realities of harm. Therefore, I will simply apologize for any instance where my usage is jarring, hurtful, or misguided and promise to continue listening and learning. I sincerely hope that my choices help facilitate a positive reading experience and that any instances where I have erred do not detract significantly from anyone's ability to find meaning and value in this text.

# On the Cover Art

Statement by Brandy Smith and Christi Jay Wells

For the past two years, Brandy and Christi Jay have been dance partners in the social and competition blues dancing scene. That relationship is a particularly profound way to build, through physical touch, a shared understanding of dance and music. Severed from this connection (at time of writing) by the COVID-19 pandemic, working together on this book cover has proved to be one vital way to both maintain and expand the scope and depth of our collaborative relationship as artists.

In the process of co-conceiving this cover, Christi Jay sent Brandy a draft of the full book, and she took particular inspiration from Katrina Hazzard-Donald (neé Katrina Hazzard-Gordon)'s concept of "The Jook Continuum" and from Christi Jay's description of it in the book's first chapter as "as a spectrum to make visible the continuities among African American dance and movement practices as they adapt to emergent contexts that offer varying amounts of literal and figurative room for bodies to move." Brandy took individual words and concepts from that passage—"spectrum" "making things vulnerable" "movement practices" "adapt to emergent" "room for bodies to move"—to form a conceptual basis for the artwork.

This passage also inspired Brandy to choose collage as a medium. By crafting the individual figures such that they could be placed in a range of backgrounds and orientations, Brandy embodied in the process of the work's creation the notion of "emergent contexts that offer varying amounts of . . . room for bodies to move." Riffing on the ideas of emergence and variation, Brandy wanted to be able to have dancers and musicians she could put into a range of spaces (backgrounds) such that she and Christi Jay could choose together the iteration of this flexible piece that would work best for the book cover. In addition, using collage and photographing the work from above creates natural shadows, which contributes to the sense of "emergent" figures. To craft these figures, Brandy took inspiration not only from a range of photographs and film and video clips, but also from her own embodied knowledge as a practicing social dancer. Since the book is about shifts in dance and music practices—as well as in the narratives we craft about them— over time, Brandy created images that move from black-and-white to color to show the passage of time and to position the process of creation itself, and that process's core sociality, as central to the work's sense of flow and motion. That the musicians' instruments, however, remain in color points to fluidity and connection as artists within living traditions, dancers and musicians alike, speak to each other across temporal spans.

In creating the background that appears on this book's cover, the imagined venue in which to place the dancers and musicians, Brandy drew inspiration from many spaces for Black vernacular dance in a range of times and places including those discussed in the book (most notably the Savoy Ballroom and Jazz 966.) In addition, this background, and in particular its color palate, was inspired by the work of Harlem Renaissance artist Archibald Motley (to which Christi Jay introduced Brandy) and specifically the ways Motley's color palette and use of light playfully yet poignantly embody Black nightlife.

**Brandy Smith** is an award-winning mixed media artist and champion blues dancer. A native of Rockford, Illinois, her passion for art began at a young age following in the artistic footsteps of her Mother and Grandmother. Brandy uses mixed media and collage to express herself freely and emotionally. She tackles hard topics such as mental health and weight issues. She believes in not worrying about straight lines or a spill on a paper. She thinks it is more important to convey oneself, flaws and all, than to portray a false sense of self. She has been very lucky to have many inspirational people in her life including her Uncle Brian and her art teacher at Rock Valley College, Matthew Vincent.

The work in process. Artist Brandy Smith holding the jazz musician figures for the *Between Beats* cover art.

# 1

# Jazz Music and Its Choreographies of Listening

Like many jazz scholars, I spend a lot of time engaging in critical historiography, contemplating the sedimental layers of ideology that jazz's histories have accumulated over time and how those striations affect our view
of the past.[1] But, there is one moment in my life that sticks out when I truly
felt the gravity of jazz historical narratives. When I say gravity, I mean precisely that: it pulled me off my feet and planted my ass in a chair. At the 2013
American Musicological Society annual meeting in Pittsburgh, a live band
performed Ted Buehrer's painstaking transcriptions of Mary Lou Williams's
compositions and arrangements. My friend Anna and I lindy hopped our way
through some of Williams's best charts from the 1920s and 1930s: "Walkin'
and Swingin'," "Messa Stomp," and "Mary's Idea."[2] About halfway through the
concert, the band took up "Scorpio" from Williams's *Zodiac Suite*, and I felt
that groovy bassline throughout my legs and hips as delightful pockets of
rhythmic dissonance invited me (and I presume also Anna, though I haven't
asked her) to keep dancing ... but we didn't. The music still felt "danceable," but
we'd moved from 1938 to 1944, and I felt a shift inside myself as I questioned
whether letting my hips respond to that bassline would still be appropriate.
As the band crossed the "bebop moment": that early 1940s boundary separ-
ating jazz-as-pop from jazz-as-art, I felt the socially inscribed choreography
that governed and shaped the conditions of possibility for movement shift be-
neath my feet.[3] Suddenly, to shake my hips felt far less respectful than to sit

[1] Portions of this chapter previously appeared as Christopher J. Wells, "'You Can't Dance to It': Jazz Music
and Its Choreographies of Listening," *Daedalus* 148, no. 2, special issue "Jazz Still Matters," eds. Ingrid
Monson and Gerald Early (Spring 2019): 36–51. Reproduced here with the permission of MIT Press.

[2] Anna Reguero DeFelice of SUNY Stony Brook, a fantastic dancer whom I met in New York City's swing
dancing scene long before either of us became a musicologist. The performance in question was Indiana
University of Pennsylvania Jazz Ensemble, "Mary Lou Williams: Selected Works for Big Band," American
Musicological Society Annual Meeting, Pittsburgh, Pennsylvania, November 7, 2013.

[3] The period in the early/mid 1940s when the Zodiac Suite was composed was, of course, a time of sig-
nificant personal, community, and artistic change and growth for Williams herself, as detailed beautifully
by Tammy Kernodle and Farah Jasmine Griffin, *Soul on Soul: The Life and Music of Mary Lou Williams*
(Boston: Northeastern University Press, 2004), 81–146; Farah Jasmine Griffin. "Rollin' with Mary Lou
Williams." In *Harlem Nocturne: Women Artists and Progressive Politics During World War II*, 133–186.
New York: Basic Books, 2013.

*Between Beats*. Christi Jay Wells, Oxford University Press (2021). © Oxford University Press.
DOI: 10.1093/oso/9780197559277.003.0001

and listen quietly, performing those entrained non-movements that project serious, rigorous listening.

Had Anna and I continued dancing, might we have disrespected the legacies and wishes of great African American jazz musicians like Williams, Dizzy Gillespie, or Duke Ellington? As Ellington wrote in 1931:

> The music of my race is something more than the "American idiom." It is the result of our transplantation to American soil and was our reaction in the plantation days to the tyranny we endured. What we could not say openly we expressed in music, and what we know today as "jazz" is something more than just dance music.[4]

Yet, this is not the complete quote. Ellington goes on, embracing dance as a guiding metaphor for the African American experience: "It expresses our personality, and, right down in us, our souls react to the elemental but eternal rhythm, and the dance is timeless and unhampered by any lineal form."[5] For Ellington to frame his music in terms of a dance that is "timeless and unhampered by any lineal form" is to express the sort of confluence of sound, body, and spirit that musicologist Samuel Floyd would later articulate as a central point of resonance between African American music-making and West African epistemologies. Floyd articulates this position, via historian Sterling Stuckey, through the ring shout. As Floyd explains, "in the world of the slaves, the ring shout fused the sacred and the secular, music and dance; it continued the African and Africa-derived tendencies to eschew distinctions between religion and everyday life, between one performance medium and another."[6] One way to reconcile Ellington's ostensible contradiction is to consider that, in claiming jazz as "something more than just dance music," Ellington notably employs the word dance as an adjective. More to the point, he uses it as part of the music industry-specific collocation "dance music" that is less a descriptor of musical quality or of whether listeners do or don't move to it and more a signifier of his ensemble's implicit placement in the spatialized hierarchies of culture and the foreclosures or opportunities such placement yields for him and his band. In 1931, the label "dance music" told you that the music in question was to be played in a ballroom rather than a concert hall, that it belonged to a certain tier of lowbrow

---

[4] Duke Ellington, "The Duke Steps Out," 1931, reprinted in *The Duke Ellington Reader*, ed. Mark Tucker (New York: Oxford University Press, 1993), 49, as cited in Lisa Barg and Walter van de Leur, " 'Your Music Has Flung the Story of "Hot Harlem" to the Four Corners of the Earth': Race and Narrative in *Black, Brown, and Beige*," *Musical Quarterly* 96 (2013): 431–432.

[5] Ellington, "The Duke Steps Out," 49.

[6] Samuel Floyd, *The Power of Black Music: Interpreting Its History from Africa to the United States* (New York: Oxford University Press, 1995), 6.

or middlebrow entertainment, and that those playing it should expect to be paid less and afforded less respect than their peers playing "concert music." In distancing himself and his music from "dance music" status, Ellington works within the branding project he and his manager Irving Mills had laid out to position him as a serious composer worthy of serious attention. Thus, even as he honored the "dance" central to African American life, Ellington's stated disposition toward "dance music" helped align his performance of seriousness with an emergent ideological formation through which jazz music critics and other ostensibly elite listeners could differentiate themselves from regular, dancing fans.[7]

Ellington's prose evinces a deft and creative navigation of space and context, and in this it shares kinship with the nineteenth-century ring shout practices that form the basis of Floyd's aesthetic system. As a practice that embodied West African corporeal values yet still functioned within the Christian church, the ring shout required the deft syncretizing of dance-like practices that could very specifically not be named dance-as-such. As practitioners moved profoundly in the ring, they were mindful not to cross their feet, as only then would their movement constitute the sin of dancing in church; the spiritual "Ezekiel Saw the Wheel" admonished ring shout practitioners, "better mind my brother how you walk on the cross! Your foot may slip and your soul get lost." Nevertheless, this singular prohibition was simultaneously generative in "the upper-body dancing of African provenance" as well as the hand, foot, and body percussion available to ring shouters.[8] Viewed through this lens, perhaps jazz musicians' move toward the concert hall and away from "dance music" creates one more layer within the "jook continuum" laid out by Katrina Hazzard Donald (née Katrina Hazzard Gordon) as a fluid spectrum that makes visible the continuities among African American dance and movement practices as Black people adapt to emergent contexts that offer varying amounts of literal and figurative room for bodies to move.[9] Such navigations of the connections between dance and music, as well as the systems of value that

[7] In discussing the music of the Beatles during the 1960s, and the predominantly white male critics' preference for it over James Brown and other artists producing "black dance music," Elijah Wald writes that "critics, by their nature, want to hear music that is not only functional but interesting—after all, they need to listen to it carefully and find something to say about it. So when straightforward dance music is turned into something more complex and better suited for seated listening, they naturally see this as a step forward." Wald also highlights the gendered nature of this dynamic, as male critics have long ascribed the status of serious and careful listener to themselves and that of frivolous dancing "fan" to young women. Elijah Wald, *How the Beatles Destroyed Rock 'n' Roll: An Alternative History of American Popular Music* (New York: Oxford University Press, 2009), 251, 98.

[8] Floyd, *Power of Black Music*, 37.

[9] Katrina Hazzard-Gordon, *Jookin': The Rise of Social Dance Formations in African American Culture* (Philadelphia: Temple University Press, 1992), x, 63–119.

surround them, form the core of this book, which chronicles and interrogates the ever-shifting relationship between jazz music and Black vernacular dance.

## Choreographies of Listening

African American jazz audiences during the interwar period were particularly mindful of the intersection between seated listening and the projection of rigor and dignity. A series of events targeting Black audiences in Atlanta during the late 1930s specifically bifurcated the venue both spatially and temporally to enable, yet keep separate, both seated listening and dancing listening. Advertisements in the *Chicago Defender* and the *Atlanta Daily World*—Atlanta's primary Black newspaper—promoted dance parties that also featured a separate "concert hour" where no dancing was allowed. The first such concert was held at Sunset Park in July 1938 and featured the Jimmie Lunceford Orchestra. The *Defender* reported that the Lunceford event separated dancing time from concert time: "During the concert hour before the 'jam session,' Lunceford entertained the crowd with what could be considered a floor show, but was styled as a concert hour—no dancing was allowed. At 9:30 o'clock, swing-time begun continuing until 1:30 o'clock."[10] Two similar events were held at Atlanta's City Auditorium, the first of which, also in 1938, featured Cab Calloway's band. Advertisements made clear that from 9 to 10 p.m. there would be "NO DANCING, in order that you may hear Cab at ease" with assurances that "at ten o'clock sharp, he will get 'hotcha' and 'jam it' until one-thirty o'clock the next in the morning" (figure 1.1).[11] The following year, City Auditorium hosted Count Basie's orchestra, offering a concert half-hour with "POSITIVELY NO DANCING" following a patrons' interview in the lobby (figure 1.2).[12]

To understand why these Atlanta concerts were exceptional, and why these audiences may have desired to enact the seated posture of serious listening, we must consider that these performances were organized as racially segregated events that targeted Black audiences. The same *Daily World* article announcing Cab Calloway's 1938 appearance and its "streamlined" concert section also revealed that this would be City Auditorium's first "all colored double performance" and that "management is eager to see if Negro people really appreciate an evening all their

[10] "Harlem Band Swings Down in Atlanta," *Chicago Defender*, July 2, 1938.
[11] Advertisement, *Atlanta Daily World*, August 4, 1938. Capitalization in the original.
[12] Advertisement, *Atlanta Daily World*, May 14, 1939; and "'Cab' in All-Colored Show Week from Today," *Atlanta Daily World*, July 28, 1938. Capitalization in the original.

**Figure 1.1** Advertisement, *Atlanta Daily World*, August 4, 1938.

own."[13] While it may have been their first jazz-centered concert, the Black Atlantans attending City Auditorium were not strangers to the role expected of them: attentive audience member for a serious concert performance. The venue regularly hosted not only jazz dances but also graduation ceremonies, community pageants, and operatic and concert recital performances by Black opera singers: the kinds of events whose concordances with elite European culture musicologist Lawrence Schenbeck has situated within the broader

---

[13] "Cab Calloway's Coming This Thursday Awaited," *Atlanta Daily World*, July 31, 1938. I use the term "racially segregated" here only to suggest this event was intended exclusively for Black people, not to in any way imply parity between Black exclusion and white exclusion. The former is backed by white supremacist power structures where the latter arguably resists them.

**Figure 1.2** Advertisement, *Atlanta Daily World*, May 14, 1939.

social and intellectual project of racial uplift.[14] In fact, earlier that month, City Auditorium had staged a pageant entitled "75 Years of Progress" that celebrated the forward trajectory of Black emancipation and social advancement in the United States, and earlier in the year the venue had hosted spiritual concerts from the Tuskegee University Choir under the direction of composer William L. Dawson.[15] Atlanta's Black audiences thus already understood the specific rules governing audiences' corporeal performance in "high culture" listening spaces: by sitting down, listening intently, and responding appropriately with limited movement, Black audiences could acquire embodied

[14] Lawrence Schenbeck, *Racial Uplift and American Music, 1878–1943* (Oxford: University of Mississippi Press, 2012).

[15] Gamewell Valentine, "Pageant of Race Progress Viewed at City Auditorium," *Atlanta Daily World*, July 12, 1938; Gamewell Valentine, "Tuskegee Choir Presentation Looms Treat," *Atlanta Daily World*, April 26, 1938.

cultural capital by performing the physical rhetoric through which seated audiences communicate respect, dignity, intelligence, and sophistication.

Concerts impose a specific choreography for audiences, as musicologist Scott DeVeaux observes in his essay chronicling "The Emergence of the Jazz Concert." DeVeaux explains that, "The concert is a solemn ritual with music the object of reverent contemplation. Certain formalities are imposed upon the concert audience: people attend in formal dress, sit quietly, and attentively with little outward bodily movement, and restrict their response to applause at appropriate moments only."[16] In a concert setting, musicians and seated audience members lay claim to cultural capital by performing the movements and non-movements that mark the concert as an elite social space and the music performed as worthy of serious consideration. DeVeaux argues that the rise of the jazz concert between 1935 and 1945 was crucial to repositioning jazz as a form of serious art. As he explains, concert formats present a powerful cultural rhetoric within the United States, because of their associations with the "considerable social privilege" afforded European art music.[17] Jazz musicians' attempts to access this "considerable social privilege," however, predate the period DeVeaux analyzes. In discussing bandleader Fletcher Henderson, musicologist Jeffrey Magee situates jazz musicians' enactment of racial uplift during the 1920s as an acquisition of cultural mastery that demonstrated fluency in Euro-American concert traditions.[18]

By corporeally enacting the role of Western concert listeners, Black audiences at City Auditorium also embodied an ethic of racial uplift through specific performances of cultural mastery, situating themselves as serious, educated, and cerebral listeners. Crucially, performing the non-movements of a seated listener also signaled that Black audiences were capable of corporeal discipline, a powerful counter-statement to long-standing minstrel tropes that dehumanized Black people by portraying them and their bodies as fundamentally wild and subhuman. Corporeal discipline was thus central on numerous levels to the physical enactment of racial uplift as control of one's body was tied to positive moral values through the early twentieth-century discourse surrounding physical culture.[19] As a precursor to the American bodybuilding

[16] Scott DeVeaux, "The Emergence of the Jazz Concert, 1935–1945," *American Music* 7, no. 1 (1989): 6.

[17] DeVeaux, "Emergence of the Jazz Concert," 6.

[18] Jeffrey Magee, *Fletcher Henderson: The Uncrowned King of Swing* (New York: Oxford University Press, 2005), 27–38. I riff on Magee's argument in discussing Black jazz listeners' demonstration of aural mastery as a means of racial uplift in Christopher J. Wells, "'The Ace of His Race': Paul Whiteman's Early Critical Reception in the Black Press," *Jazz and Culture* 1 (2018): 84.

[19] David Krasner has shown that prominent Black dancers—and specifically Aida Overton-Walker—sought to rebrand Black embodiment as fundamentally dignified and an expression of control in discipline through cakewalk performances and instruction in the 1910s. David Krasner, "The Real Thing," in *Beyond Blackface: African Americans and the Creation of American Popular Culture, 1890–1930*, ed. W. Fitzhugh Brundage (Chapel Hill: University of North Carolina Press, 2011), 109–118.

movement, the concept of physical culture offered that individuals were capable of transforming their bodies through educated, disciplined labor and were able, through this work, to improve their worth and moral character. This concept became an especially potent tool for Black communities because it offered a counter-narrative to white supremacist genetic determinism.[20] It is also important to note that a still, seated listening posture draws attention *away* from one's body, presenting a space where serious sounds meet serious minds (with, perhaps, the minor concession that there are ears involved). For African Americans at this time, emphasizing their cerebral prowess and sensitive intellect was a powerful tactic for contesting oppressive stereotypes that marked Black bodies as animalistic, unrestrained, and dangerous and that sensationalized Black talent as the result of a savage and naturally gifted body rather than a rigorously cultivated mind.

I introduce these hybridized concert events, which explicitly instruct audiences about how to position their bodies for listening, to suggest *choreography* as a useful analytic lens through which to approach listening practices and engagement with music, and specifically with jazz. My use of the term choreography follows dance scholar Susan Leigh Foster, who employs the concept to consider broadly the structuring of possibilities for how bodies can move and behave within a given space. Whether planned intentionally by a single person or formed organically through gradual shifts in tacit social mores, choreography, she argues, is a "hypothetical setting forth of what the body is and what it can be based on the decisions made in rehearsal and in performance about its identity." She claims we can thus read choreographies as "the product of choices, inherited, invented, or selected, about what kinds of bodies and subjects are being constructed and what kinds of arguments about these bodies and subjects are being put forth."[21] Foster's work draws from a robust conversation in the interdiscipline of dance studies that regards bodies, whether moving or stationary, as always performative and always political.[22]

---

[20] Mark Whalan, "Taking Myself in Hand: Jean Toomer and Physical Culture," *Modernism/Modernity* 10, no. 4 (2003): 597–607.

[21] Susan Leigh Foster, *Choreographing Empathy: Kinesthesia in Performance* (New York: Routledge, 2011), 4. Foster's work includes a robust review of the trajectory of the term choreography within dance studies, and thus I will not reproduce it here.

[22] Though my discussion here centers on Foster, my thinking is also deeply informed by Kate Elswit's concept of "archives of watching" as a means to read dance spectatorship closely by blurring the dichotomization of onstage and offstage bodies in concert dance spaces, as well as Andrew Hewitt's notion of "social choreography" as "a way of thinking about the *relationship* of aesthetics to politics." Kate Elswit, *Watching Weimar Dance* (New York: Oxford University Press, 2014), xvii–xxiii; and Andrew Hewitt, *Social Choreography: Ideology as Performance in Dance and Everyday Movement* (Durham, NC: Duke University Press), 11. The essays in the provocatively titled collection *Choreographies of 21st Century Wars* also demonstrate the lengths to which this concept can be applied usefully outside of dance-as-such. Gay Morris and Jens Richard Giersdorf, eds., *Choreographies of 21st Century Wars* (New York: Oxford University Press, 2016).

Drawing from the work of choreographer William Forsyth, musicologist Nina Eidsheim applies a similar notion of choreography to singing and specifically to the intersection of race and vocal timbre. Eidsheim explains, "I understand choreography, then, as an external structural force that—with a decisive power that ranges from 'coercion' to 'suggestion'—funnels the body through certain movements and stances rather than others. It is a condition within which we carry out actions, whether those actions are considered dance or, as we will see, song."[23] As Eidsheim applies this idea of choreography as an "external structural force," and one often mediated both internally and externally by race, to singing, I seek here to illustrate choreography's role in shaping the corporeal conditions of possibility within which the fundamentally embodied act of listening takes place.

Within Black communities, socially mediated choreographies are communicated through processes of what ethnomusicologist Kyra Gaunt terms "kinetic orality." In *The Games Black Girls Play*, Gaunt defines kinetic orality as "the social training ground upon which girls create a background of relatedness to one another."[24] As Gaunt explains, kinetic orality is a form of intergenerational transfer and a cultural archiving practice for various Black social dances, stylistic particularities, and expressive practices. Gaunt makes clear, however, that kinetic orality is also a means through which African Americans communicate various foreclosures and contextual specificities, educating each other in not only the expressive potentials of Black embodiment, but also its enforced limitations within a white supremacist society. As Gaunt explains this dynamic, "black musical style and behavior are learned through oral-kinetic practices that not only teach an embodied discourse of black musical expression, but also inherently teach discourse about appropriate and transgressive gender and racial roles (for both girls and boys) in black communities."[25] Viewed through this lens, we could thus interpret the City Auditorium audience's movement between two distinct choreographies of listening—in the context of a broader midcentury move among jazz audiences toward still, seated concert listening—as a form of kinetic code switching fostered through generations of cultivated hyper-awareness of Black bodies' particular signifying potentials and dangers within a white supremacist social order.

[23] Nina Eidsheim, "Voice as Action: Toward a Model for Analyzing the Dynamic Construction of a Racialized Voice," *Current Musicology* 93 (Spring 2012): 22. Eidsheim's discussion of choreography draws heavily from William Forsythe, "Choreographic Objects," http://www.williamforsythe.com/essay.html.

[24] Kyra Gaunt, *The Games Black Girls Play: Learning the Ropes from Double-Dutch to Hip-Hop* (New York: New York University Press, 2006), 4.

[25] Gaunt, *The Games Black Girls Play*, 2.

African American choreographies of listening are thus crafted through interpersonal and intergenerational practices of kinetic orality that perform both choreopolicing and choreopolitical functions. I draw these terms from the work of performance theorist André Lepecki, who offers "choreopolitics" as a specifically resistant mode of engagement with those structures that enforce choreographic constraints. He terms those constraining mechanisms "choreopolicing" or the authoritarian containment of movement that yields "a policed dance of quotidian consensus."[26] While it is tempting to position danced listening as choreopolitical in a way that concertized, "choreopoliced" seated listening is not, it is a temptation I wish to resist. I posit, rather, that Black non-movement functions as choreopolitical resistance to overdetermined fetishizations that cast Black bodies in motion as fundamentally premodern and dangerously unrestrained. As dance scholar Jayna Brown astutely points out, "White recognition of black expressive exuberance was contingent on the codification of the black expressive body as a signature for the past, for a fictional moment of pre-industrial innocence. For black people to lay claim to the complexities of the present, both temporally and spatially, was to overstep the terms of the contract."[27] In breaking this "pre-industrial fantasy," spoiling the "fictional moment," Black performances of non-movement certainly do "overstep the terms of the contract." In denying the overdetermination of "black expressive exuberance," Black non-movement resists not only the white gaze writ large, but also the white leftist desire to mobilize Black embodiment as a site of liberation not for Black people from oppression but for white people from whiteness.[28]

Indeed, both still and moving listening practices represent African American jazz listeners' claims to corporeal agency in resistance to the various determinisms inscribed upon their bodies. Interrogating the corporeal agency of listening bodies necessarily invites a more robust engagement with ethnomusicologist Ingrid Monson's work on "perceptual agency" than space affords me here, but certainly the relationship Monson seeks to explore between the auditory and the political could productively involve both the internally experienced and externally perceivable phenomena felt and expressed

---

[26] André Lepecki, "Choreopolice and Choreopolitics: Or, the Task of the Dancer," *TDR: The Drama Review* 57, no. 4 (2013): 20.

[27] Jayna Brown, *Babylon Girls: Black Women Performers and the Shaping of the Modern* (Durham, NC: Duke University Press, 2008), 162.

[28] For more on white "slumming" and the political left, see Wells, "And I Make My Own." For its historiographic resonances, see Ingrid Monson, "The Problem with White Hipness: Race, Gender, and Cultural Conceptions in Jazz Historical Discourse," *Journal of the American Musicological Society* 48, no. 3 (1995): 396–422; and John Gennari, *Blowin' Hot and Cool: Jazz and Its Critics* (Berkeley: University of California Press, 2006).

by diverse listeners through their bodies.[29] Indeed, it is important to re-member is that embodied, danced ways of knowing are, and have long been, central to jazz as they have been to many forms of African American music. As cultural theorist Fred Moten beautifully writes in his work on the Black rad-ical tradition, "It was always the whole body that emitted sound: instrument and fingers, bend. Your ass is in what you sing. Dedicated to the movement of hips, dedicated by that movement, the harmolodically rhythmic body."[30] At the same time, I do not mean to invalidate stillness and non-movement as modes of engagement, and the power of seated Black concert listeners' still-ness resonates with the profundity to be found in recent theorizations of quiet and silence in Black life. Jazz studies and African American literature scholar Farah Jasmine Griffin has recently argued for a reclamation of quiet and still-ness in Black music, asking us to understand moments of quiet as places not of complacency but of deep resilience.[31] In addition, ethnomusicologist Matt Sakakeeny's evocative account of a silent march against anti-Black violence in New Orleans demonstrates that an explicit refusal to make a joyful noise can also resonate with poignance, as can a dignified listener engaged in active, de-fiant non-movement.[32]

Just as sound and silence can be both profound and banal, resistant and compliant, so too can motion and stillness. As Foster explains, individual performances can respond to the choreographies that purport to govern them on a spectrum ranging from conformity to subversion to total disregard. These performative responses to choreographic prescriptions both impact and are impacted by the particularity of their circumstances as, in Foster's words, "both choreography and performance change over time; both select from and move into action certain semantic systems, and as such, they derive their meaning from a specific historical and cultural moment."[33]

To see how movement's interaction with choreography influences listening specifically, it is useful to consider the socially co-authored model of listening praxis ethnomusicologist Judith Becker has termed a "habitus of listening." Building upon Pierre Bourdieu's framework, Becker offers this term as a way

[29] Ingrid Monson, "Hearing, Seeing, and Perceptual Agency," *Critical Inquiry* 34, no. S2 (2008): S38.

[30] Fred Moten, *In the Break: The Aesthetics of the Black Radical Tradition* (Minneapolis: University of Minnesota Press, 2003), 39–40.

[31] Farah Jasmine Griffin, "On Being: Quiet and Stillness in Black Music," Committee on Race and Ethnicity Critical Race Lecture at the Annual Meeting of the American Musicological Society, Sunday, November 15, 2020.

[32] Matthew Sakakeeny, *Roll with It: Brass Bands in the Streets of New Orleans* (Durham, NC: Duke University Press, 2013), 169–173.

[33] Foster, *Choreographing Empathy*, 24.

to understand the default mode(s) of listening within a particular sphere of musical practice. As Becker explains:

> Our habitus of listening is tacit, unexamined, seemingly completely "natural." We listen in a particular way without thinking about it, and without realizing that it even is a particular way of listening. Most of our styles of listening have been learned through unconscious imitation of those who surround us and those with whom we continually interact. A "habitus of listening" suggests not a necessity nor a rule, but an inclination, a disposition to listen with a particular kind of focus . . . and to interpret the meanings of the sounds and one's emotional responses to the musical event in somewhat (never totally) predictable ways.[34]

Tacit, socially constructed choreographies are often central to the process of "unconscious imitation" to which Becker refers. The habitus generated by a musical space's choreography guides how one enacts the process of listening, what sensory information is a relevant part of this listening process, and what constitutes appropriate interaction between the various participants. When applied to jazz listening spaces, choreography indexes the implicit and explicit assumptions people make about their role in the event (dancer, musician, concertgoer, etc.), how they should thus orient their body in space to communicate what it means for them to listen to the music being played (or that they are playing), and what their listening body communicates about the soundscapes and attendant values present in the space. For, as Guthrie P. Ramsey Jr. has said, "Generic labels such as 'jazz' guide listeners toward the 'proper' responses as dictated by a social contract established by the label itself."[35] Recognizing jazz music's multiple conjuncturally specific choreographies of listening as well as those audience performances that work within and against these choreographies offers a way to explore how different participants in a space (those who dance, those who music, those who spectate, and so on) enact various modes of listening that hold the potential both to affirm and to resist the constraints placed upon their bodies by the assemblages of accumulated corporeal performance and narrative conceit that form and shape, applying Becker's term, the particular "communities of interpretation" they inhabit.[36] Interrogating choreographies of listening also invites all of us to reflect on the ways we do, and specifically don't, listen and move, perhaps offering us more space to play

---

[34] Judith Becker, *Deep Listeners: Music, Emotion, and Trancing* (Bloomington: Indiana University Press, 2005), 71. Parentheses in the original.

[35] Guthrie P. Ramsey Jr., *The Amazing Bud Powell: Black Genius, Jazz History, and the Challenge of Bebop* (Berkeley: University of California Press, 2013), 20.

[36] Becker, *Deep Listeners*, 69.

within and against our own socially embedded choreographies as we consider how we listen, how else we might choose to listen, and why.

## (Inter)disciplining Intimacies in Jazz Studies and Dance Studies

A central theme throughout this book is the exploration of complex corporeal intimacies danced and musicked into existence through jazz's ever shifting conditions of possibility. Philip Bohlman and Goffredo Plastino have recently highlighted the centrality of intimacy as a constitutive force in jazz music.

> Jazz is the art of the intimate. It resides in the social and musical worlds formed from intimacy. Jazz depends on the personal and the interpersonal, the communication between a musician with something to say and the listener seeking passionately to respond. The intimacy of jazz is both performative and social; its intimacy forms at the place musical and human attributes become one. Intimacy gives structure to the music itself, as well as to the acts of the musicians who play jazz.[37]

Bohlman and Plastino locate this intimacy in the practice that has long marked jazz music's specialness, the fundamental brand signifier that differentiates it within the marketplace: improvisation. "Improvisation," they claim, "is the language of jazz's intimacy, forged from conversations and mutual understanding, the sensitivity to the places in which performers join together, reaching out to one another, thus closing the gap between them."[38] In response, I would suggest that improvisation is *a* language of jazz's intimacy, one among many. Jazz intimacies are forged as often through dissensus, negotiation, and widening gaps as they are through mutual understanding as such. Indeed, works addressing the layered exchanges involved in partnered social dancing provide a check on this idealization of intimacy. Jazz scholar Sherrie Tucker and political theorist/anthropologist Marta Savigliano make clear—through their work on the social dancing at the Hollywood Canteen and the "political economy of passion" that drives the global circulation of tango's close embrace respectively—that intimacy flows through systems of power and both provokes and responds to the full force of narrative; intimacies can

---

[37] Philip V. Bohlman and Goffredo Plastino, introduction to *Jazz Worlds/World Jazz* (Chicago: University of Chicago Press, 2016), 1.
[38] Bohlman and Plastino, *Jazz Worlds/World Jazz*, 1.

be bought and sold.[39] As cultural historian Eric Lott establishes regarding the "love and theft" of American blackface minstrelsy and as does critical theorist Homi Bhabha in his theorization of colonial mimicry more broadly, intimacies often form not despite but through systems of dominance, cultural misreadings, and deliberate disavowals.[40] Jazz music, its history, and its historiography are structured both by these intimacies and by the anxieties and disavowals they have repeatedly provoked. As I argue throughout this book, the specter of dance, whether in its coequal presence or its loudly performed absence, is central to the terms of encounter that forge and re-forge jazz's constitutive intimacies.

Musicologists have, however, long operated in an intellectual climate that includes both a deep discomfort with intimacy and a hypervigilant skepticism toward pleasure. In her discussion of musicality's proximity to sexuality as an area of intimate contact with formative potential for one's identity, Suzanne Cusick offers a series of rhetorical questions that suggest how the choreography of Western concert listening offers us an all-too-comfortable out from dealing explicitly with the proximal circulations of both sex and music within the "power/pleasure/intimacy triad":

> if [sex] is then *only* (only!) a means of negotiating power and intimacy through the circulation of pleasure, what's to prevent music from *being* sex, and thus an ancient, half-sanctioned form of escape from the constraints of the phallic economy?
>
> Is that why we have so many intellectual barriers in place to prevent thinking about music as *like* sex, or as having the capacity to *represent* sexuality and gender? Is that why, in the Euro-American traditions anyway, we have such a history of anxiety about music's power "to ravish"?
>
> Are all musicians sexual deviants, in that we *all* negotiate in the power/pleasure/intimacy triad in ways that are outside the phallic economy of compulsory/genital/reproductive sexuality?
>
> [. . .] If music IS sex, what on earth is going on in a concert hall during, say, a piano recital? When the pianist is on a raised stage, in a spotlight while we are in the dark . . . are we observers of a sexual act? Are we its object? Why, exactly, are we in the dark?

---

[39] Sherrie Tucker, *Dance Floor Democracy: The Social Geography of Memory at the Hollywood Canteen* (Durham, NC: Duke University Press, 2014); Marta Savigliano, *Tango and the Political Economy of Passion* (New York: Westview Press, 1995).

[40] Eric Lott, *Love and Theft: Blackface Minstrelsy and the American Working Class* (New York: Oxford University Press, 1993); Homi Bhabha, "Of Mimicry and Man: The Ambivalence of Colonial Discourse," *October* 28 (Spring 1984): 125–133.

> Does the . . . kinkiness of these questions account for the extremely rigid social
> codes surrounding concert decorum for all concerned?[41]

The concert hall's choreographed stillness and the stage-focused lighting design supporting it aid us in performatively erasing our own bodies from the space, fueling what musicologist Susan Cook has called "enculturated somatophobia": a tool that simultaneously alleviates momentarily and reinforces structurally our collective sense of discomfort both with our own bodies and with proximity to the bodies of others.[42]

When I use terms such as "our," "collective discomfort," and "bodies of others," it is important that I not only acknowledge but also center the unvoiced presence of race and racism in Western concert culture, including its choreographies of listening. In his powerful essay, "Black Concert Trauma: Why Blacks Don't Go to Orchestra Concerts," conductor Brandon Keith Brown explicates the gauntlet of microaggressions Black concertgoers endure:

> The concert hall should be as reparative, open for all to obtain spiritual suste-
> nance. Instead, it's a shored-up sonic refuge of whiteness. Concert halls are space
> for white classists to be seen, not hear and feel. My darkness breaches its white-
> ness. . . . After a lifetime of social-distancing from Blacks, white audiences unleash
> a torrent of anxiety on us in concert halls, lashing out in an all-night rondo form of
> microaggressions whose main theme is you don't belong.[43]

Brown's observations here highlight the vastly disparate pressures placed upon different bodies within the same space as two distinct choreographies are imposed simultaneously. These choreographies, however, look largely the same to those of us with the privilege not to know in our own bodies the critical difference between self-erasure for comfort and self-erasure for survival.[44]

Even as it consistently centers Black musicians, the field of jazz studies is often no better than the Euro-American concert hall in its treatment of Black

---

[41] Suzanne Cusick, "On a Lesbian Relationship with Music: A Serious Effort Not to Think Straight," in *Queering the Pitch: The New Gay and Lesbian Musicology*, eds. Philip Brett, Elizabeth Wood, and Gary C. Thomas (New York: Routledge, 1994), 79.

[42] Susan Cook, quoted in Brenda Dixon Gottschild, *The Black Dancing Body: A Geography from Coon to Cool* (New York: Palgrave Macmillan, 2003), 44.

[43] Brandon Keith Brown, "Black Concert Trauma: Why Blacks Don't Go to Orchestra Concerts," https://medium.com/all-the-black-dots/black-concert-trauma-5fa0459e5b3, accessed February 9, 2020

[44] I am white and also Jewish, and because of the latter I experienced this difference for only one brief moment in my life. I detail this experience in "Forbidden Movements, Degenerate Bodies: Black Social Dance and Jewish Resistance," in *The Oxford Handbook of Jewishness and Dance*, eds. Naomi Jackson, Rebecca Pappa, and Toni Shapiro-Phim (New York: Oxford University Press, forthcoming in 2021).

audiences. In his work on smooth jazz, musicologist Charles Carson argues that white scholars are often quick to either ignore Black audiences entirely or to treat them as monolithic and wedge them into our own pre-chosen narratives.[45] Inspired by Carson's critique, in this book I have sought to avoid conscripting Black voices to serve a single, pro-dance narrative, as many Black jazz musicians, audience members, critics, and scholars have regarded jazz music's move away from social and popular dance as a positive development. It is important to take these perspectives seriously and to highlight the nuances with which Black musicians, dancers, and audiences have long navigated discursive spaces that seek to erase them as active participants even as their art and culture are celebrated.

This tendency toward Black cultural and community erasure in white-authored works about Black music—and indeed this book is such a work—was highlighted and analyzed in the early 1960s by critic and poet LeRoi Jones (later known as Amiri Baraka) in his essay "Jazz and the White Critic." In this essay, Baraka proposes that whether of a sociological or musicological bent, the fundamental problem he introduces at the outset—that "most jazz critics have been white Americans, but most great jazz musicians have not been"—has led to a series of cultural misreadings through which white critics have consistently misunderstood both the "what" and the "why" of jazz.[46] His essay also offers a historiographic analysis of this predicament, arguing that Black people capable of accessing the literary arenas in which jazz criticism took place were likely uninterested in or actively opposed to jazz music because of their own Black middle-class values, whereas the opposite was true for white critics. As he explains:

> Most jazz critics began as hobbyists or boyishly brash members of the American petit bourgeoisie, whose only claim to any understanding about the music was that they knew it was *different*, or else they had once been brave enough to make a trip into a Negro slum to hear their favorite instrumentalist defame Western musical tradition. Most jazz critics were (and are) not only white middle-class Americans, but middle-brows as well. The irony here is that because the majority of jazz critics are white middle-brows, most jazz criticism tends to enforce white middle-brow standards of excellence as criteria for performance of a music that in its most

[45] Charles D. Carson, "'Bridging the Gap': Creed Taylor, Grover Washington, Jr., and the Crossover Roots of Smooth Jazz," *Black Music Research Journal* 28, no. 1 (Spring 2008): 1–15.

[46] Leroi Jones [Amiri Baraka], "Jazz and the White Critic," *Downbeat*, August 15, 1963, 16–17, 34; reprinted in *Keeping Time: Readings in Jazz History*, ed. Robert Walser (New York: Oxford University Press, 1999), 255–261.

profound manifestations is completely antithetical to such standards; in fact, quite often is in direct reaction against them.[47]

Baraka also critiques what he sees as jazz's growing institutional turn toward respectability as a form of "high art" as advocates in the 1950s and 1960s sought to frame the music in terms legible to Anglo-European aesthetic systems (a discursive turn discussed in depth in chapter 5 of this book). He lamented a growing domination by Western art and concert culture that he saw as highly destructive to jazz music's crucial role as a form of Black expression:

> It has never ceased to amaze and infuriate me that in the 40s a European critic could be arrogant and unthinking enough to inform serious young American musicians that what they were feeling (a consideration that exists before, and without, the music) was false. What had happened was that even though the white middle-brow critic had known about Negro music for only about three decades, he was already trying to formalize and finally institutionalize it. It is a hideous idea. The music was already in danger of being forced into that junk pile of admirable objects and data the West knows as *culture*.[48]

Baraka's words indeed proved prophetic. As musicologist Maya Gibson has observed in her thorough historiographic analysis of singer Billie Holiday's treatment in jazz discourse, "The mainstreaming and respectability of jazz has demanded a reconfiguration of its major players into heroic figures."[49] Increasingly, as Baraka both observed and predicted, Black jazz musicians were discursively canonized to serve as heroic totems—"admirable objects"—within narratives crafted to serve the discursive norms of predominantly white institutional spaces.

Baraka's concerns, specifically regarding the discursive processes that might consign jazz and its history to this gilded institutional "junk pile," are explored further in Scott DeVeaux's landmark 1991 article "Constructing the Jazz Tradition."[50] This essay catalyzed the subfield of jazz historiography to the

---

[47] Jones, "Jazz and the White Critic," 258.

[48] Jones, "Jazz and the White Critic," 260.

[49] Maya Gibson, "Alternate Takes: Billie Holiday at the Intersection of Black Cultural Studies and Historical Musicology" (PhD diss., University of Wisconsin-Madison, 2008), 4. While this quote from Gibson does effectively connect Baraka's concerns about institutionalization with the rise of canonizing "hero" narratives, my usage of it does, admittedly, oversimplify her broader position somewhat. Indeed, while Gibson does highlight a disconnect between traditions in jazz narrative formation that stem from a predominantly white field of historical musicologists and a predominantly Black field of scholars in Black cultural studies, she explicitly claims that neither group is exclusively responsible for uncritically heroic framings of Holiday.

[50] Scott DeVeaux, "Constructing the Jazz Tradition: Jazz Historiography," *Black American Literature Forum* 25, no. 3 (Literature of Jazz Issue, Autumn 1991): 525–560. My jump straight from Baraka to

point where historiographic critique rapidly became jazz studies' central conversation; it has, in many ways, remained so ever since. We are still wrestling with the issues DeVeaux raises regarding the narrative structures that shape jazz music's canon and that continue to make the music legible within academic music conservatories and other institutions whose infrastructures were built specifically to support and validate Western classical music. Throughout the 1990s and early 2000s, a series of important essays and edited collections brought more interdisciplinary perspectives to bear on this conversation as scholars interrogated not only the narrative conceits of the jazz tradition but also those tropes' relationships to the subject positions of jazz scholars past and present, as well as to which styles and groups of people dominant narratives continued to exclude.[51]

The centrality of this historiographic focus has come under scrutiny, and one notable critique comes from Sherrie Tucker, whose 2012 essay "Deconstructing the Jazz Tradition" both responds to DeVeaux's work and contextualizes jazz studies' historiographic turn within a broader movement in the humanities, influenced by post-structuralist thinkers such as Jacques Derrida, toward the critical deconstruction of narrative. Tucker suggests that jazz studies' emphasis on deconstructing narratives is itself underwritten by shifting institutional trends that support the careers of scholars working to make jazz studies a "subjectless subject."[52] While Tucker does not position this deconstructive focus as necessarily or entirely a bad thing, she does ask that we consider not only how we might tear existing narratives down, but also what new kinds of stories we might seek to tell: "we had the jazz tradition as

DeVeaux also admittedly paves over much important ground, and I do not wish in highlighting the reality of the catalytic impact of DeVeaux's essay to further marginalize Black voices or scholars. For a more thorough and nuanced assessment of the complex discursive field of Black music scholarship, a more thorough analysis of Baraka's essay and it's impact, and a needed call to action regarding the marginalization of Black voices in academic discourse, see Guthrie P. Ramsey Jr., "Who Hears Here? Black Music, Critical Bias, and the Musicological Skin Trade," *Musical Quarterly* 85, no. 1 (Spring 2001): 1–52.

[51] John Gennari, "Jazz Criticism: Its Development and Ideologies," *Black American Literature Forum* 25, no. 3 (Literature of Jazz Issue, Autumn 1991): 449–523; Monson, "The Problem of White Hipness"; Krin Gabbard, ed., *Jazz among the Discourses* (Durham, NC: Duke University Press, 1995); Krin Gabbard, ed., *Representing Jazz* (Durham, NC: Duke University Press, 1995); Robert G. O'Meally, ed., *The Jazz Cadence of American Culture* (New York: Columbia University Press, 1998); Robert G. O'Meally, Brent Hayes Edwards, and Farah Jasmine Griffin, eds., *Uptown Conversation: The New Jazz Studies* (New York: Columbia University Press, 2004); Nicole Rustin and Sherrie Tucker, eds., *Big Ears: Listening for Gender in Jazz Studies* (Durham, NC: Duke University Press, 2008); David Ake, Charles Hiroshi Garrett, and Daniel Goldmark, eds., *Jazz/Not Jazz: The Music and Its Boundaries* (Berkeley: University of California Press, 2012).

[52] Sherrie Tucker, "Deconstructing the Jazz Tradition: The 'Subjectless Subject' of New Jazz Studies," in *Jazz/Not Jazz: The Music and Its Boundaries*, eds. David Ake, Charles Hiroshi Garrett, and Daniel Ira Goldmark (Berkeley: University of California Press, 2012), 211. Tucker borrows the concept of a "Subjectless Subject" from Ann Cacoullos's discussion of the fields of American Studies and Women's Studies. Ann Cacoullos, "Feminist Ruptures in Women's Studies and American Studies," *American Studies International* 38, no. 3 (October 2000): 97.

a canon. Now we have it as an outmoded idea to repudiate. What shall we do for an encore?"[53] While calling it "an outmoded idea" may reflect the situation within certain sectors of academia at present, the jazz tradition remains a powerful narrative force driving public discourse in program and liner notes, museums exhibits, websites, magazines, introductory university courses, university jazz performance programs, and chatter from the stage between songs, to name just a few of the many venues in which the "jazz tradition" narrative is very palpably alive and thriving. I would thus say that jazz historiographers are not so much beating a dead horse (which, to be fair, is not what Tucker is saying either) as we are lightly grazing a stunningly robust thoroughbred that is more perplexed than hurt by our blows if it feels them at all. Indeed, that the new jazz studies' "wins" in the arena of scholarship have translated to so little change in any other area of jazz practice or discourse is itself a fascinating circumstance that demonstrates why the jazz tradition narrative itself remains an important object of study.

I maintain that there is much work to be done in the realm of jazz historiography, and I do think that historiography still has an important place in what, to begin answering Tucker's question, our encore as jazz scholars might look like. In her book *Charles Ives Reconsidered*, musicologist Gayle Sherwood Magee asks what opportunities exist for scholars of Ives and his music following a period of inarguable success in advocating for the composer's importance during which scholars, Magee argues, became deeply entrained in an advocacy mindset. Having largely won the battle for Ives's inclusion in the Western classical canon, Magee suggests that Ives scholarship can now explore a range of critical possibilities to be found "beyond advocacy."[54] I think that jazz historiography is at a similar point: at least in the world of academia, we've "won" the argument that jazz should not be framed principally as a contiguous lineage of geniuses, and there may thus be new possibilities available to us as we interrogate the robust staying power of the jazz tradition as well as the processes through which it was built over time and continues to do its work in a broad range of discursive arenas. For example, in my initial conceptions of this project, dance was an uncritical protagonist and Western concert culture a clear antagonist. I hope the Atlanta case study with which I opened this chapter, however, serves as a model of what framings may be possible as I seek to understand with a critical yet sympathetic eye the positive work that adaptation to a new choreography of listening offered some Black

---

[53] Tucker, "Deconstructing the Jazz Tradition," 210.

[54] Gayle Sherwood Magee, *Charles Ives Reconsidered* (Urbana: University of Illinois Press, 2008), 163–180.

audience members. What might a jazz historiography not actively focused on defeating "the jazz tradition" but rather on understanding its enduring appeal as well as its seemingly never-ending contours and nuances look like?

While historiography is perhaps not the central driving concern in dance studies that it is in jazz music studies (which is far from an indictment of that field!), there are numerous exemplary and highly innovative historiographic approaches that display dance studies scholars' tremendous facility with generating innovative approaches to discourse analysis grounded in theories of embodiment and motion. Foster's 1995 essay "Choreographing History," for example, itself treats the act of doing history as an embodied practice: a dance between the historian's body and the documentary archives left by bodies of the past:

> This historian's body wants to consort with dead bodies, wants to know from them: what must it have felt like to move among those things, in those patterns, desiring those proficiencies, being beheld from those vantage points? Moving or being moved by those other bodies? A historian's body wants to inhabit these vanished bodies for specific reasons. It wants to know where it stands, how it came to stand there, what its options for moving might be. It wants those dead bodies to lend a hand in deciphering its own present predicaments and in staging some future possibilities.
>
> To that end historians' bodies amble down the corridors of documentation, inclining toward certain discursive domains and veering away from others. Yes, the production of history is a physical endeavor. It requires a high tolerance for sitting and for reading, for moving slowly and quietly among other bodies who likewise sit patiently, staring alternately at the archival evidence and the fantasies it generates. This physical practice cramps fingers, spawns sneezes and squinting.[55]

Foster's words have strong kinship with musicologist Elisabeth Le Guin's explication of the "cello and bow thinking" that drives her practice of "carnal musicology," a formative influence on my own work.[56] Indeed, in reading Foster's prose, I feel both seen and exposed in my sense memories of butt pain and eyestrain from an endless series of seated writing sessions along with flashbacks of motion sickness at the microfilm reader. Even as I critique

[55] Susan Leigh Foster, "Choreographing History," in *Choreographing History*, ed. Susan Leigh Foster (Bloomington: University of Indiana Press, 1995), 7.

[56] Elisabeth Le Guin, *Boccherini's Body: An Essay in Carnal Musicology* (Berkeley: University of California Press, 2006), 14–37. I discuss the impact of Le Guin's work on my own thinking at length in my doctoral dissertation, Christopher J. Wells, "'Go Harlem!': Chick Webb and His Dancing Audience during the Great Depression" (PhD diss., University of North Carolina at Chapel Hill, 2014), 20–28.

it frequently, I understand deep in my bones the desire to entreat musicians, dancers, and scholars past to let me inhabit their sensory experience and feel the contours of its situatedness as well as to help me use that knowledge to sort out both my own sense of self and the broader predicaments we face in the present. I feel fairly embarrassed about all of this and sheepish to speak of it "out loud" in print, but if I'm being honest, these impulses are uncomfortable enough to drive me to erase them from my text just as concert listeners might wish to, in Cusick's sense, erase "the kinkiness of these questions" from the foreground of their listening rituals.

Though it centers the historian's own body and embodied desires in valuable ways, Foster's work does posit a problematic universalism: that historians can achieve the state of a "universal subject" and can thus viscerally understand cultural experiences beyond themselves, the colonialist roots of which dance scholar Fen Kennedy (née Fenella Kennedy) rightly critiques in a close reading of Foster's essay. According to Kennedy, Foster's work is torn between a romantically universalist position of authority and a more radical positioning of the historian's body that would invite if not demand a more inclusive view of what counts as historical scholarship and of who gets to do it. As Kennedy argues in a pointed yet hopeful analysis of Foster's work, "while her writing re-states, and even reinforces the universalist, patriarchal, authoritarian history of the field, it also provides a toolkit for transcending that authority and moving towards an egalitarian discipline that centers the individual body in the production and articulation of cultural knowledge."[57] Kennedy's dissertation itself has much kinship with my own study as they use their training in Labanotation as a springboard for far broader questions regarding how discourse in dance maps the body, not only obscuring certain nuances of movement while documenting others but also erasing whole cultural groups and movement practices. Through critical discourse analysis, Kennedy documents how the construct of "modern dance" assumes its current form in part by stripping Black social dances of their relationship with this term and discursively erasing many otherwise obvious Black influences from the predominantly white framing of American modern dance and its canon. They also show how this process informs and is inflected by dance studies' own pathway to legibility as an academic discipline. As such, their work has clear resonances with jazz music's history on multiple levels and has had a tremendous impact on my project.[58]

---

[57] Fenella Kennedy, "Movement Writes: Four Case Studies in Dance, Discourse, and Shifting Boundaries" (PhD diss., Ohio State University, 2019). This quote is from page 188, and their broader close reading of Foster spans pages 179–189.

[58] Kennedy, "Movement Writes."

Kennedy critiques Foster's self-positioning as an originary source of ideas generated from a broader dance and dance studies community, and their own work follows a lineage of dance scholars (a lineage they readily acknowledge) who have highlighted how discursive erasures have shaped racialized conceptual categories such as "Black dance." Susan Manning's *Modern Dance, Negro Dance* shows how Black choreographers were routed away from "modern dance" as a category, and Thomas F. DeFrantz—in the landmark collection of essays *Dancing Many Drums*—chronicles a discursive history of genre and categorization as he draws us into the vexing complexity of how to approach naming a field of subjects "complicated by critics who variously refer to the broad spectrum of expressive idioms practiced by black artists as 'African American dance' or the equally amorphous 'black dance,'" a historiographic interrogation in which DeFrantz also reflexively interrogates the slippages in his own deployment of terminology in reaction to different contexts and audiences.[59]

As DeFrantz centers his own positionality as a Black scholar and the "slippage" between terminologies as part of his historiographic essay, so too do other Black scholars in both music and dance studies source the epistemes that guide their work from their own experiences and cultures. Operating in musicology and in jazz studies, Guthrie P. Ramsey Jr. riffs on Samuel Floyd's formative work and his own upbringing and family life in Chicago to parse both the distinctions and the concordances between history and cultural memory as ways of knowing. For Ramsey, "the meaning of music lies somewhere in the mix and jumble of the past: in the nexus of biases, quirks, and individual rhythms of memory and the material evidence of history."[60] Drawing from her own experience and practice as a dancer as well as interviews with peers and elders, dance scholar Brenda Dixon Gottschild in many ways parallels Ramsey's approach in her book *The Black Dancing Body*. Grounding memory in embodied knowledge, Gottschild emphasizes "blood memories" to index the corporeality of intergenerational ways of knowing as she looks to geography rather than history for a lens through which to organize her multifaceted discussion of nomenclature, aesthetics, practices, and legacies in Black dance.[61]

[59] Susan Manning, *Modern Dance, Negro Dance: Race in Motion* (Minneapolis: University of Minnesota Press, 2006); Thomas F. DeFrantz, "African American Dance: A Complex History," in *Dancing Many Drums: Excavations in African American Dance*, ed. Thomas F. DeFrantz (Madison: University of Wisconsin Press, 2001), 3–5.

[60] Guthrie P. Ramsey Jr., *Race Music: Black Cultures from Bebop to Hip-Hop* (Berkeley: University of California Press, 2003), 27.

[61] Gottschild, *The Black Dancing Body*.

The resonances between Ramsey's and Gottschild's work underscores the closer conversations between jazz studies and dance studies that I hope this book can help to catalyze. In seeking to foster more substantive dialogue between these fields, my work elaborates and extends the project undertaken by Sherrie Tucker in her book *Dance Floor Democracy*. In this work, Tucker's use of "torque" turns to the leverage-tension-based partnering mechanics of the lindy hop and related social jazz dances as a generative source for theory regarding the practice of oral history, the politics of nostalgia, and the relationship between cultural memory and historiography, all central topics in so-called new jazz studies discourse.[62] Numerous jazz scholars acknowledge the need for a turn toward the body and embodiment in studying jazz, yet our (inter)disciplinary connection with dance studies—long a critical site of innovative theorization of bodies and embodiment—remains relatively threadbare. I believe this disconnect is both a conscious and an unconscious result of the fraught historical relationship between notions of "jazz" and notions of "dance music" that this book highlights and seeks to address. As such, readers may find this book less a balanced dialogue between fields and more an application of methods and ideas from dance scholars in service of historiographic questions of more central concern to jazz music scholars. When I expressed anxiety over this unidirectional flow, my editor quipped, "the faucet has long been flowing the other way."

Dance studies scholars have long been expected to know and to adopt musicological developments to a far greater extent than most musicologists, and jazz studies scholars more broadly, have felt any need to engage meaningfully with research arising from the study of dance. I do strongly hope and genuinely believe that this book has much to offer those in the field of dance studies, but I am entirely certain that dance studies has built tools that should become instrumental to the practice of jazz studies. As such, while dance-as-topic is of obvious and central importance to this book, so too is dance studies-as-field both to my own thinking and practice in researching and writing it as well as to the role I hope this text will serve in sparking further engagement among jazz music scholars, and music scholars more broadly, with dance scholars and with dance studies as a discourse. I hope we will come to see fluid collaboration between scholars of music and dance, as well as practitioners in these fields (and often they're the same people!) as invaluable and central to the interdisciplinary work of jazz studies.

---

[62] Tucker, *Dance Floor Democracy*, 11–22.

## An Exercise in Reflexive Flexing (About the Author, Extended Edition)

While I have endeavored to write this book as a project "beyond advocacy" in Sherwood-Magee's sense, as one of my book proposal's anonymous reviewers noted, there is "an intriguing tension at the center of this book," between my critique of certain discursive romanticizations and my reproduction of them as I advocate for some kind of conciliation between jazz music and the dance practices long associated with it (before they became, in many instances, actively disassociated). I do, to some extent, embrace this tension as a constitutive, even fundamental, element of the torque—the productive tension generated through counterbalance—that both holds this book's structure and propels its motion. Nevertheless, I am also very aware of the proximity of my own passions and my subject position to those of my intellectual forebears: the generations of predominantly white interlocutors whose work I critique at several points in this text. While I have mustered every bit of my entrained critical reflexivity to recognize the pull of harmful romantic and nostalgic tropes upon my thoughts and words, I suspect there remain areas where they do creep into the text itself or, perhaps more perniciously, influence the thought process underwriting my prose in more subtle ways. I hope that, if nothing else, the critical discourse analysis I model throughout the book arms readers with a set of tools to help recognize these tendencies in my own writing, even and especially in those places where I fail to recognize them myself. Nevertheless, to help arm readers appropriately, I should probably let you all know who I am and how I came to this work.[63]

The beginnings of my formal education in music and my engagement with social jazz dancing were coterminous. The spring semester of my freshman year at Guilford College in Greensboro, North Carolina, I was persuaded to join the opera scenes program and to enroll in classical voice lessons. This was also the time I began taking weekly lindy hop lessons from my fellow students who ran the campus social dance club; voice lessons and dance lessons became the highlights of my week. In March 2003, when I'd been dancing for

---

[63] I reflect critically and vulnerably on my own subject position here also to answer Guthrie P. Ramsey Jr.'s call for white scholars of to reflect upon and theorize our own subjectivities vis-à-vis Black music "with the same enthusiasm that has made the intersecting of gender, race, and class at the corner of blackness and the academy such a busy intersection indeed." Ramsey invites and encourages white scholars to take an active role in the work of crafting "accounts that, while acknowledging white privilege, move into theorizing other areas of white lived experience that will shed light on the complex reception histories of black music." I seek to answer Ramsey's call both through this discussion of my own subject position and its complexities and through my historiographic analysis of other white scholars—most notably Mura Dehn and Marshall Stearns—throughout this book. Ramsey, "Who Hears Here?," 34, 40.

two months, Frankie Manning came to Greensboro to give a series of lindy hop workshops. Manning, then eighty-eight years old, was a pioneering lindy hop dancer at the Savoy Ballroom during the 1930s and 1940s who took up teaching the dance again during the 1980s and toured globally as a much beloved dance instructor until his death shortly before his ninety-fifth birthday. Manning's Greensboro workshop inspired me to continue pursuing the lindy hop, and when I returned home to my native New York City that summer, I took thirteen hours of swing dancing classes weekly and attended social dances every chance I got. Over the next several years, I worked tirelessly on my dancing and taught regularly in Greensboro while spending my summers overseas in Sweden at the Herräng Dance Camp, an international jazz dance festival where Manning was a regular instructor.[64] I was introduced to jazz music history through jazz dance history and specifically through Manning's recollections of his own experiences dancing at the Savoy Ballroom and touring with the professional troupe Whitey's Lindy Hoppers. My first exposures to academic jazz history coursework, both in college and grad school, were perplexing and frustrating as I found that the Swing Era heroes who formed a canon in my dance community were cast as peripheral figures if discussed at all, and jazz's movement away from its role as dance music was framed as a positive signifier of the music's progress as an art form. In many ways, this book results from the years I've spent seeking to make sense of and reconcile the tension between the two spaces—one dance-centering and one dance-averse—in which I have come to understand and appreciate jazz music.

Having come to musicology and to jazz studies as a dancer, I've long viewed acting as a sort of translator between dancers and musicians as one of the ways I can best contribute to these fields. As in many fields of musicological study, jazz studies scholars, and especially those whose academic credentials come from music schools and departments, tend to come to this work from backgrounds as practicing musicians; by contrast, I approach jazz scholarship from the dance floor rather than the stage. Early on in my work as a jazz scholar, my goal was to act as an advocate for swing music and specifically for the importance of dance to the genre. My PhD dissertation on Chick Webb, drummer and house bandleader at the Savoy Ballroom, grew out of this desire as I sought to explore his music and career from the perspective of a dancing audience member. As I pursued this work, however, I also came to understand that my project would be neither accurate nor ethical without a

---

[64] I discuss Herräng Dance Camp and my experiences there in Christopher J. Wells, "Swinging Out in Sweden: African-American Vernacular Dance's Global Revival and Its Scandinavian Roots," in *SDHS 2013 Proceedings: 35th Annual Conference–Dance ACTions*, Society of Dance History Scholars, 2013, 391–398.

deep investment in the field of African American studies and in meaningfully exploring not just swing music but all of jazz history within the broader dynamic flows of Black expressive culture as it lives, breathes, and thrives in both negotiation with and opposition to white supremacist power structures.

Since taking my current job at a school of music with numerous robust programs in music performance, including both jazz studies and a brand-new performance-focused program in popular music, I have grown ever more fascinated with the institutionally negotiated narrative framings that alternately open or foreclose opportunities for inclusion in the arts education infrastructure of academic institutions. This work feels increasingly urgent as I see uncanny similarities between jazz music's institutional acceptance and the institutional trajectories of hip hop: both entered academia as objects of study for humanists and social scientists across several disciplines followed by adoption as a performance discipline in music schools, both have garnered millions of dollars in State Department funding for their utility in serving US cultural diplomacy goals, and both now have canonizing anthologies produced by the Smithsonian Institution. As hip hop and other multi-disciplinary, dance-inclusive arts practices navigate ever-shifting institutional conditions of possibility, the importance of chronicling and interrogating jazz music and jazz dance's points of confluence and severance becomes all the more immediate in the constructive lessons and cautionary tales this history offers.

In addition to these pressing concerns in my professional life, my interest (my constant preoccupation even) with the role of institutions and discourses in shaping our available corporeal modes of being—which bodies, and in which states those bodies, are included or excluded—is also highly personal. After years of wrestling with something, I didn't quite know (wouldn't quite *let* myself know) what, it finally became clear to me in the spring of 2018 that living my life as a man had never felt right and was no longer tenable. I have since transitioned to a non-binary, trans-feminine identity (I go by the more feminine nickname "Christi Jay" rather than "Christopher J." and my pronouns are they/them/theirs). In addition, recent conversations with childhood friends have resulted in further revelations about my childhood environment, particularly regarding a number of leftist male intellectuals who used the status and trust their performatively radical politics afforded them to either abuse or license the abuse of numerous women and children. While I once thought my particular historiographic fascination with the damage caused by ostensibly well-meaning leftist white men was a cautionary letter to myself (and in many ways it still is), I now have more clarity that these impulses are likely deeply ingrained tools of survival, tools that afford me a sense of kinship with both the perpetrators and the victims of the rhetorical and institutional violence I regularly encounter in my research.

## Units of Action: Organization of the Work

This book's title—*Between Beats: The Jazz Tradition and Black Vernacular Dance*—offers a road map of the book's goals and alludes to the logic of its organizational design. "The jazz tradition" aligns both my object of study and my critical historiographic toolbox with DeVeaux's work and with the myriad ways it has influenced my own scholarly contributions and the field of jazz studies more broadly. The term is also used by Black studies scholar Eric Porter to identify a formation with which jazz musicians themselves have had to wrestle during time periods predating DeVeaux's 1991 essay. Even for the numerous musicians who have expressed public and/or private ambivalence toward the term "jazz," it still "denotes a particular process by which music and musicians have been discursively and economically positioned."[65] Porter explains:

> As the discourse about the music evolved in different social contexts and around new ways of playing jazz, musicians found themselves and their music celebrated and disparaged in changing ways. Musicians who chose to express their ideas in public would come to terms with the idea of the "jazz tradition" and its formal and ideological components.[66]

In keeping with Porter's analysis, this book names "the jazz tradition" as its object of study, in part to reflect that "jazz music" is an unstable, ever-changing conceptual category guided as much by shifts in discourse, in power relations, and in mass market forces as it is by developments in musical sound or in approaches to music-making.

Notably, however, my title does not use the term "jazz dance" to denote the dance practices and forms principally under discussion throughout the book, as that term has in many ways ceased to index the social and popular dance

---

[65] Eric Porter, *What Is This Thing Called Jazz?: African American Musicians as Artists, Critics, and Activists* (Berkeley: University of California Press, 2002), xxi. "The Jazz Tradition" is also the title of a prominent book by jazz critic Martin Williams, whose explicit project of canonizing great jazz artists helped build the narratives many jazz scholars now seek to deconstruct. Martin Williams, *The Jazz Tradition* (New York: Oxford University Press, 1970). Another important book that deconstructs this canonic framework's emphasis on individual jazz heroes is Tony Whyton's *Jazz Icons: Heroes, Myths and the Jazz Tradition* (Cambridge: Cambridge University Press, 2010).
[66] Porter, *What Is This Thing Called Jazz?*, 53.

practices of Black communities. DeFrantz explains that while "jazz dance" used to be coterminous with "black vernacular social dances," it has gradually shed that association as Black popular dance forms have developed in association principally with Black popular music genres disarticulated from the formation "jazz." As DeFrantz explains the term's contemporary usage, "by now, jazz dance doesn't imply contemporary black social dance movements at all. Instead, it implies a codified movement form based on the extrapolations of (mostly white male) American choreographers and teachers."[67] Dance educator Patricia Cohen frames contemporary jazz dance practices specifically in terms of their growing disconnection both from any collaborative relationship with musicians and from the African American communication practices and socialities that formerly shaped jazz dance's development.

> Most of today's self-identified jazz dance classes have lost the sense of community and challenge, vocalization, call-and-response, "aesthetic of the cool," and improvisation. Using live music has become increasingly rare, eliminating the dancer-musician dialogue. The resulting contemporary or theatrical jazz dance blends some of the kinetic elements of vernacular jazz with the influences of ballet and modern dance, while eschewing most of the social elements.[68]

Both Cohen and DeFrantz point to "jazz dance" as an increasingly amorphous identifier, DeFrantz claiming that "an open secret about jazz dance today is that there is no discrete jazz dance technique . . . teachers create their own system of jazz dance, usually determined by their own individual movement preferences and taste in music."[69] Cohen, though she promotes and defends the form, still acknowledges to some extent this amorphousness and the anxiety it provokes among jazz dancers and jazz dance teachers, offering that "we will continue to ask, Where's the jazz?"[70]

Among many possible formulations, I frame my subject in this book as "Black vernacular dance." "Black" identifies the forms of dance on which I focus here as an assemblage of movement practices created and practiced principally by African Americans, and the term "vernacular" denotes my specific focus on social and popular dance. My usage of the term "Black vernacular dance" also follows the work of dance scholars Jacqui Malone and Jayna

---

[67] Thomas F. DeFrantz, *Dancing Revelations: Alvin Ailey's Embodiment of African American Culture* (New York: Oxford University Press, 2006), 102.

[68] Patricia Cohen, "Jazz Dance as Continuum," in *Jazz Dance: A History of the Roots and Branches*, eds. Lindsay Guarino and Wendy Oliver (Gainesville: University Press of Florida, 2014), 6–7.

[69] DeFrantz, *Dancing Revelations*, 103.

[70] Cohen, "Jazz Dance as Continuum," 7.

Brown, who identify Black vernacular dance as the object of study in their works *Steppin' on the Blues* and *Babylon Girls* respectively. Both scholars use the term to center African American and African diasporic cultural norms and to resist what each perceives as dance studies' central focus on con- cert and theatrical dance to the exclusion of folk, popular, and social dance practices.[71] For Malone, vernacular dance is intimately connected with music, as she writes that "the evolution of these dances paralleled, influenced, and was influenced by the growth of black American music, especially jazz."[72] Malone situates vernacular dance as, fundamentally, an embodiment of mu- sical rhythm "that makes those rhythms visible," and that "derives not from 'the academy' but from the farms and plantations of the South, slave festivals of the North, levees, urban streets, dance halls, theaters, and cabarets. It is constantly changing. The changes, however, always reflect an evolving tradi- tion and a vital process of cultural production."[73] Following Malone, Brown employs the term Black vernacular dance to focus her work on "black pop- ular and social dances," or more specifically on "the most profane of black dance forms—those dances developed between the street, the club, and the popular stage."[74] My work's focus Black vernacular dance's potential to force a reconsideration of jazz historical tropes is very much aligned with Brown's claim that "black popular and social dances . . . resist containment but hold history."[75] In labeling this book's area of dance focus "vernacular," I also ac- knowledge my debt to and lineage from jazz historian Marshall Stearns even as I critique both his work and his deployment of the term "vernacular" at length in this book's fifth chapter. Finally, "between beats" is a term I borrow from a jazz dance historian whose work was formative to my thinking and highly influential within the swing dance community in which my interest in this subject was formed: the modern dancer, choreographer, and folklorist Mura Dehn. In describing jazz dance, Dehn once wrote that jazz was danced "between the beats," highlighting the "rhythmic counterpoint" and depth of intentional play dancers bring to jazz music even in those moments where someone not hip to their movement practices might think them "off" from the band.[76] Jazz musicians often use the term "in the pocket," to denote the

[71] Brown uses "Black vernacular dance" nearly exclusively while Malone uses "Black vernacular dance" and "African American vernacular dance" interchangeably, though she does use "African American ver- nacular dance" more frequently, including for her title.
[72] Jacqui Malone, *Steppin' on the Blues: The Visible Rhythms of African American Dance* (Urbana: University of Illinois Press, 1996), 1.
[73] Malone, *Steppin' on the Blues*, 2.
[74] Brown, *Babylon Girls*, 13, 16.
[75] Brown, *Babylon Girls*, 15.
[76] Mura Dehn, "The Bebop Era," unpublished typescript, Mura Dehn Papers on Afro-American Social Dance Box 1 Folder 1, 2. Jerome Robbins Dance Division, The New York Public Library for the Performing Arts.

expressive micro-timing through which musicians lag slightly behind an implied tactus, which places them "between the beats" in a way that is both barely perceptible and, from a dancer's perspective, the difference between a band that grooves and a band that doesn't.

"Between beats," as a guiding structure that shapes the book's organization and scope, is also a playful bit of riffing on Stanslaviskian acting methods. For the Russian actor/director Konstantin Stanislavsky, "beats" are "units of action" into which a text may be divided and explored, each centering a critical dramatic turn that builds the world and shapes the story. In the sense that we can conceive the jazz tradition's most robustly troped "great moments" as a series of dramatic "beats" that form a narrative, the dance-focused case studies that form this book push my historiographic footfalls between those beats, offering a new relationship to jazz's canonic time-spaces that is "a little bit off" but also critical to the specific groove I'm looking to craft, infusing the jazz tradition with discursive participatory discrepancies that invite us to dig into the corporeal heart of the matter.[77] Structurally, this book offers a series of dance-focused case studies, each corresponding to a specific narrative "beat" of the jazz tradition in a manner that asks us to question the foundational assumptions upon which that narrative move rests; I might also describe this approach as a subversive "shot-for-shot" remake of a typical jazz historical narrative. Many of my colleagues do important work expanding jazz studies' lens beyond this narrow canonic scope. Where they agitate from the margins, I support on another flank as I seek here—with dance practice and dance studies as my co-agitators—to provoke from the center.

The chapters that follow thus interrogate the choreographies of listening that shape the ever-shifting relationships between jazz music and Black vernacular dance at five of the jazz tradition's most pivotal narrative beats: the music's ostensible birth in the "cradle" of nineteenth- and early twentieth-century New Orleans; jazz's brief emergence as America's central popular music genre during the "Swing Era"; the "bebop moment" where jazz supposedly moves away from social dance and toward a future as serious modern art; jazz music's "institutional turn" toward festivals and universities and other sources of high art patronage; and finally a hopeful if uncertain and incomplete snapshot of what's been happening recently. Chapter 2 seeks to explore the quadroon balls of nineteenth-century New Orleans as a critical generative

---

[77] My use of the term "participatory discrepancies" riffs on Charles Keil's famous formulation. For Keil, "The power of music is in its participatory discrepancies. . . . Music, to be personally involving and socially valuable, must be 'out of time' and 'out of tune.'" So too, I argue, must our narrative treatments of its history and canons. Charles Keil, "Participatory Discrepancies and the Power of Music," *Cultural Anthropology* 2, no. 3 (August 1987): 275.

source of, and productive metaphor for, the discursive complex of miscegenation fantasies that mark jazz as both seductive enough to excite our sense of subversion and quintessentially American enough to serve as "America's classical music." Chapter 3 digs into the close collaborative relationship between swing-era Harlem's most iconic dance band—the Chick Webb Orchestra—and the Savoy Ballroom's best lindy hop dancers through a fluid process of shared labor that moved across and between the era's emergent social, competition, and performance contexts for partnered vernacular dance. Chapter 4 highlights the midcentury subculture of Black youth in New York City who regarded bebop as a form of popular music and developed innovative social dance practices alongside it to both trouble narrative tropes of bebop's ostensible undanceability and question the function of bebop's anti-dance reputation in its emergent status as a form of "serious art." Chapter 5 interrogates jazz music's conditional acceptance within the institutional patronage systems of festivals, government institutions, and universities by examining the relatively unsuccessful efforts of scholar Marshall Stearns—among jazz music's most effective early institutional advocates—to achieve comparable results for jazz dance. Chapter 6 focuses on my own experiences dancing at the contemporary Brooklyn venue Jazz 966 to foreground issues of intergenerational transfer and neighborhood precarity while also addressing the tremendous burden placed upon any single case study conscripted to serve the narrative function of encapsulating "jazz now."

Notable in recent work across arts and culture scholarship, especially in fields like jazz studies and social and popular dance studies that often focus on the cultural life of minoritized communities, is a move away from framing the expressive practices we study as always arcing toward "resistance."[78] Rather, music, dance, and other modes of artistic and cultural expression are increasingly understood as tools that can serve a broad range of purposes: to include but also to oppress, to heal but also to harm, to inspire but also to foreclose.[79] I thus want to clarify that I don't see dance as some kind of mythic weapon uniquely suited to felling the jazz tradition's narrative conceits in one swoop,

[78] This has been an important subject discussion at a number of recent conferences in musicology and ethnomusicology. A couple notable examples of work in this vein include Chérie Rivers Ndaliko, "Toxic Solidarity: Liberalism and the Corruption of Resistance," Annual Meeting of the Society for Ethnomusicology, Bloomington, Indiana, November 7, 2019; Tamara Levitz, "Breaking the Frame," Annual Meeting of the American Musicological Society, Boston, Massachusetts, November 2, 2019.

[79] As such, I do hope this book exists in respectful and productive dialogue with Christopher Smith's recent book *Dancing Revolution* in which he states "My fundamental premise is that participatory vernacular dance in the United States, especially dance occurring in public or quasi-public contexts, has been a tool for contesting, constructing, and reinventing social orders." Where Smith looks to propose "a historical model of street dance as both consciously interruptive and politically representative," I seek to show that this is indeed often, but critically not always, the case. Christopher J. Smith, *Dancing Revolution: Bodies, Space, and Sound in American Cultural History* (Urbana: University of Illinois Press, 2019), 18–19.

ridding us once and for all of their discursive vise grip. In addition, this book is not meant to offer any chronological series of answers to the question of whether any particular style of jazz definitively *was* or *was not* "dance music" or "danceable" in any objective way at any particular point in time. Such claims, if one finds value in making them (and plainly, I do not), can neither be made in a vacuum nor be based on musical sound alone. The question of "danceability" is ultimately a socially contingent one, and I hope that through the case studies I present here, the framework of choreographies of listening provides tools to help clarify the intersections of musical fundamentals, community norms, and spatial practices that influence whether jazz in a given place or time might be regarded as more or less of a dance music, by whom it may have been regarded as such, and the significance of the processes through which certain perspectives and stories are ultimately amplified and others muted. What my interrogation of jazz music and Black vernacular dance's intersecting histories *does* offer is a chronologically multi-sited look at a range of complex negotiations between expressive practices that are at times intimately connected and at others intentionally separated. Jazz music and dance's shifting choreographies have much to tell us about the narrative weight that concepts such as listening and dancing hold for how we understand our own bodies and the bodies of others, as well as how we might ourselves move with and against the worlds we embody and the stories we tell.

# 2

# "Its Bite and Its Feeling"

## The Quadroon Ball and Jazz's New Orleans *Plaçage* Complex

> "The story of music in New Orleans must begin with dancing. This
> was the earliest sustained musical activity there; it was always the
> greatest—in terms of effort and quantity . . . in this music mad city."
>
> —Henry Kmen

Sitting at a computer terminal at the New Orleans Public Library's Louisiana Collection, I had a thrilling research discovery moment.[1] With access to a text-searchable database of historical Louisiana newspapers, I was able to find advertisements from the 1850s for quadroon balls in the *Times Picayune*. *Success!!* In a column announcing balls of various kinds are a series of advertisements for the Washington and American Ballroom at the corner of St. Peter and St. Claude. Formerly the Globe Ballroom, the Washington and American, I discover, began giving quadroon balls weekly on Thursday nights in March 1858. The ads boast that "the proprietor of this establishment has gone to an enormous expense, and has spared no trouble to make this one of the most agreeable places of amusement in this city."[2] Toward that end, the venue's proprietor Samuel S. Smith hired the band of a Monsieur La Garito to play for the season and promised that "a superior restaurant and private eating rooms are connected with the establishment." Among the amenities for which Smith "spared no expense" was the hiring of supplementary law enforcement. The ad boasted that "an additional police force has been engaged and will be

---

[1] A portion of this chapter was previously published as Christopher J. Wells, " 'And I Make My Own': Class Performance, Black Urban Identity, and Depression-Era Harlem's Physical Culture," in *The Oxford Handbook of Dance and Ethnicity*, eds. Anthony Shay and Barbara Sellars Young (New York: Oxford University Press, 2016), 17–40. Reproduced here with the permission of Oxford University Press.

[2] Advertisement, *The Daily Picayune*, March 23, 1858, 2.

*Between Beats.* Christi Jay Wells, Oxford University Press (2021). © Oxford University Press.
DOI: 10.1093/oso/9780197559277.003.0002

in attendance, so that all who attend these Balls may rest assured that all will be mirth and gaiety."[3]

*I flash back to my first visit to New Orleans as an adult in 2010, entranced with what seemed to me then a perfect city. It was full of live music in my favorite genres, a vibrant set of walkable streets, and an architectural distinctiveness that made me feel like I was somewhere specific, somewhere unique. As I explored Frenchmen Street, I walked past a bar called "The John," about a block north of Snug Harbor where Ellis Marsalis regularly held court and the Spotted Cat and where some of my buddies play in "trad" bands. A retired police officer employed by the bar stops me as I walk past, advising me to go no further lest I leave the "safe" area and wind up somewhere "dangerous." A one man "additional police force" engaged to foreclose my entrance to the Treme, St. Roch, or Seventh Ward neighborhoods, presumably deemed necessary by the bar to ensure for myself and other white tourists that we "may rest assured" within the confines of the hyper-curated French Quarter and gentrifying Marigny "that all will be mirth and gaiety." But anyway. . . .*

*What a research find!* I scan above the ads for the Washington and American and find myself elated yet again as I discover an ad for a "Grand, Fancy Dress, and Masquerade Ball" at the Odd Fellow's Hall, well known to historians and enthusiasts of early jazz music as a venue where Buddy Bolden, jazz music's much mythologized ostensible progenitor, would later perform regularly. Even more exciting as a scholar writing a book on dance history—and a little out of my usual depth in searching for exactly what my "nineteenth-century New Orleans" topic for this book should be—was a series of advertisements for dance academies that appeared just below those for balls. An ad for Madame DeBar's Dancing Academy announces that "The Ladies of New Orleans are respectfully informed that the above academy is now open, where all the Fashionable Dances will be taught including the celebrated BERNADINE QUADRILLE and LANCIER."[4]

---

[3] Another advertisement, *The Daily Picayune*, March 23, 1858, 2. Well after completing this chapter, I found that historian Nick Douglas had written a piece for *Afropunk* in 2016 deconstructing these same advertisements. I want to cite his work here and make clear that while I stand by the arguments I make throughout this chapter, I also acknowledge, with respect, that Douglas both takes a somewhat harder line in claiming quadroon balls were myths or fabrications than I do here and that he draws upon substantial research and family knowledge in making that case. I do, however, agree entirely with his conclusion that "Continuing to retell the fanciful myths about the quadroon ball only serve[s] to paper-over another injustice of slavery—the use of slave women for sex and sex trade—with a convenient and white-male-centric fantasy." The Race Card [Nick Douglas], "Know Your Black History: Deconstructing the Quadroon Ball," *Afropunk*, October 27, 2016. https://afropunk.com/2016/10/know-your-black-history-deconstructing-the-quadroon-ball/, accessed October 10, 2020.

[4] Yet another advertisement, *The Daily Picayune*, March 23, 1858, 2. Capitalization in the original.

**Figure 2.1**  Image reproduction from advertisement, *The Daily Picayune*, March 23, 1858, 2. Reproduction by Grey Armstrong.

On the left-hand side of each ad is a small, simple silhouetted figure, presumably to help readers identify the subject matter. For the balls and dance academies, it is a woman in a petticoated gown dancing with a man in a coat and tails (figure 2.1).

*Oh, that's definitely going in the book! How do I get a higher quality image? Might the* Times-Picayune *re-scan it for me? Do I need to have an artist re-render it? (That'd probably be pretty cheap.)* As I skim down the column to see what other treasures I might find, comes a huge gut punch. I notice that the happily dancing couple has been replaced by a single figure holding a bindle on a stick (figure 2.2).

The ads were no longer for dance parties but for cash rewards:

FIFTY DOLLARS REWARD—The above reward will be given for the apprehension and return to the subscribers, or in jail, of the Negro boy SAMEDI, belonging to MME. F. Turpin...

**Figure 2.2** Image reproduction from advertisement, *The Daily Picayune*, March 23, 1858, 2. Reproduction by Grey Armstrong.

FIFTEEN DOLLARS REWARD—Ran Away on the 4th March, a black slave man by the name of Joe . . .

Negroes for Sale: Just arrived with a large and choice lot of Maryland and Virginia Negroes. . . .

ONE HUNDRED NEGROES FOR SALE AT FOSTER'S SLAVE DEPOT.[5]

That the advertisements for parties, dance lessons, and slaves for sale or capture appear in the same column of classified ads in an 1858 New Orleans newspaper is simultaneously more and less jarring than it should be: less jarring because the casual advertising of human chattel for purchase can never

[5] Some more ads, *The Daily Picayune*, March 23, 1858, 2. *Very* different . . . but how different really?

be jarring enough and more jarring because I know what year this paper is from, and I should know what to expect.

As a lindy hop dancer for most of my adult life and as a professional historian of the music and dance of the Swing Era, this archival moment is an important reminder of the dangers of "time machine thinking" or romanticizing the past as one explores, enacts, and celebrates its expressive culture. As dancer and cultural theorist Grey Armstrong wrote of white Americans involved in historically reproductive dance subcultures in a poignant post on his blog *Obsidian Tea* entitled "Dance Communities and Time Travel":

> They idealize the dress and hairstyle that they think is associated with these dances. And yet amongst the fervor Black Americans find themselves isolated, uncomfortable and giving side eye. Part of the issue is clearly a cultural one. White American culture loves to preserve things. They love to create time capsules of the past and dig deep to find more material that creates a better picture of the thing they love so they can preserve it. While in Black Culture the ideal is the exact opposite. You learn the foundations of the thing then you find your own style with in it. You take the original idea, dance, music and expand on it innovating and making it better as time goes on. But I'm a strong believer that part of this cultural difference comes from the fact that for Black Americans there is nothing in the past for us. The only thing you can do is continuously improve your own life and the lives of your children. The only thing that is in the past is more pain, more racism, and being treated as less than human. So, no, many of your Black counterparts are not going to be interested in being vintage or 1920s Dance or a sock hop.[6]

Armstrong's point has resonance not only for white swing dancers or for practitioners of so-called Dixieland or "trad jazz" music, but also for white practitioners of other forms of African American music and dance and for those of us who study its history.

While we might aspire otherwise, many tellings of jazz music's history either explicitly or implicitly celebrate *both* the dancing couple at a quadroon ball and the runaway slave fleeing with a bindle, for these images are intimately connected within the racialized circulatory system of antebellum exchange. As historian Diana Williams points out, "descriptions of the antebellum balls conjured an elaborate choreography of physical intimacy and

---

[6] Grey Armstrong, "Dance Communities and Time Travel," *Obsidian Tea: A Blackness and Blues Blog*, May 24, 2019. https://obsidiantea.com/2019/05/24/dance-communities-and-time-travel, accessed January 30, 2020.

social distance—not unlike the situation under slavery."[7] Jazz historical accounts of the music's origins frequently trade upon a celebratory "melting pot" framing of America's miscegenated history to position jazz music as a living embodiment of neoliberalism's pluralist gambit: jazz comes to symbolize overcoming racialized systems of injustice as it simultaneously validates those systems' existence, positioning them as necessary conditions of possibility to produce those special "mixed" elements that make certain art forms, and especially jazz, uniquely and fundamentally American. As a lecturing jazz professor once asked a room of two hundred students when I was in graduate school: "without slavery, could we have had Duke Ellington?" The audacious conceits that might lead us to ask such a question of jazz, however, are fundamentally tied to narrative strategies that reframe domination as benevolent exchange. These narrative strategies function within a system historian Emily Clark terms the New Orleans "*plaçage* complex." For Clark, the *plaçage* complex developed from an assemblage of exoticized miscegenation fantasy tropes that created a perpetual feedback loop between narrative and enactment through which the idea of the quadroon ball came to shape both romanticized visions of, and lived experiences within, the city of New Orleans.[8]

The discursive power of quadroon balls affixed the idealized and fetishized body of a quadroon woman (a light-skinned free-born woman of mixed-race ancestry) to New Orleans' performance within the American imaginary of a state of temporal stasis as a cultural time capsule. As Clark explains in her book *The Strange History of the American Quadroon*, "sequestering the quadroon figuratively and literally in the Crescent City shaped American identity and historical narrative in subtle but powerful ways, effectively turning New Orleans into a perpetual colonial space in the national imagination."[9] Clark's work makes a massive contribution to an already vibrant twenty-first century scholarly discourse revisiting the subject of quadroon balls, where scholars have not only carefully parsed the differences between historical evidence of the balls and the many likely exaggerated or outright fictitious accounts, but have also advanced interpretations of the balls that offer quadroon women social and political agency beyond their traditional framing as passive "tragic mulatto" archetypes.[10] Where Clark extends this work is in laying out how the

---

[7] Diana Williams, "Can Quadroon Balls Represent Acquiescence or Resistance?," in *Gendered Resistance: Women, Slavery, and the Legacy of Margaret Garner*, ed. Margaret Garner (Urbana: University of Illinois Press, 2013), 126.

[8] Emily Clark, *The Strange History of the American Quadroon: Free Women of Color in the Revolutionary Atlantic World* (Chapel Hill: University of North Carolina Press, 2013), 148.

[9] Clark, *Strange History*, 9.

[10] Notable sources in this discourse include Williams, "Can Quadroon Balls"; Kenneth Aslakson, "The 'Quadroon-Plaçage' Myth of Antebellum New Orleans: Anglo-American (Mis)Interpretations of a French-Caribbean Phenomenon," *Journal of Social History* 5, no. 3 (2012): 709–734; Monique Guillory, "Some

rhetorical power of quadroon balls, through the *plaçage* complex into which they were imbricated, formed and maintained a narrative feedback loop where exotic miscegenation fantasies traded upon the same logics of racial domination that built and maintained the American system of chattel slavery. This narrative loop also drove the rhetorical coding of nostalgia for ostensibly benevolent white dominance over the bodies and cultural production of peoples of color while simultaneously prompting New Orleans's ballrooms and brothels to adapt to, accommodate, and enact those very fantasies. As Clark explains, what we are dealing with is not a simple "fact vs. fiction" issue but a more complex and dynamic relationship between narrative and praxis:

> Contemporary observers and historians alike have treated quadroon balls and the *plaçage* complex as relatively static, fixed phenomena. Scholars recognize the commodification of sexual fantasy and white mastery embedded in them but have missed the narrative circularity that continuously reinvented the quadroon and repurposed her for new markets and for shifting political objectives.[11]

Most notably, at least for my purposes here, Clark identifies the quadroon ball as a precursor to jazz in its role as the principal generative source of national and international fascination with New Orleans. Though she discusses in some detail the *plaçage* complex's hand in shaping the choreographies of exchange in Storyville, the officially sanctioned turn-of-the-century red light district from which jazz ostensibly emerged, in-depth discussion of the complex's connection with jazz music and its discourses is, quite understandably, beyond her scope. Here, I look to build on Clark's work by demonstrating how jazz as practice, history, and historiography—replete with both explicit and implicit miscegenation fantasy tropes—is and long has been firmly imbricated within the discursive feedback loop of the New Orleans *plaçage* complex to which the quadroon balls gave rise.

Regularly highlighted as jazz's place of origin, the city of New Orleans itself is the central protagonist in "melting pot" tales of jazz's birth. From textbooks and academic scholarship to university syllabi to public lectures and documentary films—and perhaps most tellingly in the city's own tourism literature—New Orleans is proudly hailed as jazz music's singular point of

---

Enchanted Evening on the Auction Block: The Cultural Legacy of the New Orleans Quadroons" (PhD diss., New York University, 1999); Floyd Cheung, "'Les Cenelles' and Quadroon Balls' 'Hidden Transcripts' of Resistance and Domination in New Orleans, 1803–1845," *The Southern Literary Journal* 29, no. 2 (Spring 1997): 5–16.

[11] Clark, *Strange History*, 180.

origin. To offer a few examples: the first entries in Robert Walser's *Keeping Time* anthology are from New Orleans musician Sidney Bechet and the New Orleans newspaper the *Times-Picayune*. The course description for "Jazz 101: A Beginner's Guide to Jazz" at Jazz at Lincoln Center's "Swing University" (JALC's "higher-education program" to "help you become a better listener") promises that students will learn "the history of the music and cultural movements that helped create the conditions necessary to engender Jazz's birth in New Orleans."[12] The first volume of Ken Burns's ten-volume *Jazz* documentary series is entitled "Gumbo," and it proudly proclaims early on that "jazz grew up in a thousand places, but it was born in New Orleans."[13] The Louisiana Office of Tourism's website features a story entitled "History of Jazz Music: Birthplace New Orleans," which claims that any disputes over the music's point of origin were settled in New Orleans' favor by Don Marquis's 1978 book *In Search of Buddy Bolden*.[14]

The centering of New Orleans as jazz's birthplace, however, began far earlier than Marquis's work, as many critics in the 1930s and 1940s were fixated on a revival of so-called Dixieland or traditional New Orleans–style jazz. Among the critics who, in Scott DeVeaux's words, "narrowly identified the music with a romanticized notion of folk culture," was Hughes Pannasié, whose 1938 book *Le Jazz Hot* alleged that jazz prior to 1926, in DeVeaux's words, "was characterized by an upward arc from the 'chaos' of the Ur-styles of New Orleans through the agency of musicians like Louis Armstrong."[15] Such framings of New Orleans canonize the city both for its cultural importance and also for its ostensible provincialism, operating within a broader paradigm of romanticized folkloric discourse whose primitivist fascination with Black life in the American south, historian Karl Hagstrom Miller argues, has close ties to the logics that produced the gross stereotypes of nineteenth-century American blackface minstrelsy.[16]

Without necessarily disputing the "truth" of jazz's roots in New Orleans, jazz scholars have more recently offered critiques of the narrative function

[12] "Swing University: About the Program" and "Swing University Single Classes," *Jazz at Lincoln Center Jazz Academy*, <https://academy.jazz.org/swing-university, https://academy.jazz.org/swing-university-single-classes, accessed January 28, 2020.

[13] *Jazz*, volume 1, "Gumbo" directed by Ken Burns (Burbank, CA: Warner Home Video, 2000) DVD, 87 min.

[14] Jan Ramsey, "History of Jazz Music: Birthplace New Orleans," *LouisianaTravel.com*, Office of Louisiana Tourism, n/d, https://www.louisianatravel.com/music/articles/history-jazz-music-birthplace-new-orleans, accessed January 29, 2019.

[15] Scott DeVeaux, "Constructing the Jazz Tradition," *Black American Literature Forum* 25, no. 3 (Autumn 1991): 529, 532.

[16] Karl Hagstrom Miller, *Segregating Sound: Inventing Folk and Pop Music in the Age of Jim Crow* (Durham, NC: Duke University Press, 2010), 5–6; Benjamin Filene, *Romancing the Folk: Public Memory and American Roots Movement* (Chapel Hill: University of North Carolina Press).

that New Orleans serves within stories of jazz's formation as a distinct musical genre. As historian Bruce Boyd Raeburn shows, the stories of jazz's "born in New Orleans" status that we continue to reproduce stem from a particular connection between history, criticism, and revivalism forged by communities of predominantly white "hot" record collectors in the 1930s and early 1940s.[17] In revisiting those stories with a critical eye, several scholars highlight the "melting pot" tropes of jazz's origins as particularly problematic. Ethnomusicologist Travis Jackson calls the common trope of locating Black/creole encounter as jazz's source of origin an "especially pernicious" and oversimplified story, made all the more so by its ubiquity. As Jackson explains, "many writers reproduce a narrative in which a moment of contact, the throwing together of rough-hewn, streetwise Black musicians with their more 'refined' Creole counterparts in late nineteenth-century New Orleans, sparks the emergence of jazz."[18] Sherrie Tucker further criticizes the tropic focus on Storyville brothels as jazz's ur-source. She finds this narrative gravity particularly troubling because it advances a hyper-sexualized birthing narrative—steeped in misogyny and patriarchy—where jazz was "delivered into the steamy ambiance of exotic prostitutes by a handful of irrepressible and ingenious male musicians" who "created jazz as the bawdy background music for the city's booming sex industry of the early 1900s."[19] Tucker thus cautions that

A focus on early jazz that cannot see its way out of Storyville brothels feeds a problematic tendency to always equate jazz with sex—an association with racist underpinnings that needs to be carefully examined, not uncritically reproduced. This "creativity-born-in-a-brothel" narrative obscures the complexity of the history of [the] New Orleans sex industry as well. It is difficult to see power imbalances, economics, and politics when the commodified female bodies of Storyville are seen only as a sexy backdrop to sexy music.[20]

Tucker's and Jackson's critiques are fundamentally intertwined, as both the romanticization of interracial exchange and the fetishization of "creativity-born-in-a-brothel" are rooted in colonial miscegenation power fantasies whose associations with New Orleans can themselves be traced back to the nineteenth century and the alluring rhetorical power of the quadroon ball.

[17] Bruce Boyd Raeburn, *New Orleans Style and the Writing of American Jazz History* (Ann Arbor: University of Michigan Press, 2009),
[18] Travis Jackson, "Culture, Commodity, Palimpsest: Locating Jazz in the World," in *Jazz Worlds/World Jazz*, eds. Philip V. Bohlman and Goffredo Plastino (Chicago: University of Chicago Press, 2016), 387.
[19] Sherrie Tucker, "A Feminist Perspective on New Orleans Jazzwomen," New Orleans Jazz National Historical Park, National Park Service, 2004, 59.
[20] Tucker, "New Orleans Jazzwomen," 60.

## "Far Removed from Reality": The Quadroon Balls as Myth and Praxis

The most common, if deeply mythologized, contemporary understanding of quadroon balls is that they were dance parties, simultaneously elegant and raucous, that served principally to facilitate a particular quasi-legal and highly choreographed ritual of racialized sexual exchange. As the story goes, the balls were attended principally or exclusively by white men and light-skinned mixed-race women (quadroon creoles), who sought to form relationships with one another. Unable to marry across race lines, quadroon women would seek semi-formal arrangements exchanging dedicated, long-term social and sexual companionship for financial support via contracts ostensibly negotiated by the quadroon women's mothers, who functioned as de facto madams for their progeny. positioning this exchange as the balls' central purpose renders the dancing itself a kind of marketplace-cum-audition process for the white men present to effectively "sample the wares" and for the quadroon women to display their elegance, refinement, and of course their bodies. For white men, the allure of these balls, in addition to the sort of music and dancing present elsewhere, was the reputed exceptional beauty of quadroon women and the prospect of a relationship that paired the sexual, social, and domestic comforts of marriage with an attendant guarantee of impermanence.[21]

In his in-depth study of music in early New Orleans, musicologist Henry Kmen wrote that "no facet of early New Orleans has intrigued writers more than the famed quadroon balls. Consequently, a few facts have been embroidered with much myth to construct a legend far removed from reality."[22] The issue, however, is more complicated than simply reality vs. falsehood, as actual practices and lived experiences prompted the spinning of fantastical stories, the tropes of which in turn reshaped both the balls themselves and a number of related social spaces. That said, scholarship over the past two decades has done much to help parse this relationship and offer substantial nuance to our understanding of the balls as they functioned both in practice and in narrative. The rough consensus history as it currently stands is thus: quadroon balls emerged from the tricolor balls held in late eighteenth-century New Orleans. These balls were called "tricolor" because they welcomed white, Black, and creole guests. They were sponsored by Don Bernard Coquet and Joseph Antonio Boniquet, who were, despite city officials' reticence, able to gain exclusive licenses to hold mixed-race public balls in New

---

[21] Hazzard Gordon, *Jookin'*, 59–61.
[22] Kmen, *Music in New Orleans*, 42.

Orleans in exchange for supporting an important but financially struggling public theater, the maintenance of which the city felt was necessary to maintain public morale and civic culture.[23] While appeals were made to cancel the balls, citing principally the indecency of slaves attending with free people and alleging that the only manner in which slaves could afford admittance was to steal from their masters, Coquet and Boniquet overcame these objections by threatening to close the aforementioned theater if they could not support it with the income generated through their wildly popular tricolor balls. After 1803, when the United States took control of New Orleans as part of the Louisiana Purchase, Governor William Claiborne chose the path of tolerance for public balls—including those with reputations for disorder and indecency—to avoid unrest among a local populace with French and Spanish cultural allegiances and a fierce skepticism regarding American intervention in their established way of life.[24]

The quadroon ball's emergence from the practice of tricolor balls came about through new social conditions owing not only to the Louisiana purchase, but also to a coterminous influx of Saint Dominguan refugees in the aftermath of the Haitian Revolution. The years from 1804 to 1810 saw a massive influx of refugees to New Orleans, reaching over 4,000 by mid-1809. Fearing a reprise of the Haitian Revolution, a fear itself informed by works of fiction that vividly described Haitian men as particularly dangerous brutes, the territorial government restricted migration of Haitian refugees to women and to those under age fifteen, creating by policy a strong demographic imbalance that led to a large number of single, mixed-race women in need of work or other forms of financial security as well as domestic companionship.[25] The relationships of convenience and the sex work opportunities they found were curated by white men's expectations, informed again by works of literature, of exotic and sexually skilled Dominguan mulatto women, stereotypes to which female refugees often adapted as a survival strategy.[26]

Born of these dynamics were the quadroon balls, the first of which were sponsored by August Tessier, an actor and dancer by trade who was himself a native of France and a refugee from Port-au-Prince living in a long-term, marriage-like relationship with a free woman of color with whom he had two children.[27] Tessier rented Coquet's hall and began to hold his own events, drawing upon Saint Dominguan conventions that were at the time

---

[23] Monique Guillory, "Some Enchanted Evening," 23.
[24] Kmen, *Music in New Orleans*, 3–4.
[25] Aslakson, "The Quadroon-*Plaçage* Myth," 716.
[26] Clark, *Strange History*, 58.
[27] Clark, *Strange History*, 60, 62.

new to New Orleans. Accessing an exotic orientalism from the outset, Tessier renamed the venue the *Salle Chinoise* and began offering balls for free women of color and white men.[28] While the idea of excluding only men of color was new to New Orleans, the concept drew from long-held Saint Dominguan practices and proved quite popular, quickly spreading through several other promoters to a range of venues.[29] Notably, where New Orleans' French and Spanish governments granted exclusive monopolies to individual dance promoters, under the American free-market system, any enterprising person was welcome to start their own dances modeled on Tessier's successful concept.[30] Enthusiasm for quadroon balls continued to grow coterminously with the growing popularity of dance events in New Orleans more broadly, as the number of public ballrooms increased from roughly fifteen in 1805 to more than eighty by 1841.[31]

As the quadroon balls grew in number, so too did the romanticized accounts about them authored by numerous antebellum travel writers who chronicled their experiences in New Orleans. Along with depictions in works of fiction—including two plays in 1842 whose plots focused on quadroon women—a series of fantastic accounts of travel in New Orleans continued to spread a specific set of narrative tropes about quadroon balls that came to form the New Orleans *plaçage* complex. While literary depictions of quadroon balls grew more numerous, this growth did not result in a broader range of perspectives as, much like American blackface minstrelsy, stories of quadroon balls continued to reproduce a set of tropes that had solidified in the 1820s.[32] Many travel writers who discussed quadroon balls never attended one themselves and based their stories on second- or third-hand accounts. They weaved tales of enticingly sinful spaces full of elegant decadence tinged with provincial exoticism, values with which the quadroon woman's body was itself discursively imbued. These authors' works both spread national awareness of quadroon balls and created a set of expectations for those travelers who would come to New Orleans anticipating entertainments that matched the fantastical descriptions they had read.[33]

---

[28] Guillory, "Some Enchanted Evening," 27.

[29] Guillory, "Some Enchanted Evening," 28; Clark, *Strange History*, 58–60.

[30] Aslakson, "The Quadroon-*Plaçage* Myth," 721.

[31] Kmen, *Music in New Orleans*, 6–7.

[32] Clark, *Strange History*, 160; Aslakson, "The 'Quadroon-*Plaçage* Myth," 710–714. The 1820s origin of several blackface minstrel archetypes to which I allude here is discussed in depth in Barbara Lewis, "Daddy Blue: Evolution of the Dark Dandy," in *Inside the Minstrel Mask: Readings in 19th-Century Blackface Minstrelsy*, eds. Annemarie Bean, James V. Hatch, and Brooks McNamara (Hanover, NH: Wesleyan University Press, 1996), 257–272.

[33] Clark, *Strange History*, 149.

In both the antebellum wave of narratives about quadroon balls and in the consumer expectations those narratives fostered, the lines became blurred between quadroon balls themselves, along with the system of exchange they ostensibly offered, and two other forms of sex commerce in New Orleans: prostitution and the "fancy maid" slave trade. The desire for the companionship, sexual and otherwise, of quadroon women, influenced by romanticized tales of quadroon balls, spilled over into New Orleans brothels as madams and light-skinned sex workers of color—many of whom were themselves Saint Dominguan refugees—shrewdly worked with these tropes to accommodate the expectations white male travelers brought with them to New Orleans. In addition, the rise of quadroon balls was accompanied by a spike in the desire for "fancy maids": light-skinned enslaved women purchased both to serve as domestic servants and to be sexually exploited, and truly the more appropriate term is raped, by their masters.[34] In turn, stories of quadroon balls often conflated second-hand anecdotes from the balls themselves with those of brothel encounters or of "fancy maid" slavery, the growth of which the balls had influenced. Though quadroon balls developed a reputation as dangerous sites of fights and duels and as operating grounds for prostitutes, these were traits they shared with whites-only balls marketed to working-class white audiences, events that failed to generate comparable levels of cultural mystique.[35] Indeed, quadroon balls in specific would prove to have a large impact on the marketing and presentation strategies of those Storyville brothels in which jazz ostensibly developed.[36]

In her careful study of quadroon balls, literary scholar Monique Gillory offers two compelling dialectic renderings of the balls and their significance, highlighting that the balls "represent highly charged sites of unprecedented sexual and racial confluence which would have seemingly undermined slavery but was made possible through it."[37] This formulation could as easily describe both the "born into brothels" romanticization of Storyville that Tucker critiques and the implicit necessity of slavery itself to shaping jazz music's resistant possibilities (*I hear that professor's voice again*: "without slavery, could we have had Duke Ellington?") When Gillory further claims that the balls represent "super abundant spaces of unimaginable possibility and potential; in one sense, an avant-garde utopian vision and in another, a perversely racialized sexual fantasy," she may as well be describing representational

---

[34] Williams, "Can Quadroon Balls"; Clark, *Strange History*, 162–164.

[35] Kmen, *Music in New Orleans* 32–33.

[36] Clark outlines the quadroon balls and the attendant *plaçage* complex on spaces of explicit sex work in New Orleans, including the formation of Storyville, in depth in *Strange History*, 180–185.

[37] Guillory, "Some Enchanted Evening," 21.

potentials that continue to shape our understandings and our framings of the jazz tradition.[38]

## "The Most Cosmopolitan of Provincial Cities": New Orleans as Miscegenated Body

Quadroon balls receded in frequency but grew in both infamy and nostalgic romanticization after the Civil War. Longing for "the old plantation" became a tacit lament for slavery's end in the reconstruction south, an implicit coding that remains active to this day. Fueling this white southern longing through a narrative feedback loop of discourse and practice, quadroon balls' reputation as simultaneously disreputable and irresistible grew in the 1870s when they became the center of a political sex scandal surrounding the Louisiana gubernatorial election. Ironically, this scandal's fallout contributed to the circumstances in the US Congress that shortly thereafter facilitated the very compromise that bought Rutherford B. Hayes the US presidency at the expense of reconstruction in the American south. This compromise, which resulted in the withdrawal of federal troops from southern states, paved the way for a wave of white supremacist retribution that would entrench Jim Crow segregation for much of the following century as well as the systemic white supremacy its enduring legacy continues to feed.[39] The quadroon balls' sustained appeal was at the same time ensconced within the same plantation nostalgia tropes that drove minstrel shows throughout the nineteenth century and also characteristic of a particular discourse forming about New Orleans that situated the city simultaneously as a simulacrum of everything good about the "old south" and as always already tinged with a foreignness that would forever keep it distinct from the rest of the United States. As such, it acquired a peculiar dialectic location as both margin and center that has yielded a specific mystique the city still maintains.

Among the many postbellum travel narratives that underscore New Orleans' unique status within the broader discursive constructs of plantation nostalgia is Charles Dudley Warner's 1886 piece for *Harper's*, which exemplifies the concentric narrative circles that link the quadroon woman's body, the quadroon ball, and New Orleans' character as a city more broadly. Warner articulates the duality fundamental to the city's appeal when he claims that "New Orleans is the most cosmopolitan of provincial cities. Its comparative

---

[38] Guillory, "Some Enchanted Evening," 21.
[39] Clark, *Strange History*, 180–183.

isolation has secured the development of provincial traits and manners, has preserved the individuality of the many races that give it color, morals, and character."[40] New Orleans' cosmopolitan isolation appealed to Warner as the city's palpable air of difference provided an exotic respite from what he saw as the increasing homogenization of American cities during the industrial revolution. In that vein, Warner writes that New Orleans "contains a valuable element of variety for the republic. We tend everywhere to sameness and monotony."[41] He attributes New Orleans' potential as an antidote for, or at least a palliative to, this monotony explicitly to the city's creole population. In describing New Orleans' "transitive state," Warner laments the degree to which the values of the American north's fast-paced industrial culture was overtaking this southern city's creole uniqueness. He situates creole culture as the living embodiment of a simpler time that prioritized the innocence and pleasure of domestic life, a precarious and aging zeitgeist he locates in the body of the antebellum creole woman:

> The Creole had gayety, sentiment, spirit, with a certain climatic languor, sweetness of disposition, and charm of manner, not seldom winning beauty; she was passionately fond of dancing and of music, and occasionally an adept in the latter; and she had candor, and either simplicity or the art of it.[42]

His piece discusses quadroon balls principally in terms of their danger as sites of duels, a rhetorical move increasingly common following their role in the aforementioned 1876 political scandal, acknowledging that "the quadroon and the octoroon are the staple of hundreds of thrilling tales" while also highlighting that such tales emphasize and underscore themes of tragedy emerging from New Orleans' history of interracial encounter.

> Possibly no other city of the United States so abounds in stories pathetic and tragic, many of which cannot yet be published, growing out of the mingling of races, the conflicts of French and Spanish, the presence of adventurers from the old world and the Spanish main, and especially out of relations between the whites and the fair women who had in their thin veins drops of African blood.[43]

In this passage, the quadroon woman's body—both her "fair" exterior and the miscegenated inner workings of her circulatory system—comes also to house

---

[40] Charles Dudley Warner, "New Orleans," *Harpers' New Monthly Magazine*, December 1886, 190.
[41] Warner, "New Orleans," 194.
[42] Warner, "New Orleans," 193.
[43] Warner, "New Orleans," 192–193.

those "pathetic and tragic" narrative logics that mark New Orleans' alluring distinctiveness.

Warner's descriptions of New Orleans more broadly throughout the piece underscore this dynamic. He emphasizes New Orleans' shabbiness, offering a fairly derisive description of its cityscape until he makes clear that its dirtiness is the source of its charm. For Warner, New Orleans' unkempt, "dirty" side appeals to some simultaneously shameful and profound aspect of human desire that taps into deeply felt, ostensibly universal truths:

> I suppose we are all wrongly made up and have a fallen nature; else why is it that while the most thrifty and neat and orderly city only wins our approval, and perhaps gratifies us intellectually, such a thriftless, battered and stained, and lazy old place as the French Quarter of New Orleans takes our hearts?[44]

Warner's commentary on the French Quarter might well have been written fifty or one hundred years later for the degree to which it encapsulates little-changed tropes regarding New Orleans, and the French Quarter specifically, as a space to simultaneously revel in and reflect on the those commonly held shortcomings of the human condition that bind us to the corporeal pleasures we *do* want rather than the transcendent purity we *should* want.

The trope of our "fallen nature," embracing bodies, and the guilt we carry for and within them, as a source of and subject for profound reflection is echoed in Wynton Marsalis's sexualized framing of jazz's New Orleans origins. As Marsalis explicates the tangible and the symbolic importance of Storyville brothels as the ostensible site of jazz's birth:

> New Orleans was the hot bed of that type of sexual activity, and we weren't puritan. In jazz music, it says, this is what we do and it's beautiful. And it's also terrible. Then, jazz is real; it deals with that man and that woman, it deals with depraved things, because the musician saw all of these things. That's what gives our music its bite and its feeling, and that's what the world wanted from our music.[45]

As Marsalis's words demonstrate, the cultural romanticization of New Orleans as both a site of difference from American culture writ large and an origin point for its enlivening cultural practices, jazz most notable among them, is an iterative social dance: a process of give-and-take between the city itself and all those who would reimagine it to suit their own needs and desires.

---

44  Warner, "New Orleans," 186.
45  Wynton Marsalis in Burns, "Gumbo."

Among New Orleans' most notable dynamics is the city's ability to perpetually rebrand, repackage, and sell to visiting consumers various packaged iterations of its own mythos through the symbolic economy that drives its music and tourism industries. As anthropologist Helen Regis explains, jazz as a form of music developed and stewarded by New Orleans residents of color is central to the city's symbolic economy but not uniquely so, as "the cultural productions of the urban Black working-class communities are increasingly featured as the principal asset distinguishing New Orleans from other tourist destinations and conference centers. Creole cuisine, historic architecture, blues, gospel, rhythm and blues (R&B), and, above all, jazz have long drawn travelers from throughout the world to New Orleans."[46] This dance between local Black cultural production and global tourist consumption produces a system of commodified exchange as driven by racialized power dynamics as the *plaçage* complex logics it reproduces.

The iterative choreography of romanticization and auto-romanticization through which New Orleans both fuels and accommodates the expectations of those drawn to visit the city is a cycle that itself traces its origins to well before the ostensible birth of jazz. Among the first sites to elicit such romantic fascination was the quadroon ball, for, as Clark argues, "through the medium of the fictional quadroon, New Orleans was imaginatively construed as a place apart in the American polity, the only place in the nation where the strange fruit bred of slavery and white desire grew and met its inevitable, tragic destiny."[47] Like the alluring bodies of fictionalized quadroon women, New Orleans is constructed in jazz history narratives as a unique, peculiar space. It is rendered the only site where the conditions of possibility to create a music such as jazz could have existed, thus casting the hybrid music that resulted as another "strange fruit bred of slavery and white desire" whose destiny, while triumphant rather than tragic, is no less inevitable. To position New Orleans as both a cultural melting pot and a hyper-sexed site of miscegenated exchange, Burns's *Jazz* documentary turns to a quote from New Orleans musician and culture bearer Danny Barker:

People from all of the world came to New Orleans—pirates, adventurers, gamblers, exiles, criminals, Frenchmen, Spaniards, Germans, Englishmen, Irishmen, Indians, Chinese, Italians, West Indians, Africans. In the hundreds of tenements in the rear of

---

[46] Helen Regis, "Blackness and the Politics of Memory in the New Orleans Second Line," *American Ethnologist* 28, no. 4 (November 2001): 754.

[47] Clark, *Strange History*, 147.

the Front Street buildings, there were people of all nationalities living side by side. And there was a whole lot of integrating going on.[48]

The inflection and code-switching the actor voicing Barker uses for his final sentence plainly positions "a whole lotta integratin'" as a sexual euphemism, further underscoring the *plaçage* complex and its miscegenation logics' dual role in jazz's origin story: they position the music as simultaneously an exotic product of alluringly sinful origins and as the sonic realization of America's wholesome melting pot idealism. Though he was among the first to rigorously research the quadroon balls and debunk many myths about them, Henry Kmen's framing of eighteenth- and nineteenth-century New Orleans as a site of unique musical importance is instructive regarding this type of thinking and merits quoting here at length:

> Moreover, if the outstanding characteristic of America today is its successful amalgamation of many and varied nationalities and cultural traits, then New Orleans was truly, in this important respect at least, a pioneer city of modern America. Here, very early, diverse cultural groups met and slowly fused their cultures into something new, something American. New Orleans had not only the French, Spanish, Anglo-American, Irish, and German groups, but also the largest Negro population, both slave and free, of any American city. All brought with them a musical tradition or instinct or both. Add to these, West Indian music imported by refugees and visitors, the music of England and Italy heard in operas and concerts, and American folk music brought in from the hinterland by the Mississippi River sailors. These were the ingredients poured into the musical melting pot that was New Orleans.[49]

While Kmen does not make explicit here who contributed a "tradition" and who contributed an "instinct," centuries of plainly racist discourse fill in these details for him (whether he would wish them to or not). The thoroughly raced undertones he deftly skirts in this moment are at the heart of the white supremacist discursive legacies that have long structured and continue to structure, almost inescapably so, those moments of cultural encounter that we must no longer mischaracterize as equal and freely given "exchange." The racialized dichotimization of "tradition" on the one hand and "instinct" on the other also accesses the Cartesian logics through which jazz music's points of difference from Western classical music are fixed to the provincial and ever-presently corporeal circumstances of the music's birth even as its birthplace

---

[48] Danny Barker, quoted in Burns, "Gumbo."
[49] Kmen, *Music in New Orleans*, vii–viii.

ostensibly plants the very seeds that would one day offer jazz its path to cultural transcendence as both a form of high art and a living testament to American exceptionalism.

Even after decades spent placing historiographic critique at the center of jazz studies—a trend that has itself become an object of consternation even among those who continue to engage in it—the seductive pull of New Orleans as a unique site of interracial mixing still permeates jazz scholarship even when neither sexuality nor Storyville are featured as overt sites of fetishization. In musicologist Thomas Brothers's formulation, jazz was forged through the heroic local border crossings of uptown Black musicians "crossing Canal street" and encountering openminded "Creole rebels" interested in playing with them.[50] Musicologist David Ake, even as he exercises the utmost self-awareness and caution in articulating the issue's complexity, still seeks the "New Orleans Creole" in hopes this figure's mixed-race identity might offer a unique and necessary set of tools to help jazz scholars reconcile the simultaneous ethical necessity and essentialist limitations of a Black/white racial binary.[51] While both look to center a group of people—creoles of color—whose identities and critically important contributions to jazz music might otherwise be erased from jazz discourses, even such critiques of creole erasure necessarily access the "tragic mulatto" archetypes of which quadroon ball narratives were a formative element as creole bodies are still discursively manipulated to serve broader miscegenation-inflected tropes of "crossing" and "exchange."

Such understandings of jazz as a fundamentally miscegenated art form trade upon the same colonizer logics that framed the positioning of quadroon bodies and the strategies that drove Franco-Spanish practices—quadroon balls and the "fancy maid" slave trade among many others—as tactics of imperial dominance. Like the bodies of quadroon women, jazz itself becomes positioned as the perfect fusion: an exhilarating, soulful African rhythmic essence paired in ideal proportion with the ostensible "improvements" of European intellectual and material culture, specifically necessary to structure

---

[50] Thomas Brothers, *Louis Armstrong's New Orleans* (New York: W. W. Norton, 2006), 186–196.

[51] David Ake, "'Blue Horizon': Creole Culture and Early New Orleans Jazz" in *Jazz Cultures* (Berkeley: University of California Press, 2002), 10–41. While not jazz scholarship per se, I would extend parts of this critique to Christopher J. Smith's framing of "creole synthesis of black and white body vocabularies" as a necessarily resistant or subversive process of interracial and intercultural exchange in the vernacular dance practices of the United States. Though I don't dispute that there are elements of, or potentials for, "a subtle underclass resistance" in eighteenth and nineteenth century interracial dance spaces, I do think his assertion that at New Orleans's tricolor balls, "Dance was the engine, the attraction, and the mechanism for cultural exchange at many levels of intimacy, intensity, and longevity" downplays the racialized power dynamics of white dominance that both at the time and since have bolstered white supremacy across lines of class to a far greater degree than they have class solidarity across lines of race. Smith, *Dancing Revolution*, 77, 121, 122.

the music's otherwise "uncageable" African essence. This idealized process of cross-cultural blending produces jazz music: a fascinatingly alluring and quintessentially American hybrid always already available to both titillate and nurture the generations of white male jazz writers whose privilege binds them within the *plaçage* complex's discursive feedback loop as firmly as it did their nineteenth-century forebears. As literary scholar Floyd Cheung claims that quadroon balls are "powerful hidden transcripts of domination," so do I argue that, in similar ways and for similar reasons, the stories of jazz's New Orleans birth are as well.[52]

## "High Yaller" in Harlem: Plantation Nostalgia in the Jazz Age

In 1927 in New York City's Times Square, Club Alabam (not to be confused with the famous Los Angeles venue of the same name) presented an after-theater revue entitled "Magnolia Gal" that promised "a Broadway night of 'Deep River' days." Advertising in the *New York Times* boasted the show would be "pulsating with dazzling displays of inimitable Negro talent" and, most notably, "alive with the gorgeous gaiyety [sic] of the Quadroon Ball."[53] Club Alabam went so far as to claim their revue would offer New York City's theater-going public "a Quadroon Ball *every night* now! With all the thrills—with all the beauty of old New Orleans."[54] The show's ads featured various renderings of a gentleman in coat and tails courting an exotically dressed masked woman. The exchange between this couple—like the discourse surrounding the balls themselves—towered over the plethora of promised variety entertainment—the "dazzling displays of inimitable Negro talent—below them (figure 2.3).

With an ornate oval frame surrounded by pairs of slender dancers in suits and gowns, the advertisement closely resembles the ball invitations of nineteenth-century New Orleans. Another advertisement with similar artwork (figure 2.4) promised performances from Al Moore and Fredi Washington, "America's foremost colored dancing team, in a series of original and spectacular interpretive dances" as well as "Prima Donna" Julia Mitchell, "the vivacious little high-brown whose versions of 'Vanities' and 'Rangood Wedding' are high lights of the show."[55]

---

52  Floyd D. Cheung, "*Les Cenelles* and Quadroon Balls," 7.
53  Advertisement, *New York Times*, February 26, 1927, 13.
54  Advertisement, *New York Times*, March 2, 1927, 29.
55  Advertisement, *New York Times*, March 17, 1927, 27.

**CLUB ALABAM'**

44th Street Theatre Bldg.
*Just West of Broadway*

**Figure 2.3**  Image from advertisement, *New York Times*, February 26, 1927, 13.

Staged by Jack Conner and featuring songs from the popular Canadian songwriter Lieutenant Gitz Rice, the show also offered a number entitled "High Yaller," which explicitly accessed the light-skinned colorism driving Harlem's "high yellow" chorus girl shows, themselves steeped in antebellum plantation nostalgia.[56] The show's advertising specifically highlighted "High Yaller" as "Alabam's new sensation! A palpitatin', agitatin', high steppin' tune— led by ALBERTA PRYME and pranced by a high-kickin crew of high brown beauties! It's just *one* of the high spots in CLUB ALABAM's 'Magnolia Gal', that *indisputably* different after-theatre revue that hits the high mark in hilarity—every night!"[57]

---

[56] Advertisement, *New York Times*, March 2, 1927, 29. "High Yellow" was a common term at the time to refer to especially light-skinned Black women, specifically those who could pass or nearly pass for white.

[57] Advertisement, *New York Times*, March 8, 1927, 23. Capitalization and italics in the original.

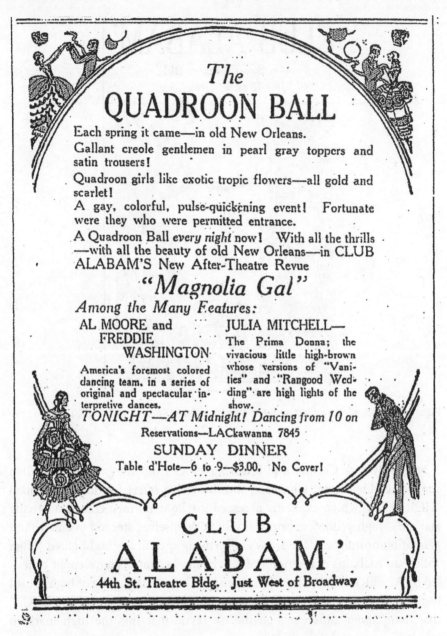

**Figure 2.4** Advertisement, *New York Times*, March 17, 1927, 27.

In *Babylon Girls*, Jayna Brown traces a clear through-line from the touring "picanniny acts" of the mid-nineteenth century, informed by "British and American literature that featured mulatto, quadroon, and octoroon concubines," and the *plaçage* complex logics that underwrote them, through hit revue shows of the 1890s such as *The Creole Show* and *The Octoroons*.[58] In the early twentieth century, Brown follows these miscegenation fantasies, grounded in nostalgia for antebellum New Orleans, through the so-called coon shows and Cakewalk exhibitions where, "performing in various gradations of skin tone, black burlesque dancers were figures linking the eroticized fantasies of the Louisiana octoroons, urban immigrant women, and various female colonial subjects."[59] In the 1920s, light-skinned chorus girls, notably including Fredi Washington, appeared in the hit show *Shuffle Along* (1921) as well as a range of revues, "Magnolia Gal" clearly among them, that took inspiration or outright borrowed liberally from the miscegenation pageants of the 1890s.[60] This created an ecosystem of signification for light-skinned performers such as Washington, where

> The chorus girls' light skin—both "real" and imagined—troubled concepts of an authentic black "folk" by raising the fleshly ghost of miscegenation. The best assessments from white critics considered the chorus a refreshing mixture of the modern and the primitive, while many gave a sly nod to the titillation of interracial desire and the erotic history of a master's access.[61]

The chorus girl–driven revue shows of the 1920s thus represented a simultaneous nostalgia for a romanticized antebellum south and a direct continuation of a contiguous discursive lineage through which the real or imagined miscegenated ancestry of Black performers fueled a pernicious American admixture of a master's access and a master's benevolence. This admixture of convergent white supremacist forces validated unfettered white access to Black bodies and Black cultural production.

Traces of "Magnolia Gal's" imbrication within a broader system of miscegenation nostalgia in the popular entertainment complex of late "Jazz Age" New York City are present in Fredi Washington's performance two years later in the 1929 sound film *Black and Tan*. In the film, a vehicle for Duke Ellington that featured his composition "Black and Tan Fantasy," Washington portrays a headlining show dancer who is also the live-in love interest of Ellington, who plays himself as an ambitious young composer struggling to pay his rent. Out of a desire to support Ellington in realizing his dreams as a composer, Washington returns to dancing despite a heart condition that ultimately proves fatal as she—like the "chosen one" in Stravinsky's *Rite of Spring*

---

[58] Brown, *Babylon Girls*, 53.
[59] Brown, *Babylon Girls*, 122.
[60] Brown, *Babylon Girls*, 203.
[61] Brown, *Babylon Girls*, 195.

the decade prior—publicly dances herself to death to the accompaniment of Ellington's orchestra. Her performance accesses tropes of the "tragic mulatto," and the specific version here might be termed a "high yellow feminine sacrifice" as this designation would access the intersection of colorism and primitivism that shaped dancing floorshows at the Cotton Club, a venue the eroticism of whose oft mythologized spectacles is itself forever linked with the genesis of Ellington's unique "jungle" soundscape.[62]

The cinematic narrative that shapes this film bears a strong relationship with the lived experiences of Harlem show dancers. Accommodating white slummers' exotic fantasies exacted both a physical and a spiritual toll on Harlem chorus dancers. Writing for the *Baltimore Afro-American*, a Black newspaper, columnist Ralph Matthews lamented the physically and socially demanding grind through which these performers gave life to the Cotton Club's primitivist spectacles:

> Harlem is synonymous with torrid, tempestuous rhythm, uncontrolled levity—and the public gives no quarter. The fact that the poor performer is dead on his feet means nothing at all to the gay night-lifer, who has slept all day and crawls out of his cozy bed and comes to Harlem for a night of slumming and levity. The playboys want gaiety. They see before them only little dynamos of high yellow flesh, dancing, singing, prancing, trucking. From their vision, blurred with liquor, are hid the tired little eyes, the aching joints, the weary hearts that belong to these human puppets of the showman's world.[63]

Matthews's sharp critique sympathetically explicates the spiritual toll exacted upon those women, and yet both the tone of this sympathy and his colorful descriptions of the "tired little eyes," "aching joints," and especially "the weary hearts" of these "little dynamos of high yellow flesh" are themselves replete with tropes of the tragic mulatto. The fetishization of "high yellow" Cotton Club dancers is also reflected in the memoirs of Timme Rosenkrantz, the Danish baron whose recollections of his Harlem soujourns include an anecdote where pianist Fats Waller "served up" three Cotton Club chorus girls, all clad in black stockings, to perform a belly dance for Rosenkrantz's

---

[62] Kimberly Hannon Teal addresses Ellington's "jungle" style as a consistent thread in his oeuvre rather than an aesthetic confined to his Cotton Club years in "Beyond the Cotton Club: The Persistence of Duke Ellington's Jungle Style," *Jazz Perspectives* 6, no. 1–2 (2012): 123–149. Nate Sloan both highlights the slavery nostalgia overtones of the Cotton Club's décor and also points out that Ellington's music has been "re-canonized" in spite of—but perhaps also because of—these associations. Nate Sloan, "Constructing Cab Calloway: Publicity, Race, and Performance in 1930s Harlem Jazz," *Journal of Musicology* 36, no. 3 (Summer 2019): 371.

[63] Ralph Matthews, "Looking at the Stars," *Baltimore Afro-American* May 2, 1936, 10.

farewell party. These women were rendered through dance a banquet of malleable flesh to be bought and sold, for as Rosenkrantz recalls Waller to have
said, " 'Timme,' he announced, 'here's the meat, I hope you've got the knives
and forks.' "[64] Waller's jape is a hauntingly literal anticipation of bell hooks's
framing of Blackness as an enlivening cultural spice enticing whites into
"eating the other," and Rosenkrantz's writing itself echoes the travel writing
tradition of nineteenth-century visitors to "exotic" American places.[65] This
narrative tradition is further reproduced in contemporaneous jazz periodicals.
Musicologist Howard Spring points out that writing in early jazz magazines,
most notably *Melody Maker* and other European titles, had strong stylistic influence from nineteenth-century colonial travel writing, the same paradigm
that shaped both ante- and postbellum accounts of quadroon balls.[66]

The *plaçage* complex's movement from the quadroon balls through the Jazz
Age does not, however, tell the full story of the women whose bodies circulated within its economy of signs, as a broader look at Fredi Washington's life
and career makes clear. Dramaturge and playwright Cheryl Black's careful
study of Washington's life and work demonstrates that one should not type-
cast Washington herself within the "tragic mulatto" archetypes she often
performed.[67] While she was subject to such typecasting, Washington was able
to use her various turns on stage and screen as a "tragic mulatto" to establish a body of work as a dramatic actress, a status at the time foreclosed to
most Black performers, who would be considered nearly exclusively for musical and comedic roles. In the early 1930s, Washington would star in feature
films including *The Emperor Jones* (1933) opposite Paul Robeson and, in her
most famous screen appearance, as Peola Johnson in 1934's *The Imitation of
Life*, a film that dealt explicitly with such themes as racial prejudice, colorism,
and "white passing." In her own writing, Washington was explicit that unlike
her *Imitation of Life* character, she had no desire to "pass" and was proud of
her identity as a Black woman. Washington would later work as an advocate
for Black performers before transitioning into a full-time columnist and activist in the 1940s.[68] I share these details of Washington's story to underscore

---

[64] Timme Rosenkrantz, *Harlem Jazz Adventures: A European Baron's Memoir 1934–1969*, adapted and
edited by Fradley Hamilton Gardner (Lanham, MD: Scarecrow Press, 2012), adapted from *Dus med Jazzen.
Mine jazzmemoirer. En bog om jazz—og andet godtfolk*, 1969.

[65] bell hooks, "Eating the Other: Desire and Resistance," in *Black Looks: Race and Representation*
(Boston: South End Press, 1992), 21–39.

[66] Howard Spring, "Changes in Jazz Performance and Arranging in New York, 1929–1932" (PhD diss.,
University of Illinois Urbana-Champaign, 1993). In explaining his use of *Melody Maker* in his own research, Spring makes this point about European jazz publications and a narrative travel writing tradition.

[67] Cheryl Black, "Looking White, Acting Black: Cast(e)ing Fredi Washington," *Theatre Survey* 45, no. 1
(May 2004): 19–40.

[68] Black, "Looking White, Acting Black," 21–33.

that the light-skinned, mixed-race women who circulated within the *plaçage* complex's pernicious ecosystem of tropes and stereotypes, and who at times enacted its proscribed fantasies, nevertheless lived full and complex lives in excess of the narratively circumscribed "tragic mulatto" characters they often portrayed. Washington was not the only light-skinned Black woman in the nineteenth or twentieth century—or of course at any point before or since—to hold a complex relationship with and nuanced understanding of the dynamic tension between her own agency and the specific conditions of possibility available to her.

## Conclusion

The mythic legacy of the quadroon balls continues to resonate throughout jazz's history and discourse, for as Gillory argues and as Clark's work further reinforces, "the malleable social dynamics inherent in these dances imbibe them with a cultural currency across historical planes."[69] If we shift our focus away from the ostensible origins of jazz-the-music, from a point of contact between Black and creole musicians, and toward the origins of "the origins of jazz"-the-discourse, from ongoing and interweaving points of contact between a miscegenated object and the white male desire to consume and dominate it, jazz's relationship to the narrative circularity surrounding the quadroon balls and their mutual imbrication in the *plaçage* complex become still more apparent. And yet, as the nature of the *plaçage* complex makes clear, the very dichotomization I have proposed here between the music and its narratives is a fundamental impossibility, and really that's kind of the point.

Jazz's music, its dance, its stories, and its historiography cannot be cleanly separated into discrete subjects of inquiry and critical analysis, for they all drink from the same well of cultural tropes, and their histories are fundamentally intertwined. The tropes generated by the romantic travel narratives that fetishized quadroon balls informed the broader colonialist miscegenation fantasy through which New Orleans became both America's cultural wellspring—the birthplace of its jazz—and its perpetually provincial other. Those tropes also informed and influenced late antebellum and early postbellum social events in New Orleans, Club Alabam's 1927 stage revue in midtown Manhattan, and the broader complex of minstrelized nostalgic plantation shows accompanied by the bands of Duke Ellington, Chick Webb, and others in late 1920s/early 1930s Harlem. Quadroon balls and their

---

[69] Guillory, "Some Enchanted Evening," 23.

mythologization influenced the sex work practices that permeated Storyville in the early twentieth century and thus surely influenced the conditions in which Buddy Bolden, Mamie Desdunes, and other formative jazz musicians made their music. Going further, the literal quadrilles and waltzes that the musicians in Monsieur La Garito's band would certainly have played, and to which New Orleanians danced, at the Washington and American Ballroom in 1858 must hold some connection to the quadrilles and waltzes Buddy Bolden's band played, and to which New Orleanians danced, in 1898.[70]

In explicating their place in the multiply miscegenated circulatory system of American identity, Williams observes that "Antebellum stories of the quadroon balls did important cultural work in articulating the terms of American citizenship in a republic based on white male privilege."[71] The privilege-reinforcing baton these stories forged has been passed to postbellum nostalgia for an earlier New Orleans, to the salacious enshrinement of Storyville as jazz's origin point, and certainly to the narrative conceits that fuel the jazz tradition more broadly. Nothing about this discursive lineage, including the linearity I have just outlined, is clean. Critically, Williams further highlights that narrativized *plaçage* relationships implicitly positioned quadroon women to become American citizens via principles of nineteenth-century liberalism and specifically liberal contract theory. Just as Burns, in his film series' opening gambit, positions jazz music as "born out of a million American negotiations," Williams points out that for quadroon women, to enter into contractual relationships was, in the nineteenth century, to participate in the forging of American identity.[72] Through his concept of "Blacksound," musicologist Matthew Morrison identifies the multiple legacies that blackface minstrel performance has left not only on the soundscapes of American popular music but on fundamental notions of American citizenship.[73] To Morrison's incisive analysis of the minstrel stage as a site of identity formation where white Americans forged the very notion of whiteness through "the expressive ways in which Irish and other white Americans performed improvised versions of themselves in blackface," I would add that the real and imagined site of the quadroon ball, and through it the *plaçage* complex, helped to write the "hidden scripts" of race in America by routing the nation's idyllically conjured "melting pot" through the white supremacist power dynamics of

---

[70] Lawrence Gushee draws heavily upon dance cards to connect nineteenth-century popular dances, including the waltz and quadrille, with the earliest jazz performers in "The Nineteenth Century Origins of Jazz," *Black Music Research Journal* 22 (2002): 151–174.

[71] Williams, "Can Quadroon Balls," 126.

[72] Williams, "Can Quadroon Balls," 122.

[73] Matthew D. Morrison, "Sound in the Construction of Race: From Blackface to Blacksound in Nineteenth Century America" (PhD diss., Columbia University, 2014), 3, 121–122.

miscegenation fantasy. This connection is underscored by jazz's mid-century imbrication—one might say its conscription—into Cold War–era cultural diplomacy as a disingenuously anti-racist totemic signifier of American citizenship itself.[74]

Where DeVeaux highlights and problematizes "the seductive badness of an originary Storyville" as "the vernacular lifeblood of jazz authenticity," the choreographed contractual exchanges of quadroon balls, both in practice and in narrative, have provided a necessary fuel source for the metaphors of sexual exchange that form the discursive engine of jazz's birth narrative by conjoining elements of alluring seduction with the dialectic of white dominance-as-benevolence and democratically licensed, ostensibly consensual exchange across racial lines.[75] Cheung argues that white dominance through miscegenation, due to Anglo American taboos against it, could be expressed only indirectly via "hidden transcripts," such as those facilitated through the quadroon ball.[76] That jazz's "hidden transcripts" also include a conflation of sexual liberation, American exceptionalism, and white supremacy—both despite and because of taboos against articulating these desires explicitly—is apparent in the layered "crossing" metaphors that shape our collective celebration of jazz's origins and continue to score the obfuscated choreographies through which mixed-race bodies, both real and imagined, both articulate and obscure the miscegenation-driven fantasies upon which those originary narratives rest.

[74] Morrison, "Sound in the Construction of Race," 77.
[75] Ronald Rodano, "Myth Today: The Color of Ken Burns Jazz," *Black Renaissance; New York* 3, no.3 (Summer, 2001): 42–54.
[76] Cheung, "*Les Cenelles* and Quadroon Balls," 14–15.

# 3

# "Lindy Hopper's Delight"

## The Chick Webb Orchestra and the Fluid Labor of Whitey's Lindy Hoppers

In September 1935, Harold Taylor, a correspondent for British jazz magazine *The Melody Maker*, was on assignment in New York.[1] Somewhat by accident, he stumbled upon Chick Webb and his orchestra doing a live broadcast for NBC. Taylor offered this thick account of the experience:

> I was wandering through the National Broadcasting Studios in the R.C.A. Buildings, New York, just looking around at the fine sights, peering in at rehearsals, listening to broadcasts, trying to find Ray Noble, and generally giving the National Broadcasting Company a thorough going-over, when I walked into a studio full of fifteen Negro musicians beating the hell out of *Singing a Vagabond Song*. There in the centre of the band was a short man on a high stool with his shoulders hunched over a mess of drums, his head in the clouds and his hands going like fury. It was none other than that uptown drummer Chick Webb, rehearsing his band for the four o'clock broadcast over the N.B.C. network.... The amusing part to watch of the broadcast was the clowning of the boys in the band throughout the whole broadcast. One fat little trumpeter danced around the soloists who were improvising and made faces at them. He couldn't sit still; every time the brass had some ensemble work to do, he stood up and pretended he was playing first trumpet with the utmost difficulty, writhing and waving his trumpet around. After the program I met that swell little gentleman Chick himself, and complimented him on the fine performance the band had just given. "No," he said, "that was no good. You come down to the Savoy tonight and hear what we can really do. It's a big night to-night and we'll show you some jazz." So down we went to Harlem and up to the Savoy to hear what Webb can really do, since if they were just fooling back in the studio, they must really send it down when they get swinging with the dancers in the Savoy.[2]

---

[1] Portions of this chapter were previously published as Christopher J. Wells, "'And I Make My Own': Class Performance, Black Urban Identity, and Depression-Era Harlem's Physical Culture," in *The Oxford Handbook of Dance and Ethnicity*, eds. Anthony Shay and Barbara Sellars Young (New York: Oxford University Press, 2016), 17–40. Reproduced here with the permission of Oxford University Press.

[2] Harold Taylor, "The Genial Chick Webb—A Broadcast and a Dance Session Described by Harold Taylor," *Melody Maker*, January 9, 1937, 2.

*Between Beats*. Christi Jay Wells, Oxford University Press (2021). © Oxford University Press.
DOI: 10.1093/oso/9780197559277.003.0003

Taylor's account offers our only surviving trace that Webb himself was aware of what many have stated since: that, as jazz critic Gary Giddins has put it, "those who heard him live insist that records hid his genius."[3] In his autobiography, Count Basie recalled of playing opposite Webb at the Savoy that "I just went somewhere and found me a place so I could sit and listen. If you never got to hear that band live, you really missed something."[4] Indeed, Webb's reputation as a dancer's musician was such that Duke Ellington's recollections of Webb in his autobiography focus primarily on Webb's sensitivity to the Savoy's dancing public:

> The reason why Chick Webb had such control, such command of his audiences at the Savoy ballroom, was because he was always in communication with the dancers and felt it the way they did. And that is probably the biggest reason why he could cut all the other bands that went in there.[5]

Ellington's perspective reinforces the most significant piece of Webb's legacy according to his peers: that his band was at its best when playing for dancers. Furthermore, Ellington's choice of words is significant: not that Webb *heard* the music the way they did, but that he *felt* it. In Harlem ballrooms, the emerging style of jazz that would come to be called "swing" was a music processed and evaluated kinesthetically through active participation as dancers responded individually and collectively to the music with a constant flow of ever-changing moves, rhythmic variations, and new dance styles. The common plane on which swing musicians and dancers could communicate was kinesthetic engagement; dancing and playing music are both, at their core, specific, cultivated practices of movement. Just as Webb felt the dancers' energy, they in turn felt his band's music and responded in ways that inspired the band. When asked why she sounded her best at the Savoy, Webb's star singer Ella Fitzgerald explained, "the Lindy Hoppers give me inspiration; I always feel they are my friends and always pulling for me."[6] As Taylor's anecdote, Ellington's commentary, and Fitzgerald's account make clear, recordings offer a relatively poor accounting of what Chick Webb's band "could really do," given that the circumstances of these recordings' creation were so detached from the dynamic, collaborative interactions between swing musicians and

---

[3] Gary Giddins, *Faces in the Crowd: Actors, Writers, Musicians, and Filmmakers* (New York: Da Capo, 1996), 111.

[4] Count Basie with Albert Murray, *Good Morning Blues: The Autobiography of Count Basie* (New York: Da Capo, 2002), 209.

[5] Duke Ellington, *Music Is My Mistress* (New York: Da Capo, 1973), 100.

[6] Ella Fitzgerald, quoted in Roi Ottley, "Popularity Runs in Cycles, Says Savoy Exponent of Swing," *New York Amsterdam News*, February 13, 1937, 10.

**Figure 3.1** Chick Webb (1909–1939) smiling from behind a set of drums with a set of drum sticks in his hand. The bass drum has a picture of Webb painted as a king on its side. Metronome/Getty Images.

their dancing audiences that shaped the sociality of the Savoy Ballroom (figure 3.1).

Jacqui Malone has argued that "It is impossible to study the evolution of African American vernacular dance in North America prior to 1950 without also studying the music of black Americans. The dancing was a visualization of the music and the musicians 'danced with sound.'"[7] Malone's assertion is

[7] Jacqui Malone, *Steppin' on the Blues: The Visible Rhythms of African American Dance* (Urbana: University of Illinois Press, 1996), 37.

particularly apparent in the relationships between swing bands and dancing audiences during the 1930s. During this time, the collaborative dynamic between musicians and dancers was both mediated and catalyzed by the commercial marketplace, as a band's success in ballrooms was defined largely by its ability to keep the dancers on the floor. As a regular part of making a living, Swing Era dance musicians were expected to construct a rhythmic framework and musical space that sparked dancers' energies and inspired their steps, spins, and improvisations. Dance musicians, therefore, recognized their role within a ballroom landscape that included, in fact depended on, enthusiastic and collaborative participation from dancers. Through this mutual exchange, musicians and dancing audiences co-created soundscapes where participating bodies negotiated social dynamics to forge shared spaces for communication, collaboration, and catharsis. Recollections from bandleaders, sidemen, critics, and dancing audience members affirm the centrality of these spaces to Chick Webb's music and thus the necessity of understanding that music through dance. Yet, these accounts leave much to be explored to conceptually "flesh out" the richly corporeal experiences their words only hint at. What did it feel like to dance to Webb's music? How did dancers listen with and through their bodies? What creative movements did they contribute to the ballroom soundscape and how might they have influenced what the band created?

The idea that such a dynamic relationship between musicians and dancers existed is far from controversial; it is near a consensus opinion in swing music scholarship across fields such as jazz studies, dance studies, and American studies that dancing audiences were central to the musical and cultural phenomena that have come to define the Swing Era. There are generally two streams of academic scholarship that interrogate this relationship. The first stream, housed primarily though not exclusively within musicology and dance studies, emphasizes musicians' collaborative connections with professional performing dancers. Work in this vein includes Brian Harker's discussion of Louis Armstrong's relationship with the eccentric dance team of Brown and McGraw, Todd Decker's work on Fred Astaire's interactive relationship with jazz musicians on both stage and screen, and Brenda Dixon Gottschild's analysis of African American ballroom team Norton & Margot's navigation of the racial dynamics of the Swing Era's professional landscape.[8] This research

---

[8] Brian Harker, "Louis Armstrong, Eccentric Dance, and the Evolution of Jazz on the Eve of Swing," *Journal of the American Musicological Society* 61, no. 1 (Spring 2008): 67–121; Todd Decker, *Music Makes Me: Fred Astaire and Jazz* (Berkeley: University of California Press, 2011); Brenda Dixon Gottschild, *Waltzing in the Dark: African American Vaudeville and Race Politics in the Swing Era* (New York: Palgrave Macmillan, 1999).

provides substantial insight into the social and professional negotiations across various professional landscapes through which dancers and musicians forged creative connections, but it tells us less about amateur dancing audience members and their role in these processes of musician-dancer collaborative innovation. Foregrounding the experiences of professional performers to the exclusion of amateur dancers exacerbates the problem of a media archive that skews our perspective on Black social dance practices. As Thomas F. DeFrantz explains:

> [H]and-made, extravagantly detailed, expert versions of Black social dances . . . inevitably develop. These versions bear little resemblance to the dance that was briefly practiced by a larger population. But these physically burnished, expert demonstrations become the sedimented archive that stand for the dance in later generations. . . . Black social dance in heavy circulation distends well past any an easily scalable "social." The important point here: depictions of Black social dance inevitably celebrate its most extravagant practitioners, rather than the anonymous people who gave rise to the forms.[9]

The second stream, much of it coming from scholars in fields such as American studies, history, and English, seeks to give voice to the "anonymous people" whose erasure DeFrantz highlights. Toward that end, studies in this stream emphasize the relationship between dancing audience members and swing bands, tending to do so metaphorically through broader social analyses of American culture in the 1930s. Works that adopt this approach include Lewis Erenberg's analysis of swing dancing as an expression of extended adolescence brought on by the Great Depression and Gena Caponi Taberry's work situating the "jump" as an expressive phenomenon in African American culture across dance, music, and sports.[10] While it often makes important large-scale connections that traverse and inform multiple more specific contexts,

---

[9] Thomas F. DeFrantz, "Bone-Breaking, Black Social Dance, and Queer Corporeal Orature," *The Black Scholar* 46, no. 1 (2016): 71. Indeed, this chapter exemplifies some of the issues DeFrantz highlights as it relies substantially on the accounts of two specific lindy hop dancers, Frankie Manning and Norma Miller, who rapidly became high-level professional lindy hop dancers in the 1930s and have been central figures in the contemporary global lindy hop scene (often mischaracterized as a "revival"). Their published autobiographies, and numerous oral history interviews (including original interviews I conducted with each of them while researching my doctoral dissertation on the Chick Webb Orchestra). I have thus designed this chapter to feature the specificity of their experiences and that specificity's broader importance rather than attempt to characterize the experiences of Black social dancers more broadly.

[10] Lewis A. Erenberg, *Swinging the Dream: Big Band Jazz and the Rebirth of American Culture* (Chicago: University of Chicago Press, 1998); Gena Caponi-Tabery, *Jump for Joy: Jazz, Basketball, and Black Culture in 1930s America* (Amherst: University of Massachusetts Press, 2008). I should note, however, that Erenberg's work often flattens distinctions of race and racialized experience, presenting a different but perhaps even more problematic means of erasing the anonymous voices of African American social dancers.

this work often avoids unpacking the challenging, fine-grained dynamics of how dancers interacted with musicians and impacted swing music's development in favor of an emphasis on swing as a mass cultural phenomenon where dance was but one expression, albeit an important one, of the era's distinctly modern, industrial zeitgeist.[11]

My aim in this chapter is to offer a case study that both unites these streams of discourse and also offers one pathway, rooted in Harlem's Savoy Ballroom, through which musician and dancer interactions during the Swing Era moved dynamically between contexts that blurred clear distinctions between amateur and professional dance. In so doing, I hope also to offer some additional nuance to the evolutionary narrative suggested by Malone, who writes:

> The dances that began on the farms, plantations, levees, and urban streets of colonial America evolved through minstrelsy and moved onto the "stages" of traveling shows, vaudeville, musical theater, cabarets, and night clubs. The development and growth of this country's preeminent vernacular dance paralleled the evolution of African American music and took a giant leap forward in the twenties, thirties, and forties, when the connections between black singers, dance acts, and jazz musicians revolutionized American culture.[12]

Malone's assessment here underscores the coterminous development of jazz music and dance practices in interwar America, and the broader study of jazz dance and big band music in which this passage appears broke new ground in articulating the shared co-creative process through which these forms developed. Still, the implication of an evolutionary migration of dance practices from social to commercial contexts tells only part of the story. The landscape for participation in popular culture during the 1930s, and especially popular dance, was shaped by complex intersections between amateur and professional spheres of cultural production. The decade's mass media landscape informed new processes of collaborative inspiration through which new modes of musicking and dancing informed each other, and the flows between folk practices to the realm of professional art and entertainment were far from unidirectional. As Katrina Hazzard Gordon has said of nightlife in urban Black communities, "the jook continuum imparted a distinct identity to the new forms. Rent parties, honky tonks, after-hours joints, membership clubs,

---

[11] Joel Dinerstein, *Swinging the Machine: Modernity, Technology, and African American Culture between the World Wars* (Amherst: University of Massachusetts Press, 2003) and Kenneth J. Bindas, *Swing, That Modern Sound* (Jackson: University of Mississippi Press, 2001).

[12] Jacqui Malone, *Steppin' the Blues: The Visible Rhythms of African American Dance* (Urbana: University of Illinois Press, 1996), 106.

dance halls, and night clubs existed simultaneously and cross-fertilized each other."[13] As this cross-fertilization occurred between Black cultural venues with diverse orientations toward official spaces of commerce, each with its own dynamic flows between the spheres of "amateur" and "professional" practice, so too did Black cultural production extend its reach into emergent media landscapes such that the virtuosic music and dance featured on stage and screen increasingly influenced everyday social practices on ballroom floors and urban streets (and on farms and levees as well).

Fluidity of exchange across spheres of amateur and professional practice in many ways defined the Chick Webb Orchestra's approach to music-making as the primary house band throughout the 1930s at the Savoy Ballroom, where they forged a uniquely potent connection with lindy hop dancers. Their collaborative relationship traversed nimbly through the interconnected contexts of nightly social dancing, formal and informal competitions, and commercial performances for stage and screen. Webb played nightly for the Savoy's social dances, which ran from early evening until 2 a.m. or later as his band was tasked with keeping the ballroom's massive block-length dance floor full and with motivating those crowds to return nightly. On Saturday nights, the band played for lively competitions where the ballroom's most skilled dancers pushed the extremes of their own, and each other's, abilities. Finally, Webb's band accompanied the lindy hop's transition into a form of professional stage dance, as the ballroom's owner Moe Gale frequently packaged Webb's band with the Savoy's top dancers for shows at the Apollo and Paramount theaters and to tour on a Northeastern circuit known as "the round robin."[14] Webb's music thus had to connect with dancers on multiple levels. On the "macro" level, his band was responsible for maintaining the dancing energy of the entire ballroom as he played in concert with the movements of thousands of dancing bodies. On the "micro" level, the band forged close one-on-one connections with the relatively small group of elite dancers who pushed the lindy hop to new creative heights.

Central to my interrogation of this close connection is an unpacking of the relationships among three distinct yet interlocking modes of, and contexts for, Black vernacular dance: social, competition, and performance. Lindy hop scholars Terry Monaghan and Karren Hubbard offer this tripartite division as a guiding framework for interpreting the lindy hop, identifying these as the

[13] Hazzard-Gordon, *Jookin'*, 124.
[14] Norma Miller, interview with the author, Herräng, Sweden, July 2011. Jacqui Malone discusses a nearly identical, very likely the same, Black touring circuit called "'Round the World," consisting of theaters in New York, Baltimore, Philadelphia, and Washington, DC, some of which are the same as those mentioned by Miller. Malone, *Steppin' on the Blues*, 93.

dance's three "major modes."[15] Monaghan and Hubbard present these three modes as distinct, but they also argue that the modes fluidly informed each other, as "however far apart these activities appeared to be outside the ball-room, the essence of each artistic achievement was infused back into the general mix when the core Savoy Lindy Hoppers returned to the Savoy."[16] As Monaghan and Hubbard observe, the dynamic exchange between the lindy hop's major modes was grounded within the Savoy Ballroom, specifically through the labor of the Savoy Ballroom's elite dancers. As house band leader for much of the 1930s, Webb and his band enjoyed a uniquely close relationship with this crowd of dancers that spanned and traversed these major modes of social, competition, and performance dancing.[17]

## Webb and His "Jungle Band": Performing Closeness, Enacting Distance

Born and raised in Baltimore, Maryland, William Henry "Chick" Webb came to New York City in 1924 with his friend and collaborator, guitarist John Trueheart. As Webb traveled in the same musical and social circles as Duke Ellington and Coleman Hawkins, journalist Burt Korall has claimed that through these associations, Webb "learned the folkways of the New York scene."[18] In mid-1929, Webb's band took over for Duke Ellington's as the house band at the Cotton Club. Located on Lennox Avenue at 142nd Street, the Cotton Club was the most famous and iconic segregated venue in Harlem. In 1925, it adopted a similar whites-only policy to its chief competitor Connie's Inn, the Harlem nightclub that had initiated the practice of marketing specifically to "downtown" white visitors and segregating the venue to cater to them exclusively.[19] In taking over for Ellington at the Cotton Club, Webb stepped into the same role through which Ellington had launched his career with

---

[15] Terry Monaghan and Karen Hubbard, "Negotiating Compromise on a Burnished Wood Floor: Social Dancing at the Savoy," in *Ballroom, Boogie, Shimmy Sham, Shake: A Social and Popular Dance Reader*, ed. Julie Malnig (Urbana: University of Illinois Press, 2009), 129.

[16] Monaghan and Hubbard, "Negotiating Compromise," 129.

[17] My analysis here is also indebted to recent work in musicology and dance studies applying history and theory from labor studies to American music and dance at midcentury. Specifically, Fen Kennedy ties Fordist labor ideology to the social and concert practices that discursively yielded "modern dance," and Kirsten L. Speyer Carithers explores the various types of "interpretive labor" asked of performers of experimental compositions. Fenella Kennedy, "Before We Became Modern: The Slow Drag from Black Partner Dancing to Concert Stages," in "Movement Writes: Four Case Studies in Dance, Discourse, and Shifting Boundaries" (PhD diss., Ohio State University, 2009), 27–77; Kirsten L. Speyer Carithers, "The Work of Indeterminacy: Interpretive Labor in Experimental Music" (PhD diss., Northwestern University, 2017).

[18] Burt Korall, *Drummin' Men: The Heartbeat of Jazz, the Swing Years* (New York: Oxford University Press, 1990), 12.

[19] Ernest Varlack, "Theatre Gossip," *Baltimore Afro-American*, July 13, 1929, 5.

colorful, exotic compositions to accompany the club's salacious floor shows. Ellington's style, now remembered through compositions like "East St. Louis Toodle-oo" and "Black Beauty," took on the moniker of "jungle music" to emphasize its titillating alterity. The label also signified the exoticization of those scantily clad Black dancing bodies whose otherness and consumability the music itself helped to construct.[20]

Indeed, Webb's earliest surviving recordings evince his engagement with Ellington's "jungle music" style. In October 1929, Webb and his band, under the moniker "The Jungle Band," recorded two sides for Brunswick: the up-tempo Charleston tune "Dog Bottom" and the slower blues number "Jungle Mama." The latter recording contains many sonic signifiers of Ellington's jungle style. Its most prominent "jungle" element is the extended trumpet solo (0:14–1:02) in which Ward Pinkett displays the pitch bending, growling effects, and muted timbres popularized by the Ellington band's trumpeter Bubber Miley.[21] In fact, "Jungle Mama's" introduction and opening series of trumpet choruses mirror the formal plan of Ellington's most famous vehicle for Miley's playing: "East St. Louis Toodle-Oo." In both pieces, an eight-bar ensemble introduction creates an ostinato that subsequently supports a two-chorus trumpet solo. In addition, "Jungle Mama's" tempo and persistent, steady guitar strumming are virtually identical to Ellington's 1931 recording "Echoes of the Jungle," and the ensemble's riff-based and interactions with the trumpet soloists are also extremely similar. The sonic resonances of "Jungle Mama" with, among other Ellington recordings, "East St. Louis Toodle-oo" predate and perhaps anticipate Cab Calloway's evocation of the song in his iconic 1931 recording of "Minnie the Moocher." Calloway's hit coincided with the start of his own Cotton Club residency, and musicologist Nate Sloan has argued that the tune "suggests the same miasmic, mysterious mood telegraphed by Ellington's 'jungle style,'" and the stylistic hallmarks of "East St. Louis Toodle-oo" in particular.[22] Whether Calloway followed Webb's model directly or simply made a similar choice for similar reasons, it is clear that the specter of Ellington's soundscape extended beyond his band's physical

[20] Christopher J. Wells, "'And I Make My Own': Class Performance, Black Urban Identity, and Depression-Era Harlem's Physical Culture," in *The Oxford Handbook of Dance and Ethnicity*, eds. Anthony Shay and Barbara Sellars Young (New York: Oxford University Press, 2016), 17–40. Kimberly Hannon Teal addresses Ellington's "jungle" style as a consistent thread in his oeuvre rather than an aesthetic confined to his Cotton Club years in "Beyond the Cotton Club: The Persistence of Duke Ellington's Jungle Style," *Jazz Perspectives* 6, no. 1–2 (2012): 123–149.

[21] The Jungle Band, "Jungle Mama," *Chick Webb: Spinnin' the Webb—The Original Decca Recordings* (GRP Records, 1994), https://open.spotify.com/track/05YC9CxtyMSJ6t5WB5to5K?si =YkZ-ueIzQ7mgYvoWLbvKqg.

[22] Sloan, "Constructing Cab Calloway," 382.

presence between the Cotton Club's walls, shaping the sonic expectations to which the bandleaders who followed him adapted.

Webb was well prepared for his entrée into the Cotton Club by his experience working at the Rose-Danceland (not to be confused with the more famous Roseland Ballroom) the year prior. In January 1928, the band began a regular engagement at the Rose-Danceland at 209 West 125th street near Seventh Avenue. According to the *Baltimore Afro-American*, Webb's band was a mainstay at the venue throughout the late 1920s, and its white clientele considered the band a gem within an otherwise underwhelming establishment. The *Afro-American* quoted an account from *Variety* describing the Rose-Danceland as "the wooziest of creep joints," although it became a platform for Webb's band to enhance its reputation.[23] Embracing its role as a "creep joint," the venue distinguished itself through its late hours—it was open until 3 a.m. where similar venues closed at 1 a.m.—and through its promise of attractive Black female "taxi dancers" who charged a per-dance fee to the Rose-Danceland's white male patrons. The *Variety* report described the taxi dancing as "a tariff dance idea of a dozen crawls for a dollar with an army of 'hostesses' on hand to entertain the visiting fleet."[24] The presence of taxi dancing facilitated mixed-race socialization, albeit mediated by commercial exchange, without integrating the venue. So long as Black women's bodies were presented as commodities to be rented for entertainment, this risqué, ostensibly dangerous, and subversive interracial contact posed no genuine threat to white supremacy within the social orders of New York City and of the United States more broadly. However, while Black female cabaret and taxi dancers may have rendered themselves commodities for white male pleasure, this performance served their own ends as well. Even when enacted through a gestural vocabulary built from primitivist stereotypes, such performances functioned discursively as critiques of Harlem's normative moral values and class hierarchy.[25] As theatre historian Shane Vogel argues, Black female

---

[23] "Webb's Orchestra Is Mainstay of Rose Danceland," *Baltimore Afro-American*, January 7, 1928, 7. In addition, a 1929 article refers to Webb's Harlem Stompers as "regular favorites at Rose-Danceland." Maurice Dancer, "Webb's Harlem Stompers, Sterling New York Band, to Play in 'Dew Drop Inn,'" *Pittsburgh Courier*, March 23, 1939, A3.

[24] "Webb's Orchestra Is Mainstay," 7.

[25] Jayna Brown argues that through such "racialized gestural vocabularies," Black female dancers could "shape and redefine their bodies as modern." Though I generally agree with Brown's argument, I do want to read her idea of "racialized gestural vocabularies" through Sherrie Tucker's observation that white performers often operated with a "working vocabulary of blackness." The performative tropes that Black women performers deployed in cabarets likely both expanded and was also shaped by a racialized "working vocabulary of blackness" that affirmed white customers' expectations and satisfied their desires. As cabaret performers and taxi dancers deployed these signifiers in a professional context, the language "working vocabulary" is particularly apt. See Brown, *Babylon Girls*, 3, and Sherrie Tucker, "Beyond the Brass Ceiling: Dolly Jones Trumpets Modernity in Oscar Micheaux's *Swing!*," *Jazz Perspectives* 3, no. 1 (2009): 18.

performers in Harlem's cabaret scene were "cultural workers" who "used the cabaret to critique the racial and sexual normativity of uplift ideology and to imagine alternative narratives of sexual and racial selfhood."[26] While working under the white male gaze, such dancers were simultaneously contesting the Black middle-class gaze by offering alternatives to the conservative articulation of bodily comportment with moral value that at the time dominated the discourse in Harlem's public sphere.[27] Furthermore, like the Black male bouncers and other service workers whose labor itself—owing to both their literal servitude and performative enactment thereof—affirmed white desire and white dominance, Black women working as dancers also profited financially from this industry and through it found an alternative to other forms of service work that rendered them invisible support structures propping up white society. By both manipulating and reshaping white constructions of Black female bodies, cabaret performers and taxi dancers shaped the corporeal conversations through which systems of exchange, power, and representation were negotiated within Harlem's "creep joints."

As the house band, Webb's ensemble provided the soundscape that bolstered and narrated the Rose-Danceland's corporeal economy of signs. *Variety* described this 11-piece iteration of Webb's group as "the best colored dance band in New York" and emphasized that the Rose-Danceland was a "common dance hall" whose success could be credited to Webb's orchestra. They praised Webb's band for "playing the colored man's jazz az iz [*sic*]. It's the Caucasian element that knows jazz az iz that has converted an impossible loft into a shrewd moneymaker."[28] This review suggests that Webb understood, as did Ellington in developing his "jungle style," that for white audiences, Black music's appeal was based on a perceived authenticity contingent upon the sonic and corporeal performance of difference.[29] By emphasizing sonic otherness through exotic harmonies, rough timbres, and syncopated rhythms, Webb, Ellington, and other Black musicians in Harlem's segregated venues constructed a sonic enactment of racial distance that established, in the minds of white patrons, a sense of undiluted, authentic Blackness. This was the "colored man's music"

---

[26] Shane Vogel, *The Scene of the Harlem Cabaret: Race, Sexuality, Performance* (Chicago: University of Chicago Press, 2009), 3.

[27] Vogel, *Scene of the Harlem Cabaret*, 11.

[28] "Webb's Orchestra Is Mainstay," 7.

[29] David Krasner argues, via Bert Williams and George Walker's use of blackface and Aida Overton Walker's cakewalk classes for upper-class whites, that African American performers at the turn of the century traded upon discourses of authenticity bound up in the broader emergence of American brand marketing to reclaim minstrel archetypes and gradually modify and repurpose them as vehicles through which to express Black dignity. David Krasner, "The Real Thing," in *Beyond Blackface: African Americans and the Creation of American Popular Culture 1890–1930*, ed. W. Fitzhugh Brundage (Chapel Hill: University of North Carolina Press, 2011), 99–123.

in its ostensibly pure and primitive form untouched by the elite trappings of white culture; this was "jazz az iz." However, this aesthetic stance maintained white dominance over Black cultural production as it positioned the discriminating white audience member as the validating arbiter of Black music and dance's unmediated racial authenticity. Self-cast in the role of subversive discoverer, white audience members became the protagonists of their own Harlem stories, performing their progressive taste and adventurous spirit by seeking out, recognizing, and celebrating Black music as they understood it, for what would be its significance without "the Caucasian element that knows jazz az iz"? Webb's performances in Jungle Alley nightclubs thus constructed race spatially by creating a simultaneity of closeness and separation through the logics of consumer culture. In effect, the clear distinction between white patrons and Black musicians, dancers, bouncers, and waiters extended the dynamics of staged performance off the stage itself into an ostensibly social dance-oriented context by constructing and maintaining a kind of racial proscenium. Even when white and Black bodies made literal contact, as in the case of taxi dancing, distance was maintained through enacted distinctions between the consumer and the consumed.

Around the time of his Rose-Danceland residency, Webb also began a relationship with the Savoy Ballroom a new Harlem venue for dance music that sought to offer an alternative to the white supremacist rules of engagement that had shaped venues including the Cotton Club and Rose-Danceland. The Savoy Ballroom opened in 1926 and reflected Black Harlemites' efforts to bypass segregated cultural spaces by building their own comparable institutions. The ballroom was a collaboration between African American community leader Charles Buchanan and white businessmen Moe Gale and Jay Faggen.[30] Faggen's involvement was no coincidence given his history as a promoter for midtown Manhattan's segregated Roseland Ballroom, as the Savoy was created to serve as a kind of uptown answer to the Roseland. The Savoy contested its downtown counterpart's segregated policies by offering a vision of utopian integration where people of all races and circumstances were welcomed.

Crucial to this positioning was the idea that the Savoy was to be every bit the Roseland's equal. Early announcements in the *New York Amsterdam News* before the Savoy's March 1926 opening emphasized that the architects behind downtown dance palaces like the Roseland and Arcadia were overseeing the new Harlem ballroom's construction and that "thousands of dollars

---

[30] Alexandre Abdoulaev, "Savoy: Reassessing the Role of the 'World's Finest Ballroom' in Music and Culture, 1926–1958" (PhD diss., Boston University, 2014), 46.

have been expended in interior decorations."[31] Despite such expenditures, the Savoy would charge the relatively low admittance fee of fifty cents. Despite its accessible price, however, it still offered the kinds of material trappings that signified wealth and elite achievement at downtown dance palaces like the Roseland, and its décor was "laid out in a manner which holds good only in the most expensive places on Broadway."[32] It boasted "ornate French mirrors, varicolored electric lights, and a reception room with costly rugs" in addition to a full staff of trained hostesses to entertain the crowds.[33] These hostesses, along with the rest of the Savoy's all-Black staff, attended a twice-weekly "School of Courtesy" to ensure that "patrons will find themselves in an environment of refinement as well as beauty second to none."[34] At the Savoy, Black patrons would have the opportunity to "sit at one of the many tables behind the highly polished rail and be served refreshments furnished by the most up-to-date caterers."[35] The Savoy also gave Black bands a space to play for integrated, though majority Black, audiences in a respectable atmosphere. In its advertising, the Savoy emphasized that it would offer Black patrons comparable entertainment to the segregated white venues in Harlem and downtown to which they did not have access:

> Thousands have found enjoyment at the Savoy since it has been opened, and to the credit of the management be it said that they have always tried to please and hold their large patronage by offering things not to be found at any other place of its kind in the city catering to Negroes.[36]

The *Amsterdam News* hoped the ballroom would "fill a long-felt want and supply that something lacking elsewhere."[37]

The Savoy's marketing of its musicians reflected its larger strategy of projecting racial uplift, and manager Charles Buchanan promoted the ballroom as a wholesome environment. In response to criticism that the Savoy over-policed patrons' comportment, Buchanan made a public statement articulating the Savoy's philosophy:

[31] "New Savoy Throws Open Its Doors to Public in March," *New York Amsterdam News*, February 24, 1926, 5.
[32] "Thousands Storm New Savoy at Big Opening Friday Night, March 12," *New York Amsterdam News* March 17, 1926, 5.
[33] "Largest Ballroom to Open Saturday," *Baltimore Afro-American*, March 13, 1926, 4.
[34] "Savoy Ballroom Now Has School of Courtesy for Its Employees," *New York Amsterdam News*, May 26, 1926, 5.
[35] "New Savoy Throws Open," *Amsterdam News*, 5.
[36] "New Savoy Throws Open," *Amsterdam News*, 5.
[37] "New Savoy Throws Open," *Amsterdam News*, 5.

Some folks have gotten the idea that the Savoy is too strict. They say that because we won't stand for a lot of necking, indecent mooch dancing and the like that you can't have a good time here. We want to tell you right now that it's a lot of applesauce. We know and so do you that the Savoy is not a fly-by-night venture, but is intended to remain here for many years to come. We just feel it's a lot nicer to live in a clean house than a dirty one and we know and so do you, nothing that isn't on the level can survive for long.

You wouldn't let your sister go to a place with indecent environment. You wouldn't want your mother to know you go there. We realize how true that is, thus we conduct the Savoy along lines that will please your mother, your sister, and you. And believe us, you can have a mighty good time here.[38]

In addition to emphasizing dignified behavior and upstanding citizenship, the Savoy boasted of its employee compensation, claiming it paid each married male employee no less than $40 per week and that musicians averaged $75 per week, roughly three times the average salary for men in Harlem.[39] Despite scant press coverage to that point, music columnist Eva Jessye reported in July 1927 that Webb's Harlem Stompers, then at the Savoy, were "the hottest 8-piece band in the country."[40] Webb and His Harlem Stompers played there regularly during most of 1927 and returned in July 1928 after an eight-month absence, presumably while the band was in residence at the Rose-Danceland.[41] In contrast to the primitivist discourse surrounding the Cotton Club, the Savoy praised its dance bands as disciplined and orderly, offering audiences a chance to "trip the light fantastic to the melodious strains emanating from a highly trained orchestra."[42]

Webb's band of the late 1920s could certainly perform melodious strains to accompany dignified social dancing just as well as they could provide a soundtrack for exotic floor shows and taxi dancing. On the other side from "Jungle Mama" of the Webb "Jungle Band's" 1929 record is the upbeat "Dog Bottom," which exhibits another musical personality entirely. Evoking a wholly different Harlem soundscape, "Dog Bottom" echoes the popular style of the Fletcher Henderson Orchestra, whose leader was a paragon of Race pride in Harlem during the late 1920s. Henderson's style of popular dance music adapted the intricate scoring practices of Paul Whiteman's orchestra

[38] Charles Buchanan, public statement quoted in "Savoy Takes Over New Alhambra Ballroom," *Pittsburgh Courier*, September 14, 1929, A3.
[39] "Savoy Takes Over," *Pittsburgh Courier*, A3.
[40] Eva Jessye, "Around New York," *Baltimore Afro-American*, July 2, 1927, 9.
[41] "Amateur Gives 'Kongo-King'," *Baltimore Afro-American*, July 21, 1928, 9.
[42] "New Savoy Throws Open," *Amsterdam News*, 5.

with the signifiers of "hot" rhythm and Black vernacular music practices Henderson acquired during his time as music director for Black Swan Records and specifically as blues singer Ethel Waters's accompanist.[43] The Henderson band molded such signifiers into an "elevated" form of intricately and cleverly scored music that projected, for Black audiences, the ideology of racial uplift. Henderson's band did not have the same kind of associations with exotic sexuality upon which Ellington's reputation was built, but their success nevertheless depended upon engagement with white culture and with white expectations of Black music. In the late 1920s, the Henderson orchestra had a long-standing engagement at the Roseland, which served as a central site to channel white youth's thirst for exciting entertainment into respectable, upper-class venues replete with crystal chandeliers and other signifiers of wealth and status. Even as he played for white audiences in a segregated ballroom, Henderson's association with this venue and its elite status reflected his and other Black musicians' emergent upwardly mobile identities.[44] Echoing the Henderson's band's sonic enactment of uplift discourse, Webb's "Dog Bottom" moves quickly from a Whiteman-esque introduction featuring a step-wise descent into a sixteen-bar section featuring a wind trio that evokes the innovative style of Henderson arranger Don Redman. This interweaving of varied instrumental groupings with full ensemble passages and brief solos was the hallmark of Redman's style. It projected an air of sophistication, cleverness, professionalism, and, most importantly, literacy that drove the reconciliation in mid- and late-1920s Harlem between popular "race music" and the ideology of racial uplift.[45] While the Savoy Ballroom's founders initially saw their venue as a site to reinforce this vision of racial uplift, the ballroom's patrons would increasingly forge a path that eschewed both the "slumming" stereotypes on display in the Cotton Club and the strict imitation of white upper classness the Roseland represented. They would craft this identity on the Savoy Ballroom's dance floor, in conversation with Webb and his band.

## The Savoy Ballroom and the Rise of Whitey's Lindy Hoppers

Shortly after the Savoy Ballroom opened its doors, its efforts to provide Black Harlemites with a high-class, Roseland-style dance palace were complicated

---

[43] Jeffrey Magee, *Fletcher Henderson: The Uncrowned King of Swing* (New York: Oxford University Press, 2005), 23–25.

[44] Magee, *Uncrowned King of Swing*, 6–7, 27–29.

[45] Magee, *Uncrowned King of Swing*, 39–71.

by a new generation of dancers, who developed a new dance that in many ways reconciled the conflicting narratives of Harlem Webb's band had navigated during the 1920s: the lindy hop. Initially principally a social dance, the lindy hop may well owe its origins to innovations developed in competition spaces. Though its origin stories vary, the most commonly accepted point of origin for the lindy hop, or at least for that name, is a 1928 dance marathon contest held at the Rockland Palace. When one reporter asked Savoy Ballroom dancer George "Shorty" Snowden what he and his partner were doing (a variation on the Charleston including "breakaways" from one's partner), he recalled recent headlines featuring Charles Lindbergh's transatlantic flight and replied that he was doing the lindy hop.[46] The dance grew in popularity throughout the late 1920s and into the early 1930s. During this time, Webb stepped into a consistent residency at the Savoy that would come to define his career throughout the mid- and late 1930s, when his became the Savoy's most famous "house band." While numerous house bands cycled through the Savoy, Webb's outfit consistently enjoyed pride of place as the band most closely associated with the ballroom and its lindy hoppers.

By 1935, the lindy hop was an accepted and highly valued element of the Savoy Ballroom's culture, which was in sharp contrast to owner Moe Gale and manager Charles Buchanan's original plans for a dance palace geared toward high-class nightlife. Throughout the early 1930s, the Savoy's patrons found means to resist and subvert the ballroom's rigid policies. Despite the Savoy management's initial reservations, the ballroom ultimately became a hub of popular dance and was central to the lindy hop's development. The lindy hop attracted young Harlem residents who exaggerated the holds and conventions of more traditional ballroom dances, infusing them with athletic, improvisational movement. At first, these developments were not welcome in the Savoy, as management feared they transgressed the dignified atmosphere for which the establishment was aiming, while dancers found strategies to both figuratively and literally evade the policing of their movements. Snowden would later recount to Marshall Stearns that he invented a traveling step to escape the ballroom's bouncers when they gave chase and that he developed his renowned foot speed through these involuntary "dances" with the ballroom's enforcers. While Buchanan initially rejected Snowden as a threat to the Savoy's "high-class" ideals, Snowden's innovative moves became so popular

---

[46] Harri Heinilä, "An Endeavor by Harlem Dancers to Achieve Equality: Recognition of the Harlem-based African American Jazz Dance between 1921 and 1943" (PhD diss., University of Helsinki, 2016), 117.

that Buchanan ultimately recognized the dancer's enormous popularity and gave him a gilded lifetime pass to the ballroom.[47]

The lindy hop Snowden and his peers developed, which came to dominate the Savoy, was a corporeal statement of participation, of agency, and of self-expression. It afforded Harlem youth otherwise marginalized within exploitive labor conditions or absorbed into essentialist constructions of their neighborhood a chance to be seen and heard in public space by their peers and on their own terms. Catering to a lindy-hopping public ultimately became a financial necessity for ballrooms. As one unsympathetic reporter noted, the dance "has developed into such a pest that some halls advertise No Lindy Hop allowed here. The result is a loss of business."[48]

Over time, the vibrancy of this emerging popular dance culture shifted the Savoy's ethos away from its reproduction of downtown elitism. Mura Dehn observed this change firsthand:

In the mid-thirties, the ballroom was invaded by youth. Gone the evening gowns, the formal dress, the grown up sophistication. Jitterbugs made their debut. Thick-rimmed glasses, thick-soled sneakers, sport jackets, sweaters. Girls in bobby socks, flaring skirts, skull caps with a long feather. Ballroom bubbling with energy.[49]

When the band found success on national radio as the first Black band with a sustaining program, *Baltimore Afro-American* columnist Allan McMillan attributed Webb's radio breakthrough to his band's pioneering ability to balance the stylistic elements of sweet and hot jazz:

There is much talk this week along Tin Pan Alley and Broadway concerning the little half-pint orchestra leader Chick Webb, who seems to have started something new so far as an innovation in music is concerned, among the sepia orchestras. He and his musical organization mix smooth syncopation and super torrid rhythm to good advantage.[50]

---

[47] Marshall Stearns, notes from interview with George "Shorty" Snowden, December 17, 1959, Marshall Winslow Stearns Collection, Box 7, Folder 22, Institute of Jazz Studies, Rutgers University Libraries.

[48] Wilbur Young, "Dances Originating in Harlem," unpublished draft of a report for the WPA Writers Project, Writers Program New York City: Negroes of New York Collection, Reel 2, Schomburg Center for Research in Black Culture, The New York Public Library.

[49] Mura Dehn, "Jazz Dance," unpublished manuscript [n.d.], Mura Dehn Papers on Afro-American Social Dance, Box 1 Folder 5, Jerome Robbins Dance Division, The New York Public Library for the Performing Arts.

[50] Allan McMillan, "Theater Chat," *Baltimore Afro-American*, September 1, 1934, 8.

Other columnists echoed this praise for Webb's stylistic synthesis during his tenure at the Savoy. In an article for the *Pittsburgh Courier* entitled "Chick Webb Likes His Music 'Sweet,' but He Can Dish It Up Plenty 'Hot,'" Floyd J. Calvin situated this quality as a product of Webb's sensitivity to the nuances of pleasing an audience, whatever their taste at the moment:

> Naturally, Chick's first interest is music. He likes his scintillating melody soft and sweet, but he admits willingly that he can dish it out plenty hot, as hot as the hottest hotcha fans like it. Yes, Chick is one guy who gives the public what it wants.[51]

It appears that, at the Savoy, the dancing public wanted everything Webb and his band had to offer. His music continued to push lindy hop dancers to new heights throughout the 1930s, and his band became synonymous with the Savoy as a space, an articulation that remains perhaps the defining feature of Webb's legacy. The larger story of Webb's musical life in Harlem, however, demonstrates the depth of this connection as the Savoy's particular assemblage of spatial practices emerged from the same complex social interweavings through which Webb's band built its sound.

Webb's band forged its voice in close collaboration with the group of elite dancers that came to be known as Whitey's Lindy Hoppers.[52] The group was named for their manager, Herbert White, who worked at the Savoy as floor manager and head bouncer before he also settled into a role as the ballroom's head talent scout for dancers. White's first moves toward creating a cooperative of high-level dancers came in 1927 during regular dance competitions at the Savoy. Drawing from his own background as a dancing waiter at various Harlem night spots, White would keep an eye on the social dance floor, looking for promising talent.[53] Once the lindy hop started gaining local and national attention, Gale and Buchanan entrusted White with assembling groups of dancers to satisfy various requests for lindy hop performances, which the Savoy's management was fielding in increasing numbers.[54] White would serve as a de facto public relations manager for the Savoy, in particular doing everything in his power to ensure the Ballroom maintained its reputation as the home of the lindy hop.

[51] Floyd J. Calvin, "Chick Webb Likes His Music 'Sweet,' but He Can Dish It Up Plenty 'Hot,'" *Pittsburgh Courier*, October 9, 1933, A9.
[52] The group's name appears variously as "Whitey's Lindy Hoppers," "Savoy Lindy Hoppers," "Whyte's Lindy Hoppers," "Whitey's Hoppin' Maniacs," and other variations. I will follow the convention throughout of referring to the group as Whitey's Lindy Hoppers, which is how they are commonly referred to in academic scholarship and in the autobiographies of troupe members Frankie Manning and Norma Miller.
[53] Abdoulaev, "Savoy," 84–85.
[54] Abdoulaev, "Savoy," 82–84.

As a trainer, White was explicit in claiming that his ideas for the dancers' performance routines came directly from the ballroom's social floor. As *Afro-American* columnist Wilbur Young reported, "when asked where he [White] got his ideas for all the new steps, he merely replied that while watching the rug cutters at the Savoy attempting some crazy steps, he makes a mental note of it. The next day at rehearsal, he unfolds this new step in its completed form."[55] White also manipulated the dynamics of the social dance floor itself, carving out the "Cats' Corner": a section near the bandstand that became a kind of social laboratory for the ballroom's elite dancers to push and inspire each other.[56] This Cats' Corner functioned as a space that was simultaneously social, competitive, and performative. Dancers engaged in improvised social dancing where they informally sought to "cut" each other in games of one-upmanship, and while any attendees were allowed to come to the corner as spectators, only those considered "elite"—as designated by White—were welcome to dance there.[57] Acceptance into Whitey's Lindy Hoppers afforded dancers free admittance to the ballroom and, crucially, the opportunity to practice at the Savoy in the afternoon. At these afternoon practices, dancers were encouraged to work on new steps and could seek more explicit instruction from veteran dancers rather than simply watching movements on the social dance floor and attempting to reproduce them.[58]

While dancers sometimes practiced to recorded music during these afternoon sessions, they could also dance to the live rehearsals of bands in residence at the Savoy. These dialogic afternoon rehearsal sessions became a crucial space for co-creative dialogue between Whitey's Lindy Hoppers and Webb's band. As the ballroom's house band leader, Webb knew better than anyone the extent to which his band's success or failure depended on keeping the Savoy's floor packed with enthusiastic dancers. Webb came to depend on the dancers rehearsing in the ballroom to offer him useful feedback. As lindy hop dancer Frankie Manning, a member of Whitey's Lindy Hoppers, later recounted to me in a 2008 interview:

[Webb] would always want to know, "hey man, how do you like this tune or how do you like this tempo?" ... But that was also a thing that musicians who worked in the Savoy looked for. They wanted to know if the dancers liked their music, and as long as the dancers liked their music, they were gonna work.[59]

[55] Wilbur Young, "This 'n' That," *Baltimore Afro-American*, June 13, 1936, 11.
[56] Franke Manning and Cynthia Millman, *Frankie Manning: Ambassador of Lindy Hop* (Philadelphia: Temple University Press, 2008), 75.
[57] Heinilä, "An Endeavor by Harlem Dancers," 121–122.
[58] Manning and Millman, *Ambassador of the Lindy Hop*, 76–77.
[59] Frankie Manning, phone interview with the author, November 2008.

The Savoy's elite dancers were thus entrusted as the Savoy Ballroom's tastemakers, both setting trends on the dance floor and representing the broader desires and preferences of social dancers to Webb in a more intimate, conversational setting.

Such conversations provided Webb a uniquely thorough understanding of what his core audience, the Savoy Ballroom's lindy hop dancers, wanted from his band. As Webb and other bandleaders were certainly aware, ballroom patrons effectively voted with their feet, and musicians unable to routinely "send" the crowd and keep them on the dance floor would not last long at the Savoy Ballroom. As lindy hop dancer Norma Miller, also a member of Whitey's Lindy Hoppers, explained this dynamic to me, "they catered to us in the ballroom. If they did not, if the dancers did not like that band, that band would not be back."[60] Harlem dance bands both before and during the Swing Era understood that drawing and maintaining crowds of dancing patrons, especially in Harlem, was vital to continued employment in ballrooms; a reputation for successful engagement with dancers meant consistent work. Absent clear directions from the ballroom's management, bands new to the Savoy were left to "feel out" the ballroom's social rhythms directly through the kinesthetic feedback they received from the crowd. Count Basie vividly describes his experience of receiving and responding to live feedback from the Savoy Ballroom's dance floor:

> You never had to worry about the manager telling you that you were playing too fast or too slow or could you bring it down a little. You played what you played. . . . And those dancers were right there waiting for whatever you wanted to play. At first they were just standing around there, just listening and waiting to find out where you were, and then they got on it. Meanwhile, Big 'Un [singer Jimmy Rushing] and I were feeling them out too. It was sort of like playing checkers.[61]

What Basie describes as a game I would call more of a dance where, as one does with a new partner, a band and a crowd connect and feel each other out. Webb's band, however, had the advantage of a regular dance partner—Whitey's Lindy Hoppers—with whom his band could practice and build a shared set of stylistic expectations and conventions over time.

---

[60] Miller, interview with author.
[61] Basie with Murray, *Good Morning Blues*, 202.

# A "Kicking-the-Ass Beat": The Sociality of Webb's "Savoy Tempo"

Webb's process of trial and error both with crowded floors of dancers in the evenings and with Whitey's Lindy Hoppers at afternoon practices resulted, notably, in a mastery of what English critic and bandleader Spike Hughes described as "Savoy Tempo." For Hughes, "Savoy Tempo" was an elastic and energetic intermingling of sonic elements that was not easily defined but could be felt and recognized by those who had experienced it, as Hughes claimed to have done on his sojourns in New York City. As Hughes attempted to describe the elusive, Savoy Ballroom-specific phenomenon, "in musical terms it is a tempo, a tone colour, a swing, above all an atmosphere captured in wax only by those who have ever deserved to play there."[62] When Webb famously battled Benny Goodman's Orchestra at the Savoy Ballroom in 1937, Helen Oakley wrote that Webb "had the edge on Benny in the fact that he provided the dancers with 'those right tempos' and due to previous experience in battling bands, he knew just how to call his sets and what to feed those people."[63] Doc Cheatham, who played trumpet with Webb's band, noted that the drummer constantly adapted his arrangements and tempos to suit the preferences of his dancing audience:

> Chick's band had the right style that suited the dancers at the Savoy. His tempos were right for them—not too fast or too slow. Remember, those lindy hoppers had a lot to do with the bands that succeeded at that place. Who was booked and who stayed on depended on them.[64]

As French critic Hughes Pannasié described this connection, the band locked in with the tempo Webb selected after the song had begun:

> He is the only one who can use the "high hat" cymbal and still please me. And the way he uses the other cymbals is wonderful. When, after a first chorus, he sets the tempo on the big cymbal, he starts swinging in such a way that all the audience at the Savoy screams [sic] with joy.[65]

[62] "Mike" [Spike Hughes, pseud.], "What Is Savoy Tempo?," *Melody Maker*, March 16, 1935, 6.

[63] Helen Oakley, "Webb Wins the Title 'King of Swing,'" *Metronome*, May 1937, 1.

[64] Doc Cheatham in Bert Korrall, *Drummin' Men—The Heartbeat of Jazz: The Swing Years* (New York: Oxford University Press, 2002), 19.

[65] Hughes Panassié, "Impressions of America December 38–February 39," *Jazz Hot* 31, April–May 1939, 11.

Pannasié's account also indicates that Webb could shift the tempo during a song, creating a more dynamic and variable effect than the relatively consistent tempos we hear on his recordings. Indeed, it was for precisely this quality that critic and impresario John Hammond criticized Webb, arguing his tempos were both too fast and too inconsistent: "in dance halls, he is given to another fault, that of playing tune after tune at a tempo which is fast enough to start with and increases right along, making dancing all but impossible."[66]

Though they were not to Hammond's taste, Webb's audience of Harlem lindy hoppers found dancing to Webb's tempos not only possible but also desirable. Indeed, the band's tempo choices were uniquely locked in with the Savoy Ballroom's atmosphere and with the embodied needs and preferences of its dancing public. His tempos pushed the ballroom's rhythmic energy to a pace short of frenetic but beyond comfortable. At the Savoy, Webb became, in Norma Miller's words, a "master of tempo" who learned how to push his band's speed to enliven the dancing audiences who in turn met his challenge by entraining themselves over time to dance the lindy hop at ever faster speeds. As Miller recalled, "and there go Chick, upping the tempo all of the time. . . . We could [dance] faster than most people, and that was Chick Webb, because the dancers loved his tempos."[67] Further positioning Webb's tempo manipulation as rooted in connections to a particular space and audience, Spike Hughes identified mastery of tempo as Webb's strongest quality and the core of his connection with dancers at the Savoy in his efforts to explicate the aforementioned concept of "Savoy Tempo." While Hughes never defined "Savoy Tempo" precisely, he did identify it on a Fletcher Henderson recording of "Hocus Pocus," which he reviewed in 1935:

The tempo is good swinging Savoy tempo, with a lift and ease, which you will understand even if you have never been fortunate enough to hear the Savoy tempo first hand. The Savoy tempo is elastic. It swings only at certain metronomic points of *Andante, Moderato,* and *Allegro ma non troppo.* But once having heard it you cannot explain it. You can only tell instinctively when it is being played and when not.[68]

One can hear this elastic tempo in Webb's 1935 recording of "Don't Be That Way," a performance in which Hughes explicitly identifies the presence of Savoy tempo.[69] This recording begins at 216 beats per minute (bpm) during

[66] John Hammond, "Chick Webb's Standard of Musicianship Too Low," *Downbeat,* November 1937, 3.
[67] Miller, interview with author.
[68] "Mike" [Spike Hughes, pseud.], "Hot Records Reviewed," *Melody Maker,* January 5, 1935, 5.
[69] "Mike" [Spike Hughes, pseud.], "Hot Records Reviewed," *Melody Maker,* July 13, 1935.

the opening ensemble chorus yet relaxes to a bpm from 203–206 during individual musicians' solos before climbing again to 216 near the end, when the full ensemble returns. While it is not a live recording, this elasticity gives the piece a sense of both anticipatory excitement and a settled, "in the pocket" groove that, when paired with Hughes's accounts, at least hints at what Webb's band could "really do."

For bands such as Webb's, flexible sensitivity to dancers' needs extended beyond individual songs to shape entire sets. Dance bands in the 1930s generally varied the tempos at which they played to give dancers variety, as too many fast numbers in a row could prove frustratingly tiring. Miller explains that Webb's tempo choices navigated the ebbs and flows of energy during an evening to keep dancers motivated and on the floor without overwhelming or exhausting them: "listen, he was king of the ballroom, he knew how to standardize his [sets] so that we could dance and so that we could rest the next number."[70] The processes through which Webb adapted his tempos to the Savoy's dancers and through which they then learned to push their dancing to match his groove represents a negotiated process Judith Becker identifies as "rhythmic entrainment," which occurs when "two or more seemingly independent processes mutually influence each other to converge in a common pattern."[71] While his tempos were often fast and pushed both his musicians and the ballroom's dancers, whatever speed Webb selected was a calculated choice made in close consultation—whether verbally during rehearsal or energetically during live performance—with the dancers. As Miller elaborates in her autobiography, "no one could push a band quite like Chick Webb could, he had what was called a kicking-the-ass-beat. The lindy hop was developed to his music."[72] This "kicking-the-ass-beat," which lay at the core of Webb's particular success as a dance musician, was fundamentally a cocreative phenomenon. Webb and the Savoy Ballroom's dancing audiences crafted this musical dynamic in close conversation, a conversation especially close for those elite dancers with whom Webb shared afternoon practice space and for whom his band played not only for social dancing (figure 3.2), but across the lindy hop's multiple expressive formats—its three major modes.

[70] Miller, interview with author.
[71] Becker, *Deep Listeners*, 127.
[72] Norma Miller with Evette Jensen, *Swingin' at the Savoy: The Memoir of a Jazz Dancer* (Philadelphia: Temple University Press, 1996), 69.

**Figure 3.2** Dancers at the Savoy Ballroom with Chick Webb, New York City, ca. 1930. Photo by Berenice Abbott/Getty Images.

## "Flag Bearers of the Savoy": Lindy Hoppers in Competition

The dialogue between Webb's band and Whitey's Lindy Hoppers extended into the many instances where Webb played for lindy hop dancers in competition settings. Frankie Manning recalled that during his first forays into the Savoy's dance contests, Webb's playing sparked his enthusiasm and creativity, making him feel that Webb was in his corner:

> Now, I danced to Chick Webb almost every single night, and we always had a lot of fun with the guys in the band, but this night it felt like they were all saying to me, "Frankie, we're going to play this for you!" Every one of them was really blowing. It was like they were telling the audience: "This is our man. We're gonna swing for this cat."[73]

[73] Manning and Millman, *Ambassador of Lindy Hop*, 99.

From Manning's account, it appears Webb played a crucial role in his victory during this battle by supporting his movements and steps with rhythmic figures on the drums and by inviting Manning to choose his own music. At that time, Webb usually played the same tune, the Fletcher Henderson Orchestra's hit song "Christopher Columbus," for each of the previous teams yet gave Manning the option to select his own song. According to Manning, who chose Henderson's "Down South Camp Meeting," this gesture signified to him that Webb's band saw him as "their man" and was determined to support and push him during the contest.[74]

Competition dancing was critical both to individual lindy hoppers' growth and to the dance's ongoing development, a vital role played by competitive formats across Black vernacular dance styles (figures 3.3 and 3.4). In rhythm tap dancing, formal and informal "cutting" contests have long been a critical vehicle for sociality and collective development where dancers would seek to both inspire and outdo one another. Dance historian Constance Valis Hill describes the cutting contests of the storied Hoofer's Club during the 1920s as "an eccentric fusion of imitation and innovation," where "young dancers were forced to find their style and rhythmic voice."[75] One finds a similar culture of social battling in hip hop dance, particularly among b-boys and b-girls (breakdancers), for whom battling is a central form of expression. As ethnomusicologist Joe Schloss has argued, these competition formats have served as critical catalysts for innovation throughout breakdancing's history, as developments that would broadly impact more casual social contexts took inspiration from the cutting-edge, boundary-pushing movements that high-level dancers would produce by consistently pushing themselves and each other.[76]

As Herbert White's account of his initial idea for Whitey's Lindy Hoppers makes clear, dance contests had been a consistent part of the Savoy Ballroom's offerings from the time of the venue's founding. Just weeks after the ballroom opened, the *Baltimore Afro-American* reported it was drawing a nightly crowd of thousands and that it featured a weekly Charleston contest.[77] By the mid-1930s, the Ballroom held a weekly Saturday night contest with a fairly

---

[74] Manning and Millman, *Ambassador of Lindy Hop*, 99.
[75] Constance Valis Hill, *Tap Dancing America: A Cultural History* (New York: Oxford University Press, 2010), 87.
[76] Joseph Schloss, *Foundation: B-Boys, B-Girls, and Hip-Hop Culture in New York* (New York: Oxford University Press: 2009), 107–108.
[77] "Tyler Visits the Harlem Theatres," *Baltimore Afro-American*, April 3, 1926, 6.

**Figure 3.3** Crowd gathered under Savoy Ballroom marquee announcing a lindy hop contest at night, ca. 1938. Photo by George Karger/Pix Inc./The LIFE Images Collection via Getty Images.

informal social format. Couples danced one pair at a time with no time limit, and winners were decided by audience applause. While entrance was free and open, most contestants who entered were members of White's group and did so only with his blessing.[78] Lindy hop contests grew in both ubiquity and broad importance during the mid-1930s, and their most significant catalyst was the Harvest Moon Ball. In response to growing racial tensions during the Great Depression, New York City mayor Fiorello La Guardia and his staff worked with the *New York Daily News* to create the Harvest Moon Ball, a citywide dance competition designed to engage young people from diverse neighborhoods, class backgrounds, and racial and ethnic groups. Preliminary contests were held at ballrooms around New York City, where a field of over 7,000 couples was winnowed to eighty-two finalists, before a planned outdoor

---

[78] Manning and Millman, *Ambassador of Lindy Hop*, 82.

**Figure 3.4** Couple competing in Savoy Ballroom lindy hop contest as a crowd looks on, ca. 1938. Photo by George Karger/Pix Inc./The LIFE Images Collection via Getty Images.

final round in Central Park on August 14, 1935.[79] When crowds for the finals exceeded the outdoor venue's capacity, the event was rescheduled for August 29 at Madison Square Garden, where 19,000 attended and 20,000 more were turned away.[80]

While Fletcher Henderson's Roseland Ballroom Orchestra played for the lindy hoppers at the contest finals, Webb's band played for the Harlem preliminaries held at the Savoy. As Norma Miller recalls, "the contest was held in front of the band shell. The band on the stage was the mighty Chick Webb Band and this was what they had been waiting for. Here the music would swing, at last they could pull out the stops and let it rip."[81] Webb's band was

[79] Gerald G. Gross, "Here and There," *Washington Post*, August 29, 1935, 6.

[80] Lucius Jones, "Society Slants," *Atlanta Daily World*, September 9, 1935, 3. The numbers varied in different reports, with Ed Sullivan of the *Washington Post* reporting 20,000 attendees and 10,000 turned away, for example. Ed Sullivan, "Broadway: Manhattan Prominade," *Washington Post*, August 31, 1935, 9.

[81] Norma Miller with Evette Jensen, *Swingin' at the Savoy: The Memoir of a Jazz Dancer* (Philadelphia: Temple University Press, 1996), 69.

**Figure 3.5** Edith Matthews and Leon James (contest winners) dancing in the finals of the first Harvest Moon Ball. Madison Square Garden, 1935.

more than capable of "letting it rip" for the lindy hop dancers, and by Miller's account they certainly did so at the Savoy's preliminaries. Webb was, however, equally capable of playing softer, sweeter styles of music, which he likely did that night to accompany preliminary contests for the more traditionally "formal" ballroom dances.[82] That said, had the Webb band given more effort to supporting the lindy hoppers, the choice to do so would have fit within the Savoy management's strategy of approaching the Harvest Moon Ball principally as a platform to feature the exceptional skill of its lindy hop dancers, who did indeed go on to sweep their division at the Madison Square Garden finals (figure 3.5).

Frankie Manning, who took second place with partner Maggie McMillan, explained that the Savoy dancers were unconcerned with individual prizes but that it was highly important that the Savoy's finalists win every prize in the lindy hop division in order to publicly affirm their collective supremacy:[83]

[82] I discuss the Webb orchestra's substantial pedigree and reputation for playing "sweet music" in addition to hot jazz in Christopher J. Wells, "'Go Harlem!': Chick Webb and His Dancing Audience during the Great Depression" (PhD diss., University of North Carolina at Chapel Hill, 2014), 108.

[83] The first-place team was Leon James and Edith Matthews, and the third-place team was Norma Miller and "Stompin'" Billy Hill. Miller and Jensen, *Swingin' at the Savoy*, 69–82.

It's a funny thing, but I never felt sorry for myself. The Harvest Moon Ball was just a contest that we needed to win for the Savoy, and we got the three top spots. It didn't faze me that someone else won first place. You see, to me, the Savoy Ballroom . . . that was the world. I was considered pretty good there, so it didn't matter what anybody else thought. As long as the Savoy thought I was good, nothing else counted.[84]

For the Savoy's lindy hoppers, the Harvest Moon Ball presented an opportunity to publicly assert ownership over Harlem's cultural production, a mission explicitly imparted to them by Herbert White. According to Miller, White offered the dancers the following "pep talk" before the Madison Square Garden contest emphasizing that it was crucial they sweep the lindy category:

You are the flag bearers of the Savoy, and you know what we expect you to do tonight. GO out there and let 'em know who we are. Let the *Daily News* report that we took it all, first, second, and third! We want all three. Remember, we don't take out any other prizes. All we got is the Lindy Hop so you better make sure it belongs to us. Do you dig?[85]

What Miller and the other Savoy dancers dug was that the lindy hop, and by proxy the Savoy Ballroom, represented Black ownership of Black popular culture.[86] While community frustration built over the predominance of white business ownership and omnipresent segregation along Harlem's central 125th Street corridor or the price gouging in overcrowded tenement housing, Black dancers in Harlem could still claim the lindy hop, which was emerging as the popular dance most closely associated with swing music, as their corporeal territory. It was one place where they were untouchable.

## "Don't Kick My Drums!": Lindy Hop Performance on Stage and Screen

Success in contests while representing the Savoy Ballroom offered lindy hop dancers both public and private validation that helped them to position themselves, or to be positioned by Gale and White, to satisfy an emerging market for professional lindy hop performance. The lindy hop arose during a period

---

[84] Manning and Millman, *Ambassador of Lindy Hop*, 90.

[85] As recalled by Miller in Miller and Jensen, *Swingin' at the Savoy*, 79. Capitalization in the original.

[86] The Savoy Ballroom was, of course, owned by a white man, but many Harlemites who frequented the ballroom, including Manning and Miller, claimed the space as "theirs."

of tremendous expansion in both the marketplace for and diversity of Black popular dance on stage during the 1930s. As Jacqui Malone explains, this decade featured a uniquely strong period of collaborative innovation between big bands and dancers specializing in eccentric, flash, adagio, and rhythm tap dancing among numerous other emerging styles of Black vernacular dance, including the lindy hop.[87] The lindy hop's commercial market followed only slightly behind the dance's development, by a couple years at most, and contest victories became powerful tools to position champion dancers as qualified professionals. Savoy dancers' championship credentials were explicitly underscored, for example, in the Corona Tennis Club's advertisement in 1930 for their annual spring dance in 1930. In their public announcement, the club boasted they had "secured as a special attraction Miss Esaline Hinton and George Snowden, winners of the Savoy Ballroom Lindbergh Hop Contest, who will give an exhibition of that popular dance."[88] George "Shorty" Snowden, a frequent contest winner often credited with inventing the lindy hop, or at least with coining its name, would be among the first to reap these benefits and professionalize the lindy hop, as he appeared on film, in the revue *Lew Leslie's Blackbirds* on Broadway, and for various local gigs performing for Harlem society parties and stage shows (figure 3.6).[89] Reflecting on his role in facilitating these opportunities, White would later frame his motivation for founding Whitey's Lindy Hoppers as principally to ensure talented lindy hop dancers would receive paid opportunities with compensation beyond mere bragging rights, given the value their virtuoso competition dancing generated for the Savoy. He explained that, per columnist Lillian Johnson, "there were so many kids around who did exhibition dances just to win cups when they needed the money that the promoters who put up the cups were getting, that he decided that the kids might as well get some of the money themselves."[90]

The opportunities for the dancers in question to earn money escalated during the mid- and late 1930s as the Harvest Moon Ball far exceeded the exposure previous lindy hop contests had afforded and offered cachet leading to professional opportunities both within and beyond Harlem. The 1937 winners reportedly drew substantial interest from Columbia Pictures and other suitors such that they were "so deluged with offers that they are bewildered by this prospect of sudden wealth."[91] The Savoy lindy hop dancers' engagement

---

[87] Malone details relationships between jazz music and jazz dance during this period extensively in *Steppin' on the Blues*, 91–110.

[88] "Corona News Items," *New York Amsterdam News*, May 7, 1930, 18.

[89] Blackbirds: "Ethel Waters to Have Her 'Othello,'" *Baltimore Afro-American*, August 30, 1930, A9.

[90] Lillian Johnson, "From Bouncer to Jitterbug Trainer," *Baltimore Afro-American*, August 12, 1939, 11.

[91] "Lindy Hop Team Is Proving Sensation," *Baltimore Afro-American*, September 18, 1937, 11.

**Figure 3.6** "Shorty" George Snowden with partner dancing the lindy hop in the film *Manhattan Melody* (1931).

at Loew's State Theater was extended after breaking revenue records to the tune of $44,000.[92] The 1938 winners—as well as the second- and third-place lindy hop couples—received a two-week engagement at Loew's State as well as a film contract with Warner Brothers–Vitaphone.[93] Due to the high-profile stage of the Harvest Moon Ball as well as the post-1935 mainstreaming of swing as a national popular music, Whitey's Lindy Hoppers increasingly gained access to a range of lucrative professional gigs including stage revues in Harlem and on regular northeast touring circuits as well as new opportunities in Broadway shows, in Hollywood films, and on international tours. Many bands during this period relied on outside agencies to book dance acts, but Savoy Ballroom owner Moe Gale managed both Webb and Whitey's Lindy Hoppers through his booking agency, Gale Enterprises.[94] Given their shared ties to the Savoy Ballroom and to Gale Enterprises, Whitey's Lindy Hoppers and Webb's orchestra frequently toured together, offering a new context for

[92] "Harvest Moon Ball Champs Deluged with Offers," *Atlanta Daily World*, September 19, 1937, 8.
[93] "Prize-Winning Lindy Hoppers Score Hit in Broadway Debut," *Chicago Defender*, September 10, 1938, 19.
[94] Malone, *Steppin' on the Blues*, 92–93. Abdoulaev, "Savoy," 79, 84.

collaborative innovation that then flowed back into the ballroom and onto the social dance floor.

Webb's band was particularly well-positioned to accompany lindy hop dancers throughout their rise to public prominence as the band had worked consistently with professional, performing lindy hop acts since the late 1920s. The Webb band appeared on film in the 1929 feature *After Seben* in which Snowden and a partner, along with two other couples, compete in a staged dance contest emceed by eccentric dancer James Barton. The band also performed for a range of stage revues throughout the late 1920s and early 1930s, most notably at Frank Schiffman's Lafayette Theater, which billed it-self as "America's Leading Colored Theatre," and for society functions at the Savoy-run Alhambra Ballroom.[95] A 1933 report in the *New York Amsterdam News* indicates the Savoy diversified its offerings by adding "hot floor shows" to rival the Lafayette. In addition, the ballroom continued and extended its business with social clubs, business the Savoy was able to attract by offering guarantees against financial losses. As the *Amsterdam News* explained:

> Fighting against the wave of depression that has carried other places of its kind under, the Savoy has instituted an elastic policy, which will permit clubs, especially the long-established organizations, to secure the place without the least chance of losing in the arrangement of their affairs.[96]

In 1934, Webb's orchestra held a regular spot at the Apollo Theater as the featured act in a series of stage revues. A June 1934 advertisement in the *Amsterdam News* details the fluid environment of professional and amateur performance—including amateur competition—in which Webb was enmeshed at the Apollo. Webb's band played in the stage revue "Hotel Harlem" featuring Emcee Ralph Cooper along with a "beauty chorus" and comedian Dewey "Pigmeat" Markham, an Apollo mainstay, followed by a screening of the film *All Quiet on the Western Front*. In addition, the Apollo featured an amateur contest on Monday nights and a "lindy hop night and shim sham contest" every Thursday following its evening revue, the winners of which were sometimes included in future Apollo shows.[97]

[95] For a substantial account of the various venues in which Webb performed during the early 1930s, see Wells, "Go Harlem!," 42–111.

[96] "Revues Topped at Dance Hall," *New York Amsterdam News*, May 17, 1933, 8.

[97] Advertisement, *New York Amsterdam News*, June 23, 1934, 6; additional contextual information from "Lindy Hop Gets Big Start at the Apollo," *New York Amsterdam News*, April 14, 1934, 6; and Advertisement, *New York Amsterdam News*, November 3, 1934, 3.

As both the lindy hop and Webb's band became synonymous with the Savoy Ballroom, Gale increasingly packaged them together for New York theaters such as Harlem's Apollo and the downtown Paramount as well as with touring productions. Norma Miller identified the circuit of northeast theaters spanning New York, Baltimore, Washington, and Philadelphia through which they regularly toured as "the round robin." The Chick Webb Orchestra's revues originating in midtown Manhattan's Paramount Theater in 1938 and 1939— toward the end of Webb's life—are particularly well documented. In summer 1938, they performed in a Paramount Theater revue entitled *The Texans*, which featured Webb's band, Whitey's Lindy Hoppers, and the comedy dance team of Chuck & Chuckles.[98] Numerous reviews of these performances highlight the crowd's particular enthusiasm for the pairing of Webb's orchestra and the Savoy's top lindy hoppers. According to an account from the *Pittsburgh Courier*'s Isadora Smith:

> A dual team of Savoy Lindy Hoppers, well coached by Herbert Whyte [sic], further tightened the knot the revue was now in. They took several encores and each was more entertaining than the last. Begging off, the Hoppers made way for another Webb jammer, sending the "cats" and jitterbugs into frenzied dancing in the aisles on the stage and in the lobby.[99]

The *Chicago Defender*'s account only underscored the extent to which Webb and Whitey's Lindy Hoppers invited corporealities not licensed by the proscenium spectator/performer divide of the stage, as dancers were inspired to bring a more familiar, and arguably more idiomatic, sociality to the Paramount.

> Standing room only all day long. . . . Chick was greeted with cheering, whistling, shouting, clapping, and stomping. . . . While the more enthusiastic jitterbugs danced in the aisles. . . . Ushers had to actually hold them in their seats. [...] the Savoy Lindy Hoppers who appeal to the thousands of Jitterbugs who attend the [Paramount] theatre.[100]

In addition to the dancers' multiple encores, these accounts highlight a kinship between amateur social dancers, professional dancers, and dance

---

[98] Kelcey Allen, "Amusements," *Women's Wear Daily*, July 26, 1938, 42.

[99] Isadora Smith, "Chick and Ella Set Attendance Record at the Paramount," *Pittsburgh Courier*, August 28, 1938, 20.

[100] "Harlem to Broadway," *Chicago Defender*, August 20, 1938, 19. Unbracketed ellipses in the original, bracketed ellipses added by the author.

musicians that transgressively frayed the Apollo Theater's proscenium layout. Audiences who had either danced alongside or admired the dancers on stage expressed kinship and participated without disrupting the performance, effectively restructuring the social geography of the theater by meeting an elite-level performative iteration of their own social dance culture with a social dancer's response. After the summer engagement, Webb, Gale, and White took this popular revue on tour, effectively bringing a performative snapshot of the Savoy Ballroom's identity to other theatrical spaces across the Northeast and Midwest. Among the tour's confirmed performances are dates at the State Theater in Hartford, Connecticut; the Stanley Theater in Pittsburgh; Toledo, Ohio; and the Newman Theater in Kansas City before returning to the Paramount for another revue in March 1939. Accounts suggest that lively crowds and standing ovations were consistent throughout this tour.[101]

While Manning consistently frames Whitey's Lindy Hoppers' relationship with Webb as intimately collaborative, Miller notes that the bandleader often viewed the dancers as a nuisance and treated them accordingly. Webb would at times employ the fast tempos for which he was known and loved to indulge his penchant for "hazing" the Savoy Ballroom's best dancers during professional performances. Miller recalls that Webb would push her troupe of elite professional dancers beyond their capabilities in professional performance contexts to get under their skin:

> We worked with him, and we'd do a twelve o'clock show, he'd hit us with a tempo that we weren't ready for half the time, he was that mean, he did it deliberately, he did shit to you that [pauses] but he was a genius, have you ever known a genius that wasn't a pain in the ass? It goes with the territory.[102]

At the same time, Miller's account of such sonic hazing also underscores Webb's awareness of dancers' capabilities, perhaps suggesting that Webb knew intimately both these dancers' expectations and the threshold of their temporal "comfort zones" such that he could push them to reach beyond their own perceived limitations. Whether or not his intention was supportive, Webb's antagonism could at times prove creatively generative to his dancing collaborators.[103] During their Paramount performances, Webb repeatedly and

[101] Billy Rowe, "Chick Webb's Band Is Forced Out of New England by Storm," *Pittsburgh Courier*, October 1, 1938, 21. "They Mowed 'em Down in Smoketown," *Pittsburgh Courier*, October 22, 1938, 21. C. C. King, "What's Doing around Toledo," *Chicago Defender*, November 26, 1938, 22. "Chick Webb Opens in Kay Cee Friday," *Pittsburgh Courier*, December 3, 1938, 20.

[102] Miller, interview with author.

[103] Ashley Pribyl explores the idea of antagonistic collaboration in her dissertation "Sociocultural and Collaborative Antagonism in the Harold Prince–Stephen Sondheim Musicals (1970–1979)" (PhD diss., Washington University in St. Louis, 2019).

animatedly expressed concern that the dancers' large, wild movements would cause them to kick over his drums or the other band members' instruments. Whether well founded or not, Webb's emphatic consternation helped spur Manning to innovate an angled presentation—where the dancers performed linear movements at a roughly forty-five-degree angle rather than straight on to the audience—that would become ubiquitous in synchronized lindy hop routines and contribute, in a proscenium stage context, to the dance's dynamic appeal.[104]

This choreographic adjustment also points to another significant innovation that became part of the lindy hop's life in its performance mode: the presence of synchronized routines. Where Snowden's generation of lindy hoppers effectively crafted a staged reproduction of a social "jam session" or contest setting in which one couple at a time would perform an ostensibly improvised dance, Manning experimented throughout the 1930s with what would ultimately become Whitey's Lindy Hoppers' core format: a series of solos by individual couples closing with a synchronized ensemble choreography. Crucially, the seeds of synchronized ensemble lindy hop can be found in the dance's social and competition contexts. The first ensemble-like move the group innovated was a coordinated entrance into "slow motion" during competitions, where each couple who was a part of Whitey's Lindy Hoppers would simultaneously begin moving at an exaggeratedly slow rate before simultaneously picking back up to tempo. The explicit purpose of synchronized "slow motion" was to draw eyes away from other couples in the Harvest Moon Ball and toward the Savoy dancers. Manning's second source of inspiration came from a piece of social choreography to Jimmy Lunceford's "Posin'," which features a regular verbal command of "everybody pose" that entreats the dancers to freeze in place during a two-bar break.[105] Inspired by seeing this phenomenon on the social floor and by social line dances such as the Tranky Doo, Manning began moving toward the synchronized ensemble routines through which the lindy hop would become enshrined on film during the late 1930s and early 1940s. In his analysis of Whitey's Lindy Hoppers' performance in the Marx Brothers' film *A Day at the Races* (1937), Musicologist Christopher J. Smith identifies strong resonances of Black vernacular dance practices as they appeared on theatrical stages, claiming that "They may be dancing on a Hollywood soundstage, but they are employing the practices and body vocabularies of the Cotton Club." Notably, Smith also describes this performance's synchronized ensemble

---

[104] Miller and Jensen, *Swingin' at the Savoy*, 106; Manning and Millman, *Ambassador of the Lindy Hop*, 161.
[105] Manning and Millman, *Ambassador of the Lindy Hop*, 103.

finale as "a literal reinactment . . . of the ritualized climax of a show at the Roseland or the Cotton Club" and convincingly ties this climactic gesture to a far longer history of stylized stage renditions of Black vernacular dance.[106] Indeed, Whitey's Lindy Hoppers' three most iconic film performances—in *A Day at the Races*, the Duke Ellington soundie *Hot Chocolate* (1941), and the Olsen & Johnson comedy vehicle *Hellzapoppin'* (1941)—all feature this performance format, complete with synchronized ensemble finales and the angled presentation Manning developed working with Webb's band at the Paramount (figure 3.7).[107]

While transitioning into their roles as professional dancers naturally made performance a central focus for Whitey's Lindy Hoppers, maintaining the integrity and quality of their dancing still necessitated keeping a connection with the creative atmosphere of the Savoy Ballroom's social dance floor. One of Whitey's troupes, seizing on the momentum from members' Harvest Moon Ball placements, did an extended overseas tour in Australia. Upon their return, Manning reflected, their dancing looked notably stale and dated as they had not remained in contact with either their own social dance skills, the core basis for competition and performance dancing, or with the dynamic innovations produced nightly on the Savoy Ballroom's dance floor.[108]

Though I have sought throughout this chapter to highlight moments of overlap and interweaving between the lindy hop's major modes—social, competition, and performance dance—I have for the most part discussed each sphere on its own terms. In addition, I have thus far framed of the major modes as discrete elements in a rough tripartite chronology where their development corresponds to roughly to the early, middle, and late 1930s. I do want to emphasize that this is largely a narrative convenience to help me explicate specific modes of lindy hop dancing as they became prominent parts of the lives of Manning, Miller, and their contemporaries among the "second generation" of Whitey's Lindy Hoppers. To properly counterbalance this, I will now turn to one case study of a specific communication dynamic between Webb and

---

[106] Smith, *Dancing Revolution*, 169–170, 184. I would, however, stop short of affirming that this performance represents "an immediate translation of street vocabularies known in black clubs to film" (169) given both the longstanding Black vaudeville traditions from which these performances draw—as Smith himself astutely highlights in his analysis—and the complex flows between venues and modes of practice I outline throughout this chapter.

[107] Robert P. Crease discusses the particular issues involved with filming the lindy hop and also offers a more extensive comparison of these filmed performances in "Divine Frivolity: Hollywood Representations of the Lindy Hop, 1937–1942," in *Representing Jazz*, ed. Krin Gabbard (Durham, NC: Duke University Press, 1995), 207–228.

[108] Manning and Millman, *Ambassador of the Lindy Hop*, 116.

**Figure 3.7** Whitey's Lindy Hoppers in synchronized performance *A Day at the Races* (1937), *Hot Chocolate* (1941), and *Hellzapoppin'* (1941).

the Savoy's elite lindy hop dancers that flowed between social, competition, and performance contexts: engagement in "catching" games of melodic and rhythmic trading. These "gotcha" moments not only traversed the three major modes of lindy hop dancing, but indeed relied specifically upon the generative lines of communication forged at and through their fluid intersections.

## Saying "Gotcha!": Dialogue, Gamesmanship, and Mirroring

In an article on dance for the periodical *Jazz Record*, Mura Dehn noted one anonymous musician's preference for playing for dancers: "When we see what we are doing we feel better and play better. It's like seeing your music mirrored."[109] Those musicians, like Webb, with especially strong reputations for connecting with dancers drew energy from seeing their playing reflected back to them in dancers' movements. Broadly, musicians depended on this give-and-take between themselves and dancers for validation, inspiration, and visual feedback. Dancers and musicians engaged in this rhythmic communication and playful gamesmanship across social, competition, and performance contexts. In multiple public interviews and in his autobiography, Manning offers a vivid account of a dance contest—a special public battle between his generation of elite lindy hoppers and Snowden's more established group—in which he and his partner Frieda Washington (not to be confused with Fredi Washington) debuted what would subsequently be enshrined as the lindy hop's first "air step": the over-the-back (a back-to-back, assisted over-the-head backflip). They developed this move in the spirit of competition, building on a lift for which Snowden and his partner Big Bea were known and one-upping them by taking it a step further. In this vivid passage, Manning describes in detail Webb's ability to both mimic his steps on the drums and to drive him to new heights of excellence:

> And then he started swinging that out for me. Boy, and he caught everything I was doing. I'd kick my foot, he'd dip, schoom. She'd twist, he'd say, too-too-too. [claps] Oh, it was great. I hear what he's playing, and what he's playing is like inspiring me to do it better or do it harder or put more into it. When I did the air step, Webb even caught the motion of it as she's coming over my back. He was saying

[109] Mura Dehn, "A Few Words about Dancing," *Jazz Record*, February 1947, 43.

te-de-de-de-de-de-de, and when she landed he said, te-de-de-de-de-de- bum. I mean, he's playing all this on the drum.[110]

In addition to Webb's facility at narrating movements through sound, Manning also describes Webb's ability, through his playing, to drive or push dancers to a higher level. In Manning's account of one of the Savoy's weekly dance contests, Webb and trumpeter Taft Jordan enhanced his and his partner's presentation on the dance floor by both reflecting and responding to his Washington's movements:

> This was one time when we *really* danced to the music, and it seemed like the band was catching everything that we were doing. Every time I kicked my leg out, Chick would say, "DJBOOM!" If I did a little swing-out, Taft Jordan would play, "BEOOOOWWW!" Frieda had one of the greatest twists of any of the girls and she could really show it off. When she was twisting around me, Chick Webb was playing "CHEEE-CHI-CHI, CHEEE-CHI-CHI" on the cymbals, keeping time with her. They'd play a riff behind me, and I'd think: *Yeah, keep up with me, guys!* I was feeling every-thing that they were doing, and the band was hitting every step that we did.[111]

Manning and Washington were dancing not only with each other, but with the entire band. These dancers experienced the Webb band's music in their bodies and responded through movement, in turn supplying the band with still more steps to "hit" and reflect in their playing. This kind of symbiotic con-versation encapsulates the relationship between jazz musicians and elite lindy hop dancers during the 1930s as they fed from each other's virtuosity to craft a common kinesthetic language that yielded visual expression from dancers and aural expression from musicians.

In this context, musicians and dancers forged within the ballroom a partic-ipatory, dialogic space where, locked in a perpetual game of cat-and-mouse, they tried to "catch" each other's rhythms and feelings and then transform them through a process of perpetual variation. Chick Webb and his band members were especially attentive to dancers on the social dance floor, and it was common for them to reflect dancers' movements in their playing. As Manning described this dynamic:

---

[110] Frankie Manning, in Jeff Kaufman, *The Savoy King: Chick Webb and the Music That Changed America*, 2012, film. Transcript. I thank Jeff Kaufman for providing me an advance copy of this transcript before the film's release.
[111] Manning and Millman, *Ambassador of the Lindy Hop*, 99.

Chick Webb would play for us. He played for the dancers. And we had this wonderful communication between the dancer and the band. And you know, like Chick,
we, we would get out on the floor and we'd be dancing and you know, Chick Webb
would focus on, oh, he'd see somebody out there dancing and they'd be doing this
step and he would catch it.[112]

By closely watching and "catching" dancers' movements, Webb inspired
them to greater virtuosity through a dynamic, escalating game of call-and-
response. As Manning clarified to me in our interview, this type of call-
and-response happened principally through close one-on-one connections
between musicians and dancers during musical solos:

When he's playing the arrangement, you've got to follow the line, . . . but when one
of the musicians would take a solo and you were dancing, that's when he would
improvise, he'd try to I'm not saying all musicians did that but Taft [Jordan, Webb's
trumpet player] was pretty good at it, he watched the dancers and he'd try to catch
what they'd do. It's like an inspiration to the dancer and it's also an inspiration to
the music. Sometimes maybe he can come up with a little riff or a little cut in the
music that he can use.[113]

Such mutual inspiration through live interaction with dancers suggests that
musicians' "solos" were in one sense anything but, as they created a space
to communicate with dancers that became fundamental to the dance floor's
sociality.

The sonic traces of such collaboration likely continue to exist both on record and in many of the common riffs and licks that comprise jazz musicians'
vocabularies, just as the kinetic traces are no doubt still present in a range
of American popular dances. While claiming concordances between these
artifacts is often at best an exercise in informed conjecture, one rhythm
Manning scatted to me during our interview also appears on a radio transcription of a 1939 live performance by Webb's band of the Count Basie an-
them "One o'Clock Jump": four straight unsyncopated beats stated and then
repeated at twice the speed (figure 3.8).

Webb plays this figure in the closing two bars of a wind trio chorus as an
accent preparing the tune's closing series of vibrant shout choruses (02:25–
02:28). According to Manning, this was the rhythm of a step he had struggled
to perfect and that Webb "caught" when he finally nailed it during a contest:

[112] Frank Manning, transcript of interview prepared for Ken Burns, *Jazz*, 1995. http://www.pbs.org/jazz/
about/about_transcripts.htm.
[113] Manning, interview with author.

**Figure 3.8** Rhythmic transcription of Webb's "fill" in "One O'Clock Jump," radio transcription from the Southland Ballroom, 1939.

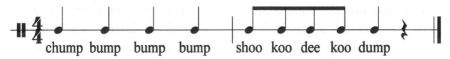

**Figure 3.9** Transcription of Frankie Manning scatting a step rhythm, phone conversation with the author, October 2008.

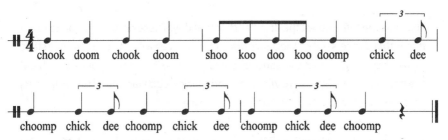

**Figure 3.10** Transcription of Frankie Manning scatting Webb's response to his step, phone conversation with the author, October 2008.

I had been trying to learn this step in a rehearsal, and I know the step went something like CHUMP BUMP BUMP SHOOKOO DEEKOO DUMP [figure 3.9], that was the kind of rhythm of the step. Then I got in the contest, and Chick Webb's band would play, and I was trying to do that step, and the first time I kinda messed it up, and then I tried to do it again and when I tried to do it a second time, Chick caught it! 'Cause he would play CHOOK DOOM CHOOK DOOM SHOOKOO DOOKOO DOOMP CHICK-DEE CHOOMP CHICK-DEE CHOOMP CHICK-DEE CHOOMP [figure 3.10]. I just remember that because, I remember I said "man I can't get this damn thing!" [laughs] And then when I heard Chick doing that, I said "oh wow, yeah!" And I'd look up at him and smile and he'd smile back. He was playing the drums and he just took his hand and pointed it at me when I looked at him, just as to say "gotcha."[114]

---

[114] Manning, interview with author.

Webb said "gotcha" to Manning as a gesture of kinship, allegiance, and mutual support. Throughout this chapter, we have seen the relationship between personal identity and group affiliation expressed in the numerous instances where Manning felt Webb's band knew he was "their cat" and felt motivated to support him. In at least one instance, Webb appears to have developed a lick in communication with Manning for which he subsequently found broader use.

Though in this case it manifested in a competition environment, the professional competencies upon which this social "catching" dynamic was built were grounded in skills Webb and other drummers developed in a performance context. The ability to "catch" dancers' steps was a particularly important marker of competence for professional jazz drummers, and it came specifically from the world of nightclub and stage revues where Webb accrued substantial experience throughout his career in Harlem. As Manning explained to me:

> That was the thing about the drummers of that day. These drummers had to catch things that dancers did on the dance floor, whether it be a nightclub revue or a stage revue, they caught what the dancers would do. Like, if a dancer pointed his hand the drummer was right there with him, and Chick Webb was one of the drummers who could do that because he watched the dancers.[115]

Manning's account suggests that Webb's attentiveness to dancing and dancers came from his background working with dancers and comedians in vaudeville revues and nightclub shows at the Cotton Club, Lafayette Theater, and Apollo Theater, among other venues. His ability to catch dancers' steps specifically in stage revues is echoed in an account from drummer Cliff Leeman, a contemporary of Webb's, who recalled that "Without being able to read music, he managed to catch everything the comics did and underline all the key spots in dance routines. His instincts were almost infallible."[116] What Leeman saw as "instincts" were in fact a well-honed skill set, forged in performance revues and translated to the Savoy Ballroom's dance floor in both competition and social settings. Seeking to match Webb's instincts, drummer Eddie Jenkins, who commuted to the Savoy weekly as a teenager to watch Webb play and who toured with Bunny Berrigan's band in the late 1930s, developed a practice of playing for packed ballrooms by focusing his attention on individual dancers.

> Over the years I learned to pick out one team of good dancers and sort of play to them, watch their footwork and throw accents when they'd be swinging the gal

[115] Manning, interview with author.
[116] Cliff Leeman quoted in Korall, *Drummin' Men*, 27.

out or swinging back. Having played for regular tap dancers, it was fairly easy to pick up on things as they were happening instantaneously. In a ballroom full of dancers, you can single out a good couple, and just make believe you're playing for them only, it helped me learn to play for dancers for sure. . . . If you see something in motion, you're throwing accents according to whatever they're doing.[117]

Jenkins, who idolized Webb, also used his experience accompanying performances by professional dancers—rhythm tap dancers specifically—to inform his approach when playing for amateur social dancers. In both cases, he relied on dancers' movements to supply him with a rhythmic vocabulary that informed his practice as a musician, just as dancers no doubt relied on his playing as a generative source for their own creative expression. It is also notable that the music Jenkins played for a full dance hall was informed by the attention he fixated on a single dancing couple, offering a real-time parable for the broader relationship between Webb's playing for large dancing audiences and the fine-grained exchanges with individual dancers I have explored throughout this chapter.

Within the lindy hop, moments of creative rhythmic expression occur most frequently during "breakaway" moments of open posture, where each partner has more independence within the haptic partnership. A common feature of many lindy hop figures, this open posture provides both figurative and literal space for dancers to improvise and to express themselves individually even as they move with their partner. In his unpublished story, "The Lindy Hop," Harlem Renaissance–era author Rudolph Fisher gives voice to this dynamic as well, indicating that dancers used the free space of the open position for both individual and collective expression before coming back together into a closed embrace:

Each had his own pet variations, which, especially while they were apart, were carried to the energetic extreme. The girl introduced alternately an agitated tap dance and a series of twisting high kicks, while the boy indulged in an elaborate Charleston, enlivened by periodic corkscrew jumps that carried him four feet from the floor. Yet these figures, wanton enough in themselves, were never wholly dissociated from the dance, always served to display either partner as the complement of the other, and so like exhibits of mating birds always drew them together again.[118]

---

[117] Eddie Jenkins, phone interview with the author, December 2008.

[118] Rudolph Fisher, "The Lindy Hop," in *The City of Refuge: The Collected Stories of Rudolph Fisher*, ed. John McClusky Jr. (Columbia: University of Missouri Press, 2008 [1932–1933]), 296.

This balance between paired and solo movement led to communication on both visual and kinesthetic levels as partners watched each other's creative expression at arm's length before connecting more solidly with each other's bodies to move as a single unit. Tap dancer James Berry expands on this concept, describing how figures from other dance steps became movements during this two-beat "breakaway" period in lindy hop patterns:

> We had a variety [of steps] to choose from because of the eras before us. Each one could break off and dance whatever occurred to them during a break in the Lindy Hop. Then come together on the beat, after two bars. Lindy was called "Breakaway" in the beginning. When you break, you are on your own to dig back.[119]

Berry's explanation invites us to read the expression "dig back" in two ways. First, one literally shifts one's weight away from one's partner, moving backward to create the dance's most extreme moment of dynamic tension in order to yield propulsion forward. This moment is, paradoxically, when one feels one's partner's weight the strongest due to the high degree of leverage tension, and yet it also when one is the most "free" to move and express oneself individually. Second, if, as Berry explains, dancers used this space to pull vocabulary from older dances, then to "dig back" is also to reanimate the steps of generations past through a corporeal enactment of cultural memory. He lists a number of such steps as he expands this description: "They did all kinds of steps in between. Ida Forsight even did a kazatsky! But back to Charleston you go. They expressed themselves in Boogie-Woogie, Camel walk, Snake Hips, Fish Tail, etc."[120] As dancers use this space to simultaneously activate older movements, carve a personal style, and create new steps through exploration and innovation, their dynamic closely parallels the "intermusicality" Ingrid Monson highlights as a central method through which jazz rhythm section players communicate.[121] According to Manning, this principle also birthed the synchronized lindy hop choreography that he claims emerged from his experimentations with the two-bar breaks in Jimmie Lunceford's "Posin.'"[122] Across a range of contexts, dancers listen actively as participants, responding to musical sound that is not passively absorbed but acted upon in the moment through embodied reflections, embellishments, variations, and interjections.

---

[119] James Berry with Mura Dehn, "Jazz Profound," 6–7.
[120] Berry and Dehn, "Jazz Profound," 7.
[121] Monson, *Saying Something*, 97.
[122] Manning and Millman, *Ambassador of Lindy Hop*, 99.

## Conclusion

Several years ago as I was finishing up my graduate studies at the University of North Carolina at Chapel Hill, I attended a concert by Congolese musician Kanda Bongo Man, one of the Democratic Republic of Congo's most popular artists. As Kanda Bongo Man emerged, he immediately encouraged the audience to get up, move to the front of the auditorium, and dance, resisting in the process the room's proscenium architecture and the seated listening posture it prescribed. As I spent the night dancing, I felt the band's drum rhythms triggering my movement, and I danced steps I'd never danced before as I watched the Congolese dancers on stage and let motion vision and kinesthetic empathy lock my movements to theirs. One series of moments struck me most of all: Kanda Bongo Man began shouting "Pesa, Pesa!," which cued the drummer to initiate a cymbal crash that anticipated the upbeat of alternate measures. Every time this crash came, the band and the Congolese audience members stepped abruptly forward with a thrust of their right shoulder in time with the cymbal. After several repetitions, the entire crowd had "caught" this movement, and we all repeatedly "hit" this moment together. For me, this experience encapsulates the participatory dynamics I've outlined throughout this chapter: it arose through a combination of regular "danceable" rhythms and a playful syncopated "catching" game created a sonically, visually, and kinetically linked moment shared among professional musicians, professional dancers, and an amateur dancing audience. When I chatted with the drummer after the show, bonding over our shared experience of this cymbal moment, it was apparent that, to paraphrase Ellington's appraisal of Webb, he felt it the way I did.

While I often think about this experience when conceptualizing the dynamic relationship between Webb's band and the Savoy Ballroom's lindy hoppers, to claim in the present to "feel" Webb's music would be to enact on some level the sort of time travel fantasy that I, drawing from Grey Armstrong's analysis, cautioned against in the previous chapter.[123] Expressing a similar predicament regarding space rather than time, Spike Hughes, who made several overseas trips from Britain during the 1930s to visit the Savoy, explains the gap between his experiential relationship with Webb's live music-making and the listening experiences of others. Responding to an Oxford University

---

[123] Though at the same time, this kind of reciprocal physical relationship with the past is central to "carnal musicology" and "cello and bow thinking" advanced by Elisabeth Le Guin in her study of Luigi Boccherini's cello music. Elisabeth Le Guin, *Boccherini's Body: An Essay in Carnal Musicology* (Berkeley: University of California Press, 2005), 24–26.

student, who charged that critics frequently overrated Webb's records Hughes
responded, "I suggest to Mr. Miller and the others that they should be good
little boys, work hard, save up and visit Chick Webb in his home surroundings. They'll know what we're talking about then."[124] In defending Webb's
music, Hughes explained that

> To me the music that [the Chick Webb Orchestra] makes belongs not to records
> or to the radio, but to a softly lighted ballroom with an enormous dance floor
> surrounded by tables occupied by gay, laughing, chattering dark figures. It is music
> for dancing, and such dancing as only those who have seen it can possibly imagine-
> lithe, vivid, brightly-clad Lindy-hopping creatures swinging their way around the
> dance floor, oblivious of time and place, of everything except their own graceful
> movements and the music coming from the dim platform at the end of the room.
> This is what these recordings by Chick Webb mean to me. What they mean to you
> I neither know nor can I possibly imagine. The listener who has never seen Chick's
> small form raised above the band, playing his drums so quietly beating his high-hat
> cymbal for the gut-bucket choruses, will probably hear [Let's] Get Together as an
> ordinary swing tune.[125]

To be sure, the barriers to visiting Chick Webb in his home surroundings
as Hughes entreats are far more substantial for us than they were for this
Oxford student: transatlantic air and sea voyages were available in the 1930s,
while, at time of writing, time machines continue to elude us. Furthermore,
that Hughes would refer to a predominantly Black group of dancers as
"lithe . . . Lindy Hopping-creaures" underscores the primitivism, exoticism,
and anti-Blackness that inevitably underwrite fantasies steeped in revivalist,
time travel thinking. Yet, we can still place the available historical material in
dialogue with an understanding built both from experience dancing the lindy
hop, a living dance still done to this day, and from applying what we know of
the communicative dynamics of Black vernacular dances and jazz improvisation more broadly.

As DeFrantz reminds us, and as I discussed earlier in this chapter, these
challenges are compounded by the fact that the surviving historical materials,
and certainly the surviving iconography, reflect a "received archive" skewed
toward elite practitioners in performance contexts rather than the social

---

[124] "Mike" [Spike Hughes pseud.], "Sayings of the WEAK," *Melody Maker*, April 10, 1937, 5.
[125] "Mike" [Spike Hughes pseud.], "Hot Records Reviewed: Chick Webb's *Unsophisticated* Music
Making," *Melody Maker*, May 26, 1934, 5.

dance practices typical among more casual amateurs.[126] While DeFrantz raises an important issue that should give caution to all historians of Black vernacular dance regarding careful attention to the archives we access and the erasures those archives perform, high-level practitioners have always played an influential role in the creative circulatory systems that drive Black social dance cultures. Virtuoso dancers' "hand-made, extravagantly detailed, expert versions of Black social dances," to use DeFrantz's words, may obscure simpler and more broadly practiced originary versions, but they also inspire widespread adoption and at times reduction or simplification in a cycle of give-and-take that perpetually blurs the lines between the exceptional and the everyday. As DeFrantz himself observes, "Africanist aesthetic structures of performance underpin popular forms of African American music and dance; these aesthetic structures value the unprecedented gestures of individual innovation within a movement structure recognized by the group."[127] This dynamic, I argue, extends to the relationship between Black vernacular dances and their media archives, as social dance formations from the lindy hop to hip hop to house and voguing rely and have long relied on an iterative feedback loop between social practice, competitive innovation, and performative stylization.[128] Webb's band depended upon this feedback loop as did the dancers in tandem with whom he crafted numerous innovations in rhythm.

We might look to Webb fan and fellow drummer Eddie Jenkins's strategy as a helpful window into this cyclical creative relationship between musician and dancer. As discussed earlier, Jenkins would serve dance music to a full ballroom by focusing on one couple and playing for them. On a different temporal scale, Webb's ongoing collaborative relationship with Whitey's Lindy Hoppers throughout the 1930s yielded innovative movements, rhythms, and dynamic approaches to tempo that influenced an entire ballroom full of dancers who in turn influenced other dancers just as Webb's style influenced other musicians. The lindy hop spread nationally and internationally both through social dancers at the Savoy Ballroom who brought the dance to other cities and regions as well as the soldiers who helped popularize it in Europe during the 1950s. The dance also spread through Whitey's Lindy Hoppers' and other professional dancers' appearances in Hollywood films and on overseas tours. In

---

[126] Thomas F. DeFrantz, "Figuring the Rhythm: Black Social Dance and Its Musics," keynote address, AMS Music and Dance Study Group, American Musicological Society Annual Meeting, November 4, 2016.

[127] DeFrantz, "Bone-Breaking," 66.

[128] Also central to this dynamic is the Black popular culture's circulation through mass media technologies, which in the twentieth century yielded what Mark Anthony Neal has described as "the tumultuous marriage between black cultural production and mass consumerism" that became a constitutive element of the Black Public Sphere. Mark Anthony Neal, *What the Music Said: Black Popular Music and Black Popular Culture* (New York: Routledge, 1999), 1–24.

the same vein, the sidemen in Webb's band impacted their subsequent musical projects as did the records the band produced. As new forms of music developed, influenced by Swing Era jazz, dancers in turn adapted to and continued to influence them. Such an emphasis on community collaboration across art forms and across the constructed divide between amateur and professional spheres of practice disrupts the gravity toward positioning singular musical geniuses as canonic drivers of the jazz tradition while still highlighting the specific conditions of possibility through which particular innovative actors make a strong impact. While I am of course not suggesting that the Chick Webb Orchestra's relationship with Whitey's Lindy Hoppers can or should serve as a singular Ur-source for post-1940 music and dance innovation, their multiple avenues of collaboration are broadly instructive regarding the fluidity of praxis through which forms of expressive culture develop and change in multiple venues, impacted by many voices and bodies beyond the relatively few our received archive invites us to see, to hear, and to remember.

# 4

# "Counter-Bopaganda" and "Torn Riffs"

## Bebop as Popular Dance Music

"No Dancing, Please." This sign fills the screen before the camera pans upward to an alto sax player blowing in a smokey club.[1] In this early scene from
the eighth volume of Ken Burns's extended documentary series *Jazz*, narrator
Keith David tells us that in the 1940s:

> Great jazz soloists abandoned dreams of having big bands of their own,
> formed small groups instead, and retreated to nightclubs: places too small for
> dancing. . . . The jam session had become the model: freewheeling, competitive,
> demanding, the kind jazz musicians had always played to entertain themselves
> after the squares had gone home. The Swing Era was over; jazz had moved on. And
> here and there across the country, in small clubs and on obscure record labels, the
> new and risk-filled music was finally beginning to be heard. It was called "Bebop."[2]

In the worlds of jazz music practice and discourse, bebop exists not only in
roughly the chronological center of jazz music's history (though increasingly
less so as time marches on), but also as a dominant focal point of jazz music's
aesthetics, techniques, compositional and improvisational paradigms, and
governing ideologies. As David Ake has argued, jazz history's "bop-centrism"
is so strong that it "implies that bop is not merely one stylistic branch of a larger
genre called jazz but rather that bop literally equals jazz."[3] Indeed, as Scott
DeVeaux argues, bebop's "perennial relevance" can be attributed to its con-
tinual reinscription in the present, for "bebop is the point at which our contemporary ideas of jazz come into focus."[4] DeVeaux's use of the word "point"
is important; narrative treatments of bebop frequently frame the genre, as in
the example from Ken Burns, as a singular moment of rupture. As essayist and

---

[1] Portions of this chapter previously appeared as Christopher J. Wells, "'*You* Can't Dance to It': Jazz Music
and Its Choreographies of Listening," *Daedalus* 148, no. 2, special issue "Jazz Still Matters," edited by Ingrid
Monson and Gerald Early (Spring 2019): 36–51. Reproduced here with the permission of MIT Press.

[2] "Risk," *Jazz*, dir. Ken Burns, DVD, Warner Home Video, 2001.

[3] David Ake, *Jazz Cultures* (Berkeley: University of California Press, 2002) 57.

[4] Scott DeVeaux, *The Birth of Bebop: A Social and Musical History* (Berkeley: University of California
Press, 1997), 2–3.

*Between Beats*. Christi Jay Wells, Oxford University Press (2021). © Oxford University Press.
DOI: 10.1093/oso/9780197559277.003.0004

critic Gerald Early and ethnomusicologist Ingrid Monson put it, "jazz's transition from dance to art music" at mid-century proved to be "one of the most profoundly cataclysmic changes to occur in American popular culture."[5]

This "cataclysmic" event, sometimes referred to as the "bebop moment," has become a crucial—arguably *the* crucial—narrative beat in many if not most histories of jazz music. According to cultural theorist Bernard Gendron:

> The bebop revolution has since been enshrined in the jazz canon as a contest of epic proportions, occurring at the major fault line of jazz history. Bebop is given credit for having transformed jazz from a popular dance music, firmly ensconced in the Hit Parade, to a demanding, experimental art music consigned to small clubs and sophisticated audiences.[6]

The potent story Gendron highlights here is reproduced to varying degrees in a range of jazz history textbooks, which consistently highlight jazz music's disarticulation from social dance as a central element of this shift. As music theorists Henry Martin and Keith Waters explain in their ubiquitous tome *Jazz: The First Hundred Years*, "the beboppers, however, disassociated jazz from the jitterbugging crowds of the 1930s in an attempt to win respect for their music as an art form. The radical change in tempo also certainly affected dancing."[7] Among the "key points" they use to differentiate bebop from swing are the following: "Deemphasis on dancing:—Tempos considerably faster or slower than in swing; Rhythmic pulse less obviously articulated than in swing." In his textbook, critic Bob Blumenthal offers that "unsympathetic listeners . . . predicted that any music presenting such challenges to dancers had no future."[8] While the implied conclusion one might draw is that these "unsympathetic listeners" were correct in assuming jazz could not survive without a dancing audience, highlighting this viewpoint exclusively serves to erase from jazz's history those dancers who creatively and enthusiastically met the challenges bebop music offered them.

"That's ridiculous!" This was the response I got from Sylvan "Charlie" Charles, a retired postal worker currently residing in Harlem, when I told him that many people see bebop as an undanceable music. When discussing his youth in 1940s Harlem, Charlie recalls dancing to bebop records played from

---

[5] Gerald Early and Ingrid Monson, "Why Jazz Still Matters," *Daedalus* 148 no. 2 (Spring 2019): 8.

[6] Bernard Gendron, "Moldy Figs and Modernists," in *Jazz Among the Discourses*, ed. Krin Gabbard (Durham, NC: Duke University Press: 1995), 33.

[7] Henry Martin and Keith Waters, *Jazz: The First Hundred Years* (New York: Schirmer and Thomson Learning, 2002), 174.

[8] Bob Blumenthal, *Jazz: An Introduction to the History and Legends Behind American Music* (New York: HarperCollins, 2007), 133.

the back of flatbed trucks at outdoor block parties as well as at social dances in ballrooms, nightclubs, school gymnasiums, church halls, and basements.[9] Contemporaneous periodicals and newspapers support Charlie's recollections of a vibrant social dance culture that accompanied bebop music. A 1949 article in *Our World*, that otherwise does not discuss dance extensively, features a half-page photo spread of dancers engaged in the solo "Applejack" and partnered "Bebop." As its author Dave Hepburn captions these photographs, "dig the new dances the cats are cooking. That should squash the deadpans who say bebop isn't danceable."[10] The *Cleveland Call and Post*'s M. Oakley Stafford offered a rather more detailed discussion of bebop as a form of dance music even as he expressed his ambivalence toward it:

> I'm Up To My Ears In The Bebop development . . . Now the newest phase of it . . . A few weeks ago there was only the music . . . Sharp, discordant chords, absence of tune, and that sort of thing. No one danced to it . . . Now the new development . . . They are dancing to it. They are doing what appears to be a combination of the modern dance with jitterbugging thrown in and even a step or two of ballroom stuff . . . It is so definitely to current music what the modern dance was to dancing . . . Difficult to accept . . . Angular . . . Meaningful . . . And slow to get into your affection but once there, you love it . . . Watch the up-and-coming set dance to it differently from the way they danced to jazz . . . It is definitely not jazz . . . Worth watching . . . It grows on you.[11]

Anecdotally, as Amiri Baraka (then Leroi Jones) notably recalled in *Blues People*, " 'You can't dance to it' was the constant harassment—which is, no matter the irrelevancy, a lie. My friends and I as youths used only to emphasize the pronoun more. '*You* can't dance to it' and whispered 'or anything else for that matter.' "[12] Where DeVeaux and others have reframed the ostensibly clear-cut bebop moment as a longer and more complex conjuncture of intersecting socioeconomic and aesthetic processes, I would like to draw from Gendron's summary the piece of the bebop moment's canonized history I hope to complicate in this chapter: the claim that bebop fully severed jazz's status as a form of popular dance music. More specifically, the experiences of Sylvan Charles and many others of his generation trouble the idea that bebop

[9] Sylvan Augustus "Charlie" Charles, interview with the author, January 13, 2015.

[10] Dave Hepburn, "Bebop: Music or Madness?," *Our World* 4, no. 1 (January 1949): 34–35.

[11] M. Oakley Stafford, "Informing You," *Hartford Courant*, March 18, 1948, 8. Capitalization and ellipses in the original.

[12] LeRoi Jones [Amiri Baraka], *Blues People: Negro Music in White America* (New York: William Morrow, 1963), 211–212. Italics as in the original.

music, with its fast tempos and structural complexities, was innately hostile to dancing, that the musical substance of it was to be experienced exclusively aurally and never kinesthetically.

Toward that end, this chapter offers a study of bebop dancing that focuses primarily on subcultures of Black youth in New York City, specifically in Harlem and Brooklyn, but also features accounts from other places that hint toward bebop dancing's broader ubiquity. Numerous accounts suggest it was a widely spread social practice in Black communities during the 1940s and 1950s that was not separate from the broader assemblage postwar Black popular culture but rather a constitutive element of it. These accounts invite an important question: what happens to our conceptualization of bebop and its history when we see its embodied geographies and corporealized spatial practices not as newly confined—exclusively to jam sessions in small nightclubs—but as expanded to a heterogeneous array of predominantly Black venues for sociality and cultural production along Katrina Hazzard-Gordon's "Jook Continuum": those sites Guthrie P. Ramsey Jr. calls "community theaters."[13] Much critical scholarship on bebop, including DeVeaux's work on the transition of jam sessions from private spaces to a viable commercial format or ethnomusicologist Patrick Burke's thick analysis of music-making on Manhattan's 52nd Street, still foregrounds the dynamics of negotiation between the Black musicians and white audiences. This dynamic is critical and certainly merits the rigorous interrogation it has received, but as the literature exploring it is already rather extensive, it is not my focus here.[14] Rather, in shifting the focus to social and popular dance and to spaces in which bebop was legible as popular music, I focus my attention squarely on the experiences of young Black audiences for whom dancing to bebop became a creatively generative challenge. In finding new ways to deftly navigate the fast tempos, challenging syncopations, and angular melodies that have earned bebop its "undanceable" reputation, Black youth departed from the aesthetic and political assumptions that guided previous generations and moved toward a new set of danced disavowals that spoke specifically to their own experiences and aspirations.

[13] Guthrie P. Ramsey Jr., *Race Music: Black Cultures from Bebop to Hip-Hop* (Berkeley: University of California Press, 2013), 4.

[14] DeVeaux's *The Birth of Bebop*, Burke's *Come On and Hear the Truth*, Gennari's *Blowin' Hot and Cool*, Gendron's "Moldy Figs and Modernists," Baraka's "Jazz and the White Critic," and Porter's *What Is This Thing Called Jazz?* all address this dynamic extensively, as do Kelsey Klotz, "Racial Ideologies and 1950s Cool Jazz" (PhD diss., Washington University in St. Louis, 2016) and Guthrie P. Ramsey Jr., *The Amazing Bud Powell: Black Genius, Jazz History, and the Challenge of Bebop* (Berkeley: University of California Press, 2013).

# Groping in the Dark: The Emergence of Bebop Dance Forms

Sylvan Charles first heard jazz music as a child growing up on the island of St. Croix before moving to New York City with his family. He and his friends got into bebop in the early 1940s as young teenagers through listening to records and started dancing to bebop records in church basements, at house parties, and by 1945 at massive block parties. In my discussions with him, which included dance demonstrations with partner Barbara Sidbury to music I played from my laptop, Charlie demonstrated a strong connoisseurship of bebop records and was precise when asking for the music he wanted to dance to. He wanted to hear a lot of Charlie Parker tunes including such canonic bop anthems as "Anthropology," "Scrapple from the Apple," and not just *any* recording of "Happy Bird" but "the 1952 one featuring Wardell Gray." By Charlie's recollection, two of the most popular and ubiquitous dance recordings at street and house parties were Dizzy Gillespie's "Emanon" and Tadd Dameron's "The Squirrel." Listened to on their own, the idea that either of these songs was danceable would be thoroughly unremarkable. Each features a perfectly comfortable tempo well under 200 bpm and a deep-pocketed groove supported by a walking bassline, precisely the same features that facilitated laid-back social dancing during the Swing Era. It is only when these tunes are affixed with the genre identifier "bebop" that their status as popular dance music begins to feel historically dissonant.

Largely reinforcing Charlie's recollections and other accounts from Black musicians and dancers, the phenomenon of dancing socially to bebop music was documented extensively on film and in prose by Mura Dehn. Dehn was a Russian modern dancer who engaged in a decades-long study of African American folk and popular dance from the 1940s through the 1980s. Shortly before she immigrated to the United States in the late 1920s, Dehn saw a performance by Josephine Baker in Paris that would lead her away from her roots in the technique and aesthetics of Isadora Duncan and toward a lifelong interest in the vernacular dance culture of African Americans. She spent over forty years on her film project *The Spirit Moves: A History of Black Social Dance*, which documents various styles of Black vernacular dance ranging from 1900 to 1986, from the cakewalk and Charleston to breakdancing and other early hip hop movement. With the Swiss photographer and graphic designer Herbert Matter as her cameraman, Dehn shot footage for the initial *Spirit Moves* volumes between 1950 and 1957, though she had been dancing (which she identifies as "fieldwork") in New York City ballrooms since the 1930s. The resulting film series is an unusual hybrid of ethnographic document, art film, and laboratory experiment moving between footage from dance venues such as Harlem's Savoy Ballroom and a studio set, and Dehn filmed bebop dancers in both settings as well as in other venues.[15]

While presented as a "fly on the wall" folkloric documentary of Black dance spaces, Dehn's intervention in these spaces is more pronounced than her narrative framing of her own work suggests. She remarked in the 1980s that "my contribution is to really have assembled and preserved the whole development of Black dance, presented by its greatest exponents; and presented in purity, presented as pure and as sincerely as they did it. I worked with them from the inside."[16] While she certainly worked with dancers "from the inside" in the sense that she both went to the Savoy Ballroom as a social dancer and worked with its elite dancers professionally, this relationship did not, indeed could not, yield the unmediated "purity" she claims for her documentary film work. In the 1940s, she worked as a choreographer featuring many of the same dancers she filmed for the *Spirit Moves* in jazz dance concerts and demonstrations, and her work decades later with breakdancers suggests her role in creating presentations of ostensibly unmediated Black spaces involved a high degree of intervention and mediation.[17] A documentary film about Dehn, produced in the 1980s, captures footage of her work with breakdancers. In this film, we see Dehn coaching a dancer on how he should engage in call-and-response and what kind of contrast to offer during a staged presentation mimicking a street battle, where she entreats the dancers to show more animated encouragement when one of their peers enters the cypher.[18] Indeed, her own accounts of her work filming the *Spirit Moves* reinforce the critiques Thomas F. DeFrantz has made, and which I discussed in the previous chapter, regarding a "received archive" of Black social dance skewed toward elite performers. As Dehn explains, "I wanted to film the great dancers of the Savoy ballroom. I had to get the permission from the director of the Savoy and he put us in one place. We were not allowed to roam around or to even turn around.

[15] Dehn's c.v., likely from the early 1970s, reads "Field work in Harlem, 1932–57"). "Curriculum Vitae" typescript, Mura Dehn Papers on Afro-American Social Dance, ca. 1869–1987, (S) *MGZMD 72 [hereafter "Mura Dehn Papers"], Box 20, Folder 213, Jerome Robbins Dance Division, The New York Public Library for the Performing Arts. Mura Dehn Papers, Box 20, Folder 213. Her c.v. also claims that filming *The Spirit Moves* began in 1952, though several documents in the collection claim she filmed at ballrooms in either 1950 or 1951. While I do not discuss at length here the problematic issues of representation in Dehn's films regarding issues of racialized primitivism, such critique can be found in Karen Backstein, "Keeping the Spirit Alive: The Jazz Dance Testament of Mura Dehn," in *Representing Jazz*, ed. Krin Gabbard (Durham, NC: Duke University Press, 1995), 229–246.

[16] Mura Dehn, in *In a Jazz Way: A Portrait of Mura Dehn*," produced by Louise Ghertler and Pamela Katz. Filmmakers Library, 1986.

[17] One example is a 1947 performance at Local Auditorium in downtown Manhattan featuring Dehn alongside Al Minns, Leon James, and Sandra Givens, all of whom would later appear in *The Spirit Moves*. "Mura Dehn, Negro Group in Jazz Dances," *New York Times*, April 30, 1947, 75.

[18] Dehn, in Ghertler and Katz, *In a Jazz Way*.

He put us in one place; and whoever came into that place and wanted to be photographed or filmed, that was it."[19] Thus, even in the Savoy Ballroom itself, her and Matter's filmic gaze reinforces the "Cats Corner" social architecture of the Savoy's dance floor, positioning specific elite dancers as chief exponents of social dance practices more broadly. Nevertheless, her work plays a vital role in documenting a crucial yet largely unacknowledged cultural space in which bebop dance thrived as part of an emerging postwar Black youth culture.

When asked in the 1970s about bebop's nature as "undanceable," Dehn retorted, "it was very, very danceable—it was magnificent. It was not done by white people. It was mostly done by black people, and it was done in spurts."[20] Dehn's account of bebop dancing focuses on the early 1950s, when a new generation of young people, more cynical and politically radical than those ten or twenty years older, regarded bebop as *their* popular music. Her films document young bebop dancers performing in a studio against a white screen, at the Savoy Ballroom during the popular weekly "Ladies Free Night," at the Chateau Gardens on Houston street, and at P.S. 28, a public school in Brooklyn. Dehn would later claim in an interview that schools were the current "hot beds of jazz" after the demise of major ballrooms: "Well, I would say in the schools. The kids are really the creators of Rock n' Roll, it certainly is in the bars. In the church, as another kind of expression, but they bring the contemporary church styles into movement when they get happy."[21] In her drafts for an unfinished manuscript, Dehn relays a vivid description of the attitudes of Black youth from a Mr. Bishop, an instructor of physical culture at P.S. 28:

> The post-war kids are brighter, more mature, aware of problems economic, social, political. Conditioned to present time unrest, insecurity. They don't think in terms of the future. . . . They don't want to be dominated. They are spontaneous, dynamic. I actually feel they are a better human material, conscious of their environment—good and bad. They don't go for Jazz. They are Bop fiends. If they are interested in dance, everything else becomes secondary.[22]

[19] Ghertler and Katz, *In a Jazz Way.*

[20] Mura Dehn interviewed by Maria Kandilakis, typescript, 1, Mura Dehn Papers Box 20, Folder 216.

[21] Mura Dehn interviewed by Maria Kandilakis, typescript, 7, Mura Dehn Papers Box 20, Folder 216. Dehn's work with teenagers at school dances reflected a broader strategy throughout her career as a dance researcher of working with children and teenagers to stay abreast of the most recent and "authentic" developments in Black social dance.

[22] "Mr. Bishop," quoted by Mura Dehn in "The Bebop Era," typescript, Mura Dehn Papers Box 1, Folder 6. I discuss the resonance of the "physical culture" movement in Black communities in greater depth in Christopher J. Wells, "'And I Make My Own': Class Performance, Black Urban Identity, and Depression-Era Harlem's Physical Culture," in *The Oxford Handbook of Dance and Ethnicity*, eds. Anthony Shay and Barbara Sellars-Young (New York: Oxford University Press, 2014), 21–22.

In describing the difference between the optimism that shaped dances of the Swing Era and the more Afro-pessimist mindset driving the "bop generation," Dehn would later make clear that bebop dance became a pathway for young Black people in the 1940s and 1950s to speak their experience of alienation and reject the obligation to perform happiness for the white gaze:

> The Savoy dancers, the main thing of the dance of that time of the 30s was hope. They felt triumphant. They felt recognized. They felt that they could, through dance, through music, earn a position of equality. Bebop was just the opposite; they found out throughout during the war experience that nothing is going to be given to them. They're not going to have equal rights. They're not going to be treated in the same way. Bebop is the strongest turning their back on white influence, breaking up the couple dance, breaking up all the movements and it represented the broken-up, disoriented, lost world, in which they can only rely upon themselves.[23]

Bishop and Dehn's accounts parallels Eric Lott's description of shifts in social consciousness among young northern Black people in the mid-1940s. Lott presents "bop style" as a defiant identity performed through a matrix of statements not just in music, but also fashion, language, and demeanor. Though dance is conspicuously absent from Lott's account of bebop culture in New York City, his description of "an aesthetic of speed and displacement" and a "closed hermeneutic that had the undeniable effect of alienating the riff-raff and expressing a sense of felt isolation, all the while affirming a collective purpose" align with Dehn's positioning of the culture surrounding bebop dance.[24]

These bebop dancers represented a sharp generational shift as the new music activated young peoples' bodies while older dancers resisted the change. Indeed, published accounts from jazz dancers who took up dancing in the 1920s or 1930s have largely affirmed the idea that bebop was undanceable. Frankie Manning, arguably the most influential Savoy Ballroom lindy hopper during the Swing Era, gives an account of bebop from which one would certainly surmise that it was not for dancing. Manning writes, "I went to Minton's Playhouse to hear some jazz, and I said, 'What the heck is going on?' . . . I was used to music for dancing, but this new sound was only for listening. At first, I was devastated because it was such a big change for me."[25]

---

[23] Dehn, in Ghertler and Katz, *In a Jazz Way*.

[24] Eric Lott, "Double V, Double Time: Bebop's Politics of Style," in *The Jazz Cadence of American Culture*, ed. Robert G. O'Meally (New York: Columbia University Press, 1998), 461.

[25] Frankie Manning and Cynthia R. Millman, *Frankie Manning: Ambassador of Lindy Hop* (Philadelphia: Temple University Press, 2007), 203.

Though their experiences—recounted in numerous oral interviews, in auto-biographies, and in other published accounts—serve as critical sources for the history of jazz dance, Manning and his compatriots can also be seen as analogous to the "moldy figs": those musicians dedicated to the music of an earlier generation who couldn't get hip to the new sound.[26] The *Cleveland Call and Post*'s Bob Williams expressed his bewilderment at bop dancers' movements as he acknowledged that the new style of dance's illegibility to him and his peers was, indeed, likely generational:

> Now, you'll pardon me, all of you "boppers" for my ancient tolerance and futile realization that while this new thing you call a dance seems easy enough for those of you who do it, I doubt seriously if any of the old bugs who thought they had gone modern when they learned to jitterbug can quite latch on to this one.[27]

Dehn was herself conscious of her own status as a member of this earlier generation, as she would later remark:

> During the time of be-bop [*sic*], I suddenly realized that each period [of Black vernacular dance] before or after or during is not something that is natural but something that is tremendously creative, and the person not of that generation is simply outside of it. And I was outside of the bop movement—suddenly and completely.[28]

While Swing Era dancers' reactions to bebop are an important part of its history, they should not be used to support the conclusion that the music was necessarily inhospitable to dancing. For a new generation of dancers, the challenges presented by bebop were central to their shared creativity and sociality; if the new music and its associated dances existed in tension, that tension was dynamic and generative.

The dance element of the new culture, according to Dehn, lagged behind the music by about half a decade. During World War II, Dehn claims:

> Musicians were ahead of dancers in their search of new forms. . . . In a furious assault of saxophone virtuosity the musician seems to disregard the dancer. He sweeps him off the floor, breaks his legs with irrational rhythms, stabs him with long whaling spasms, paralyzes with introvert monotony.[29]

---

[26] Gendron, "Moldy Figs and Modernists," 36–49.

[27] Bob Williams, "Bobbing Along," *Cleveland Call and Post*, July 9, 1949, 8B.

[28] "Transcript of Interview with Mrs. Mura Dehn by Maria Kandilakis," typescript, 1, Mura Dehn Papers, Box 20, Folder 216.

[29] Mura Dehn, "The Bebop Era," 2, Mura Dehn Collection Box 1, Folder 6.

This would seem on face to strengthen the claim that bebop was not for dancers, and Dehn even cites one older lindy hop dancer who likens dancing to bebop to having "to fight your way through sleet and snow."[30] Yet, she offers another reason for the lag between bebop music and bebop dance: World War II devastated both music and dance by removing so many men from bands and ballrooms, abruptly crippling the aesthetic nerve center of the thriving Swing Era. "With the advent of World War II," she writes,

> the Savoy Ballroom was left for the first time without the reassuring presence of seasoned dancers. Every one [sic] is a beginner. . . . The new generation gropes in the dark. There are no rules, there is no continuity of tradition. Everything looks awkward, like a mistake. The breaks are prolonged to any count, even eleven! The music is too fast for the unskilled youngsters.[31]

This explanation is certainly plausible given that the transition from the Charleston to the lindy hop as an adaptation to jazz's stylistic shifts late 1920s and early 1930s was spearheaded, most accounts suggest, by the innovations of the Savoy Ballroom's best dancers. It thus seems reasonable that, absent the most talented dancers and the innovations they may have generated or inspired, new styles would be slower to emerge. If Dehn's analysis is correct and there was in fact a period of relative dormancy in the early 1940s before new dance styles solidified, it would help to explain the popular perception that bebop could not be danced to, especially given that bebop histories often overemphasize the early 1940s, framing the time from roughly 1941 to 1944 as the music's most, or even only, significant period. However, while there may have in fact been a disconnect between music and dance during the canonized height of the Minton's and Monroe's jam sessions during the early 1940s, this disjuncture would prove short-lived as teenaged bebop dancers soon came into their own.

What ultimately emerged from the younger dancers' experimentation was a new style that expanded upon earlier vernacular forms, most notably the lindy hop and the applejack. First to emerge, by Dehn's account, was the Jersey bounce, an adaptation of the lindy hop where dancers compensated for bebop's quicker tempos by dancing in half-time. According to Dehn, the Jersey bounce emerged in the years between 1941 and 1943 to supplant jitterbugging as a dominant step in ballrooms in and around New York City.[32]

---

[30] Alfred Liegens, quoted in Mura Dehn, "The ABC or the Fundamentals of Jazz Dance," 3, Mura Dehn Papers Box 1, Folder 1.

[31] Mura Dehn, "The ABC or Fundamentals of Jazz Dance," 1, Mura Dehn Papers Box 1, Folder 1.

[32] Mura Dehn, "Plans for Work," unpublished typescript (n/d), 3, Mura Dehn Papers Box 20, Folder 237.

Her description of the Jersey bounce, which she calls "a hesitating, tanta-
lizing step," emphasizes a move away from the frenetic energy of Swing Era
lindy hop dancing and toward a more relaxed, nonchalant affect as "instead
of fast bouncing steps the dancers use a resistant slow step with a jitter on
each foot."[33] She asserts that this early style crystallized into the "bop lindy"
when Afro-Cuban rhythms were introduced to the music. At the same time,
Dehn claims the body movement and affect of bop lindy is very different from
mambo. She explains that "bop ignores the wiggle of hips. The movement is
directed from a stiff bounding torso into a sliding dip and then a splash of
arms and shoulders in a gesture of helpless surprise. The dancers look like
bullet-ridden birds raising themselves from a fall."[34] On a technical level,
Dehn identifies bop lindy as a 3/4 time (or "six count") step derived from the
lindy step the "jigwalk," which includes a "rock-step" and two kicks. Dehn
notes, however, that in the bop lindy's basic step, "legs are kicked backwards,
awkward and stiff; the accent is on the upbeat in the air. Steps are not of equal
duration. The motion is pulled through the hip with the grace of a goat."[35] My
own film work with Charlie and Barbara as well as my observation of older
dancers at Brooklyn dance venue Jazz 966 (which is the focus of chapter 6)
closely matches Dehn's description (though I do not wish to affirm or reinforce her practice of making reference to animals in her descriptions of Black
dancers given the primitivist tropes that discursive choice reinforces). In
Dehn's footage, I do observe many similarities with contemporaneous mambo
dancing, and the stylistic differences between 1930s lindy hop and the 1950s
bop lindy she describes, despite her protestations to the contrary, do have clear
mambo influences: extended periods of stationary time in an open position,
separation from one's partner to perform solo "shines," and sharp drops of
the shoulder. Indeed, Dehn acknowledges elsewhere that dance styles during
this period were mambo-influenced "due to great influx of Latin population
and the authentic Cuban musicians."[36] Nevertheless, her description of bop
lindy dancers' stoic affect at the Savoy Ballroom is a complete anathema to
the joyful exuberance previously associated with the lindy. Amongst the new
crowd, she writes:

> Lindy is danced with mesmerized faces and stiff limbs. During the send-out break
> the dancers part from each other with a ruthless fling. At times the intense stiffness
> is broken by histrionic shakes—compulsive staccato shakes of head and shoulders

[33] Mura Dehn, handwritten notes, Mura Dehn Papers Box 1, Folder 6.
[34] Mura Dehn, "The Bebop Era," Mura Dehn Papers Box 1, Folder 6.
[35] Mura Dehn, "The Bebop Era," 4, Mura Dehn Papers Box 1, Folder 6.
[36] Mura Dehn, Notes for *The Spirit Moves*, Mura Dehn Papers Box 21, Folder 259.

which shatter the stiff frame. They don't smile. It is a confrontation of victims entranced.[37]

Dehn's completed film includes multiple instantiations of bop lindy, the most prominent of which she shot at the Savoy Ballroom in 1951 during the weekly "Ladies Free Night." In her handwritten production notes, she identifies a young woman in a white dress and a man with a shaved head as "the main exponents of bop lindy in [the] Savoy."[38]

Around the same time, applejacking became the most prominent style of bebop solo dance, done almost exclusively by men and often in formal and informal cutting contests.[39] While individual dance steps known as the "applejack" date back to the 1920s or before, applejacking re-emerged as a solo dance craze in the late 1940s. Individual styles of applejacking emerged with varying degrees of complexity among different scenes. Dehn's handwritten movement descriptions of applejackers at the Audubon Ballroom identify a range of slides and dips as well as abrupt stops in the middle of steps, leading her to identify Audubon dancers' style as "the most modern dancing I ever saw."[40] At the Savoy Ballroom, Dehn noted, "it is danced in a broad and sweeping way, with dips and slides, with diving and skating, mostly to Boogie-Woogie music. But its off-balance pendulum fits into the torn riffs of Bop."[41] Dehn further observed, based presumably on her fieldwork in the southeastern United States, that the step revived, or at least recalled, aspects of ring shout movement from the rural south.[42] Among its greatest "exponents," according to Dehn, was trumpeter Henry "Red" Allen, who would perform the step while soloing on his trumpet.[43] In his research notes, Marshall Stearns also highlights the applejack as bebop's central dance innovation. Identifying the dance as a descendent of the "big apple" routine, Stearns explains that, "For the jazz dance always follows the music. And here, along with the new accents of what was then known as BEBOP, the jazz dance developed its own off-beat, fragmented set of steps."[44] Tap dancer Cholly Atkins, who worked extensively

[37] Mura Dehn, Notes for *The Spirit Moves*, Mura Dehn Papers Box 21, Folder 259.

[38] Mura Dehn, Handwritten outline and notes for *The Spirit Moves*, 13. Mura Dehn Papers Box 21, Folder 260.

[39] In her writings, Dehn alternately identifies it as a trend of the 1940s or early 1950s. She also notes that "girls also did Applejack—*but seldom.*" Handwritten notes for *The Spirit Moves*, Mura Dehn Papers Box 21, Folder 60.

[40] Mura Dehn, handwritten drafts for "The Bebop Era", 4v, Mura Dehn Papers, Box 1, Folder 6.

[41] Mura Dehn, "The Bebop Era," 1, Mura Dehn Papers, Box 1, Folder 6.

[42] Mura Dehn, "The Bebop Era," 2, Mura Dehn Papers, Box 1, Folder 6.

[43] Mura Dehn, Unpublished handwritten notes, 4r, Mura Dehn Papers, Box 1, Folder 6.

[44] Marshall Stearns, research notes (typescript page fragment), Marshall Stearns Collection Box 7, Folder 2. Institute of Jazz Studies, Rutgers University Libraries. Underline in the original.

with Stearns in the 1960s, claimed to have first seen the applejack in Detroit in 1940 and observed that many tap dancers integrated it into their routines.[45]

Black newspaper coverage of the emerging applejack phenomenon largely affirms Dehn's assertion that this dance, like the bop lindy, followed the Jersey bounce and further suggests that the dance became widely known and adopted via stage revues featuring the song "Applejack," popularized by Lionel Hampton in 1948 and Lucky Millender in 1949. Dolores Calvin of the *Chicago Defender* reports seeing the applejack for the first time both on stage and among the audience during a 1948 performance by Hampton in Newark, New Jersey:

> The kids were jumping to "applejack" rhythm in the aisles. . . . The ones in their seats who couldn't get to the aisles were yelling "applejack" followed by wild, uncontrollable hysterics. . . . We just sat glued to our chair, afraid to comment for fear of a hundred or more nearby juniors crashing our skull. . . . But nevertheless amazed and shocked at the goings on . . . [. . .] Then Hamp began Hamp's Boogie. . . . That too, had "applejack" steps in it which he did quite willingly. . . . The singers, Wini Brown and Roland Burton were also on the "applejack kick."[46]

Like the Jersey bounce, the applejack was a dance associated in the 1940s principally with r&b music and specifically with a popular "jump blues" hit. Indeed, Dehn frequently cites the applejack, along with the hucklebuck, as major postwar dance trends among the bebop "cools." Though she emphasizes applejack more, its appearance alongside the hucklebuck is indicative of the porous transfer between bebop and other popular music styles rooted in Black communities. The popular song "The Hucklebuck" was an r&b recasting of Charlie Parker's composition "Now's the Time" and became a significant hit for Paul Williams and his Hucklebuckers in 1949 (and later, of course, for Chubby Checker). One source of the applejack's assimilation into bebop may have been the dance team Roll and Tapp, composed of Johnny "Tapp" Smith and Johnny "Roll" McPhee. Former first- and second-place winners at the Harvest Moon Ball and Savoy Ballroom regulars during the 1940s, the pair were on tour Johnny Otis in 1951 and billed themselves as the "Original Kings of the Applejack." The pair had formerly appeared with Billy Eckstine, Woody Herman, and Lucky Millender, and the *Baltimore Afro-American* credited the pair with introducing the dance nationally on *The Ed Sullivan Show* in 1949,

[45] Marshall Stearns, research notes (typescript page fragment on lined paper), Marshall Stearns Collection Box 7, Folder 2.

[46] Dolores Calvin, "'Applejack' Replaces 'Jersey Bounce' with Dancers in the State of Jersey," *Chicago Defender* May 8, 1948, 9. Unbracketed ellipses in the original, bracketed ellipses added by the author.

adding that, "now, they have added a tinge of bop to the Applejack which gives it a terrific punch." While the pair were credited with introducing the dance nationally through their Ed Sullivan appearance, they explicitly claimed that the dance originated in Harlem at Minton's Playhouse.[47]

Now remembered as Harlem's Mecca for jam sessions and as a crucial incubator for bebop experimentation, Minton's Playhouse was also a venue for dancing, and the venue explicitly advertised itself as such in the *New York Amsterdam News* during the late 1940s.[48] Dolores Calvin of the *Chicago Defender* described a Minton's performance featuring Lionel Hampton and a "Chinese ballet dancer" whose routine included the applejack:

> She glided gracefully over the stage in a loud red outfit looking the part of a swan. . . . No applause. . . . The[n] she took off the skirt part and began a boogie. . . . The kids began screaming. . . . For a curtain call, the girl came back and Hamp said "You want her to do some more?" . . . So lucky for her the Chinese gal knew the applejack[. . .]. . . . I hate to think what would've happened if she hadn't.[49]

At the close of our interview session, Charlie emphasized to me that Minton's was a place where one regularly found bebop dancing. Though it remains central to jazz lore specifically because of the atmosphere it created for jam sessions and for the rhythmic and harmonic innovations of house band members including drummer Kenny Clarke and pianist Thelonious Monk, it is important to keep in mind that Minton's was still, in DeVeaux's words, a "legitimate nightclub" that billed itself as "The Showplace of Harlem."[50] The diversity of practices at Minton's, ranging from its oft mythologized back room jam sessions and Monk's hours of dedicated practice and solo experimentation to public social dances and novelty entertainment only bolsters what Patrick Burke has demonstrated to be equally true of 52nd Street clubs: that the formative practices of bebop music emerged not in isolation from but adjacent to and in dialogue with a broad spectrum of popular entertainment practices, which clearly included a generation of Black youth's experimentation with new forms of social dancing.[51]

---

[47] "Original Kings of the Applejack Dance Rapidly Moving to the Top," *Baltimore Afro-American*, May 12, 1951, 8.

[48] Classified ads for Minton's promising dancing appear in the *Amsterdam News* on December 7, 1940; January 18, 1941; and August 19, 1944.

[49] Calvin, "'Applejack' Replaces 'Jersey Bounce,'" 9. Unbracketed ellipses in the original, bracketed ellipses added by the author.

[50] DeVeaux, *Birth of Bebop*, 219. For a detailed look at the heterogeneity of Black music-making and community life at Minton's during this period, see also Ramsey, *The Amazing Bud Powell*, 36–38.

[51] Patrick Burke, *Come In and Hear the Truth: Jazz and Race on 52nd Street* (Chicago: University of Chicago Press, 2008), 155–160.

## "The Seat of the Cools": Bebop Dance's Venues and Geographies

While such iconic Harlem venues as Minton's Playhouse and the Savoy Ballroom played host to bebop dancing, they were not its central hubs. Dehn's written accounts and my interviews with Sylvan Charles and Barbara Sidbury independently pointed to two other venues as the main spots for bebop dancers in New York City during the late 1940s and early 1950s: the Audubon Ballroom in Harlem and the Chateau Gardens on Houston Street in lower Manhattan. The Audubon Ballroom, which Dehn described as "the incarnation of BeeBop [*sic*] in its abstract and pure form," stood at 166th Street and Broadway, roughly at Harlem's northern border; tragically, the ballroom is remembered principally as the site of Malcolm X's assassination in 1965 (the building currently houses the Malcolm X and Dr. Betty Shabazz Memorial Education Center.)[52] The ballroom had served as a dance palace and dance studio since before 1920, well earlier than the Savoy which opened in 1926. In the early 1940s, the Audubon continued to emphasize its status as an integrated dance palace, highlighting that it not only welcomed a broadly diverse audience but also that it specifically welcomed interracial couples.[53] In 1945, the Audubon advertised a hybrid "Jam Session and Dancing Party" featuring "Famous Stars of 52nd Street" including saxophonists Don Byas, Rudy Williams, and Ben Webster.[54] As with Minton's, the musicians advertised for this Audubon event reinforce the porous line between bebop's emergent "hip" underground spaces and a broader palette of Black popular entertainment that Burke highlights in his study, a practice also reflected in the Audubon's merger of two adjacent forms of participatory sociality in jazz: the dance party and the jam session.[55] Dehn's description of the venue emphasizes the affect of coolness and nonchalance associated with postwar Black youth culture:

> The Audubon Ballroom uptown is the seat of the "cools," as the Bop Generation
> is called. An enormous hall, at matinee dances it looks like a disorderly railroad

[52] Mura Dehn, Work plan for film "Epic of Negro Dance," unpublished typescript, 4. Mura Dehn Papers, Box 20, Folder 235.

[53] Photo caption beginning "Betty Johns and Bill Jones," *New York Amsterdam Star-News* June 20, 1942. The emphasis in this photo caption on interracial couples may have been a response to a news story the previous year where interracial couples were denied admittance to a private event at the ballroom sponsored by the Hispano-Americano Club. The ballroom's manager, in response, emphatically emphasized the venue's policy of non-discrimination and history of regularly and enthusiastically welcoming interracial couples. "Mixed Group Refused Admittance to Public Dance at Hall Near Harlem," *New York Amsterdam Star-News*, September 13, 1941, 20.

[54] Advertisement, *New York Amsterdam News*, April 7, 1945, 9B.

[55] *Burke, Come In and Hear the Truth*, 159, 180–181, 196–200.

station. People stand in groups here and there and in the middle of the floor. The greatest congestion is in front of the orchestra. The crowd is almost exclusively young men. In hats and long coats, unbuttoned, they stand and listen. Sometimes a solitary chair is dragged out incongruously among standing listeners, for someone to listen in comfort.

Their dedication is to the music, severe and restrained. They take in the message almost like a sermon. But it is a teaching of confrontation with oneself.

At times, not being able to suppress the inner ecstasy, one or another breaks into movement—strange, archaic posturing. Yet a most modern dance. It is dropped in the middle of a sentence without regret. The equation is resolved. These motions are a tribute to the music.[56]

In addition to hosting society parties and other formal events for Harlem clubs, the Audubon was also a site for fundraisers aligned with progressive activism. A 1946 fundraiser featured musicians associated with the integrated downtown nightclub Café Society.[57]

The uptown Audubon's principal downtown counterpart was the Chateau Gardens. Located at 105 Houston Street on the border of Manhattan's Lower East Side and West Village, the Chateau Gardens opened in the early 1950s and closed in 1959. The venue, converted from a Russian Orthodox Church, featured a red and white stone façade and boasted leather seating for at least 1,000 guests along with multiple grand pianos; it was used for dance events, weddings, and large meetings and conventions.[58] While throughout the 1950s the Chateau Gardens made frequent appearances in Black newspapers' society pages as a go-to venue for gala balls and fundraisers, one observer—city councilman and columnist Earl Brown—described it as a "drab dance hall" where he felt "crowded into a hole only a little healthier than the one the Indians put the Englishmen into in Calcutta."[59] The Chateau Gardens came to have significant political ties with progressive leftists. In 1954, it hosted the Communist newspaper *The Daily Worker*'s thirtieth anniversary party and in 1957—at the height of McCarthyism—it hosted a meeting of the American Communist Party after the organization had been turned down by at least twenty other venues.[60] This interracial gathering, which proved highly controversial and

---

[56] Mura Dehn, "The Bebop Era," 3, Mura Dehn Papers Box 1, Folder 6.

[57] Dan Burley, "Dan Burley's Back Door Stuff," *New York Amsterdam News*, June 15, 1946, 19.

[58] Per a classified ad detailing its inventory of items for sale upon the venue's closing in 1959. *New York Times*, February 8, 1959, W24.

[59] Earl Brown (Councilman), "Communist Convention," *New York Amsterdam News*, February 23, 1957, 14. Brown's feelings may have been influenced, at least in part, by his political opposition to the Communist Party.

[60] "Daily Worker's 30th Year Fete," *New York Times*, January 23, 1954, 6.

featured a counter-protest of Hungarian exiles throwing eggs at the venue's door, reflected the Chateau Gardens' explicit commitment to inclusion and exemplified the decades-old relationship between the American Communist Party and the New York City jazz scene.[61]

Dehn identifies the Chateau Gardens as a mecca for both bop dance and a related form of bop style "Avant Garde ballroom dancing."[62] She introduces the venue through a thick description of a "grand ball" in which she describes a surreal affective juxtaposition of fancy dress and introversion among the venue's young patrons:

Chateau Gardens, a dance hall downtown, is even stranger. Women in shimmering evening gowns, décolleté, with lacquered hairdos, orchids and gloves. The men [whited out: are] very young, mostly school boys—in somber "undertaker" habit with exceedingly small-brimmed hats and long unbuttoned coats. I thought it was a deliberate style but found that teenagers had money enough for a ticket, but not for the coat check.

The crowd is from Brooklyn, New Jersey—many West Indians among them. One pair performs their native courtship dance, prancing and circling each other like a haughty ostrich and a water buffalo. This evening is a special treat, with two of the most admired orchestras. But the couple dance is on the way out. Men and women pass each other as though invisible—every one absorbed in his own gesticulation. The bodies of boys move in one piece, stiff, insecure, shifty at the base. They repeat a limping footfall as though hanging suspended above the floor, a Bop "falling off the log." Some are beyond themselves with sound and motion. They are contemptuously called "soul dancers," a derogatory phrase at that time. The overall aspect of the crowd is festive. Especially the boys emphasize a ludicrous importance. Humor is replaced by irony. Insolence is absent. They are among themselves—for themselves. The satisfaction is complete.[63]

Perhaps the irony Dehn describes stems from the ambivalence with which Black youth performed socialite conventions associated both with whiteness and with Black middle- and upper-classness. While the markers of Black high

---

[61] "Kremlinites Control US Reds," *Chicago Daily Defender*, February 11, 1957, 2; "Communists Adopt New Negro Tactics," *New York Amsterdam News*, February 16, 1957, 3.

[62] Mura Dehn, Unpublished typescript outlining *The Spirit Moves: A Film History of Afro-American Dance and Theatre in 5 Volumes*, 1, Mura Dehn Papers, Box 21, Folder 259.

[63] Mura Dehn, "The Bebop Era" unpublished typescript, 5–6, Mura Dehn Papers, Box 1, Folder 6. While Dehn's use of primitivist language—using animals and "native" rituals as descriptors—is neither the focus of this chapter nor something I wish to see derail my centering of these dancers and their experiences, it is important to acknowledge that Dehn's highly problematic descriptive choices here do figure into larger tendencies, both in her own work and far more broadly among white authors, to romanticize Black bodies and Black movement as premodern and subhuman.

**Figure 4.1** A view from behind the stage of jazz saxophonist James Moody performing at Chateau Gardens with the James Moody Orchestra on September 5, 1952, in New York. Photo by PoPsie Randolph/Michael Ochs Archives/Getty Images.

society were certainly present at the Chateau Gardens, so too was an ironic distancing from any extroverted display of high-class affectation, as to "play it cool" was to simultaneously enact and eschew the performative trappings of racial uplift. This shared affective sense reflects the "critical ecumenicalism" Eric Porter argues was fundamental to bebop's social context in Black communities. Porter describes this critical ecumenicalism as an "experimental aesthetic sensibility" that, reflecting Porter's thoughts on the music itself, "may not have represented a particular, class-specific ideological stance, but it did reflect changing orientations and perspectives among working-class and middle-class African Americans, especially black youth and adults"[64] (figures 4.1 and 4.2)

[64] Eric Porter, *What Is This Thing Called Jazz?: African American Musicians as Artists, Critics, and Activists* (Berkeley: University of California Press, 2002), 57.

**Figure 4.2** Solo dancer at Chateau Gardens, early 1950s. Mura Dehn and Herbert Matter, *The Spirit Moves.*

While Chateau Gardens events hosted by social clubs and organizations feature prominently in Black newspapers' society pages, the venue did not generally post advertisements for its regular dances. This leaves us without the sort of detailed record of which artists performed there that would substantiate recollections of the Chateau Gardens as a bebop venue. That said, the venue did advertise a New Year's Eve breakfast dance in 1951 featuring a three-way "duel of drums" between Max Roach, Art Blakey, and the Duke of Iron's Trinidad Calypso Troubadours.[65] Pianist, composer, and bandleader Randy Weston confirms that such battles were a regular occurrence at the Chateau Gardens in an account largely in concordance with Dehn's narrative:

> During the beginning of the Second World War the government put a 20 percent tax on dancehalls, which had the effect of killing a lot of the great dancehalls like the Savoy Ballroom in Harlem, the Brooklyn Palace, and the Sonia Ballroom. They all closed down. But black folks loved to dance, so before that period, and even after the dancehalls closed, during the so-called bebop period, I went to dances to hear people like Charlie Parker, Billie Eckstine, and his big band. I even went to dances where Art Blakey and Max Roach would have battles of the bands, at a place

[65] Advertisement, *New York Amsterdam News*, December 29, 1951, 13.

in downtown Manhattan called Chateau Gardens. At Brooklyn dances folks would bring their own food and drink and we'd dance to bebop.[66]

As Weston implies here, jazz music and dance at the Chateau Gardens did, effectively, become an extension of the Brooklyn scene, as the ballroom's Houston Street location in lower Manhattan made it far more accessible than Harlem venues to Brooklyn's Black communities. Many Brooklyn-based social clubs and community organizations hosted events at the Chateau Gardens, and in recruiting such business, the venue explicitly advertised its location off the F train as an attractive feature for Brooklynites.[67] Barbara Sidbury, who grew up in Brooklyn's Williamsburg and Bedford Stuyvesant neighborhoods, also recalled the close-knit nature of Brooklyn's community of Black jazz musicians and dancing music fans.[68] While discussions of New York City's Black population are ubiquitously Harlem-centric, accounts from Dehn, Weston, and Sidbury all make clear that Brooklyn was a major hub of bebop dance culture among Black youth. Finally, society events at the Chateau Gardens frequently employed Calypso bands as well as musicians we might associate with the emergent popular styles "jump blues" and r&b music. These connections bolster Sylvan Charles's observations aligning bebop's audience both with the tremendous popularity of calypso music specifically and with contemporaneous Black popular music more broadly.[69]

Though to this point I have focused largely on dance spaces and practices within New York City, bebop dancing found a far greater reach, enjoying diverse iterations both across the United States and internationally. In 1948, Philadelphia's Elate Ballroom initiated a weekly dance night featuring Jimmy Heath, who through his saxophone playing drew comparisons with Charlie Parker and acquired the moniker "little bird." The *Philadelphia Tribune* encouraged its readers to "drop down to the Elate Ballroom to 'dig the Bebop.'"[70] Parker himself appeared the following year at Philadelphia's Olympia Ballroom for a joint concert/dance with Lucky Thompson, Al Haig, and Max Roach.[71] In Detroit, police raided the Club Sudan—an interracial venue marketed to teenagers—for alleged fire code violations and indecent

---

[66] Randy Weston with Willard Jenkins, *African Rhythms: The Autobiography of Randy Weston* (Durham, NC: Duke University Press, 2010), 27.

[67] Advertisements in 1950 and 1951 highlight the venue's F train accessibility, with one specifically offering directions to the venue from Brooklyn. *New York Amsterdam News*, November 18, 1950, 3; August 25, 1951, 24; and December 29, 1951, 13.

[68] Barbara Sidbury, interview with the author, January 13, 2015.

[69] Sylvan Charles, interview with the author, January 13, 2015.

[70] Ralph Holmes, "Breaking the Ice," *Philadelphia Tribune*, February 10, 1948, 8 [cont'd from 5]

[71] Huntley, "If You Ask Me…," *Philadelphia Tribune*, March 14, 1949, 12. Capitalization in the original.

dancing. The owner argued that police "could [not] make an exact account of the number of persons on the dance floor, especially when they were doing the 'bebop.'"[72] Bob Williams of the *Cleveland Call and Post* reported that bebop dancing was a popular form of outdoor diversion in suburban Solon, Ohio, observing that "the Bebop is demonstrated every Sunday afternoon for free, and without the necessity of an invitation or introduction, by several tireless couples."[73] Bebop dance also reached London in the form of "jiving," as the *Manchester Guardian* reported, "the form of music to which jiving—a somewhat refined version of jitterbugging—is usually performed nowadays is Bebop, that curiously indefinable noise which certain experts consider to be a symbolical revolt of the Negro against the white."[74]

Dehn's research also highlights bebop dancing's transmission far beyond New York ballrooms and the genres of music they featured. She describes encounters with bebop dance in Beaufort, South Carolina, and Tallahassee, Florida, while on a research trip in the American Southeast documenting movement practices in Black sanctified churches. Dehn also attended a late-night party in Tallahassee, escorted by one of her friends' maids, where she saw dancers executing the same steps to bebop music she regularly observed in New York. She interviewed one of the better dancers, a local hotel bellboy, and asked him if they were tiring of bebop; he responded "we are not finished with it yet, we are still working on it."[75] As a phenomenon, "bop dancing" was neither a unified "craze" nor a coherent style so much as an assemblage of divergent yet often intersecting localized practices that grew and changed in constant dialogue with the community theaters in which they were forged and with the various mass media apparatuses, such as films and magazines, through which specific dance movements circulated, sparking trends that inspired new localized versions. As DeFrantz explains, "black social dances emerge and recede with persistent regularity within the United States," which results in the formation of what he terms, "microclimates of dance style."[76]

A full account of the breadth and extent of bebop social dancing in Black communities across the United States is beyond the scope of this study, though I strongly encourage further research to expand our understanding of both

---

[72] Isaac Jones, "Cafe Owner Protests Raid on Be-Boppers," *Philadelphia Tribune*, February 1, 1949, 12; "Raid Interracial Teenagers Club: Liberal Policy Held Responsible by Owner," *Baltimore Afro-American*, February 5, 1949, 3.
[73] Williams, "Bobbing Along," 8B. Capitalization in the original.
[74] "Our London Correspondence," *The Manchester Guardian*, March 4, 1950, 6. Capitalization in the original.
[75] Anonymous bellboy, quoted by Mura Dehn in "Bebop Becomes a World Influence," Mura Dehn Papers Box 1, Folder 7.
[76] "Bone-Breaking," 66.

the phenomenon's broad reach and its distinct, localized iterations. Still, the styles of bebop dance that formed in New York City responded to and articulated particularities of place in a range of formal and informal spaces along the jook continuum, and it is unlikely they were unique in doing so; the particularities of spaces from a Black church in Beaufort to a late-night party in Tallahassee surely informed the microclimates of bebop dance that formed in those communities. Still, the practices across these communities likely shared substantial points of resonance as well, as Hazzard-Gordon reminds us that Black social gatherings and dance spaces in the American south are distinct from such spaces in the north but that they also share certain paradigms of aestheticized sociality that traverse the jook continuum.[77] DeFrantz further observes of "microclimates of dance style" that they "characterize time and place for varied groups along variegated axes of expression."[78] While it is clear that the movement practices of New York City bebop dancers helped construct and articulate notions of place, equally or perhaps more critical was their relationship with time. As this chapter's next section explores in depth, bebop dancers' ability to move with and manipulate time was central to the musicality and sociality that shaped their politics of style and their terms of musical encounter.[79]

## "Off Time! Off Time!": Temporal Autonomy and Hypermetric Play

Dehn's film footage from Brooklyn's P.S. 28 includes an applejacking section featuring four male dancers in the center of a jam circle of their peers. Watching this footage with Charlie, he points at the screen animatedly, exclaiming: "see! off-time, off-time!" Prior to meeting and interviewing Charlie, this same moment in Dehn's footage had been one I returned to frequently and cited in numerous presentations as an example of temporal manipulation among applejack dancers. In this moment, two young men dance side-by-side expressing wholly different time feels with their feet and bodies. One dancer performs small steps in place keeping his legs under his center while most of the action occurs in his feet and ankles. The other dancer takes larger, more pronounced steps making clearer weight shifts and covering

[77] Hazzard-Gordon, *Jookin'*, 124. As Hazzard-Gordon reminds us, the northern rent party, for example, "stems from two divergent traditions: the jook and the church social." *Jookin'*, 96.
[78] DeFrantz, "Bone-Breaking," 66.
[79] I thank one of this book's anonymous reviewers for introducing the phrase "terms of encounter" to my lexicon, and I riff on it here with gratitude.

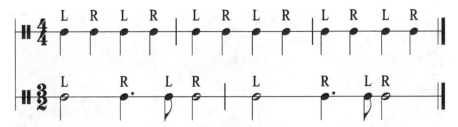

**Figure 4.3** Transcription of two dancers' footfalls during an applejack jam at P.S. 28 in Brooklyn, early 1950s. L and R = left and right footfalls. Mura Dehn, *The Spirit Moves Part 1: Jazz Dance from the Turn of the Century* (Dancetime Publications, 2008 [1986]). Transcription by the author. Prepared for publication by Alex Temple.

more ground while still dancing "in place." What both Charlie and I spot here is that the latter dancer's step pattern is organized in groupings of three while his counterpart's movement reflects duple groupings (while the pattern is continuous with no clearly articulated accent, one might transcribe it in either "two" or "four"). In addition, he dances "off time" by articulating a slower, half-time pulse in his body such that if the other dancer were moving in 4/4, he would be moving in 3/2 (figure 4.3).

This move to half-time (or "off-time" dancing) was the new style's most striking innovation. As Dehn described the phenomenon:

> Time is cut in two. Instead of fast bouncing steps there is a resilient slow stepping with multiple jitters on each foot. It travels through the erect body to a wobbling head. It is still the basic Lindy formula, but a new rhythm has emerged. A half-time off-beat Lindy. The preoccupation is to break up the beat. The position of the body becomes nonchalant, deliberately negligent. The arm which the girls in the 30's held up in a gay, triumphant salute, takes a reverse position. Palm down, the arm in front of the stomach flaps undirected. The stiff torso is swinging back and forth from the pelvis up.[80]

The ubiquity of half-time, or "off-time," applejack dancing created a range of intricate, creative temporal possibilities. More than a mere adaptation to faster tempos, the option to move in half-time, normal time, and even double-time invited dancers to phrase with and against the music at different metric and hypermetric levels, which they could move freely between. This allowed dancers not only to keep up with bebop musicians, but also to move in and out of time with them at will in a manner analogous to the tension between

---

[80] Mura Dehn, "The Bebop Era," 1–2, Mura Dehn Papers Box 1, Folder 6. Capitalization as in the original.

**Figure 4.4** Applejack Dancing at P.S. 28 in Brooklyn, 1952. Mura Dehn and Herbert Matter, *The Spirit Moves*.

"inside" and "outside" playing in a jazz solo. This layered metric play created space for complex nuances in dancers' engagement with musical rhythm and meter as, in Dehn's words, "in New York, they also dance between the beats, forming a rhythmic counterpoint with the music"[81] (figure 4.4).

By halving the pulse, bebop dancers' figures also change their relationship to the music at larger structural levels, and bop lindy, an adaptation of the partnered lindy hop, has particularly interesting hypermetric implications. Lindy hop dancing is made up of patterns of different phrase lengths, the two most common being six and eight beats (or for dancers trained in classrooms or studios, "counts") that are built from smaller two-beat chunks of movement and footwork.[82] These different figure lengths create the ability to move in and out of sync with musical phrase structure. Lindy hop dancers in the

---

[81] Mura Dehn, "The Bebop Era," 2, Mura Dehn Papers Box 1, Folder 6.
[82] I discuss this structural aspect of the lindy hop in depth in chapter 3 of Christopher J. Wells, "Go Harlem!," 112–176.

1920s and 1930s played with musical time principally at the level of phrasing but established a stable kinship by locking in with the musicians at the level of pulse. Famed tap dancer James Berry of the Berry Brothers described this aspect of lindy hopping in "Jazz Profound," an essay he composed collaboratively with Dehn in the 1970s:

> The rhythmic motion on the beat with the music has something. You feel free to do what you want and you can't get lost, because you can always come in, you can dance with abandon but still <u>you are encased within the beat</u>. <u>That is the heart of dancing</u>. Being capable of coming out and getting in. Even stop and jump in because the rhythmic beat is waiting for you.[83]

Yet, where lindy hop dancers play at the level of phrase structure, bebop dancers, in dancing off-time, extend this play to the level of pulse itself as they weave fluidly between the music's layers of metric and hypermetric structure. As eight-count lindy hop patterns already occupy two 4/4 bars in "normal time," at half-time they occupy four 4/4 bars of music. The beats in lindy hop's "eight-count" patterns effectively function as two-count units. Thus, when danced as off-time bop lindy, they effectively create four-bar hypermeasures where the various patterns' two-count movement chunks form measure-length hyperbeats. Through off-time dancing, bebop dancers worked around one of the core features of bebop music's ostensible undanceability—that it was simply too fast—by effectively cutting the tempo in half at will through their own realization of pulse. In doing so, they modified the central parameters of the long-standing rhythmic conversation between jazz dancers and jazz musicians, yielding a new world of dialogic possibilities.

Bebop dancers' shift away from a stable relationship with a steady pulse suggests that sophisticated dialogue took place between bebop dancers and bebop musicians. Kenny Clarke's accounts of developing his innovative and highly influential style share parallels with bebop dance, specifically his switch to playing half-time on the bass drum as an adaptation to faster tempos.[84] More broadly, off-time dancing paralleled similar innovations among bebop musicians, particularly "double-time" solos in slow- or medium-tempo tunes. Take, for example, Dizzy Gillespie and Charlie Parker's 1950 recording of "My Melancholy Baby."[85] Metric play is paradigmatic of this performance as Gillespie, Parker, and pianist Thelonious Monk weave in and out of the

---

[83] James Berry, "Jazz Profound," Mura Dehn Papers Box 1, Folder 21. Underlines in the original.
[84] Quoted in DeVeaux, *Birth of Bebop*, 219.
[85] The recording was released in 1952 as part of the collection *Bird and Diz* for Clef Records.

steady 130 bpm groove laid down by the drummer and bassist (Buddy Rich and Curly Russell, respectively). Parker's opening solo features a juxtaposition of melismatic double-time "playing the changes" passages that implicitly double the rhythm section's tactus with lyrical, melodic quotations that slow time back down as they return to the rhythm section's steady groove. Monk at one point leads the pair of soloists into a brief riff that could be the head of a tune at double the speed, and this is repeated to close the song. Throughout, Gillespie and Parker explore the relationship between the return from double-time to standard time and the return of discernable melodic material as each of their solos features a temporal realignment with the rhythm section paired with a melodic quotation of the head melody and, specifically, the song's titular lyric "My Melancholy Baby." Gillespie's solo notably features multiple types of play with double-time, including melismatic runs and repeated riffs, before answering Parker's earlier return to "My Melancholy Baby," and to the rhythm section's groove, in parallel with his own return. Ake has argued that, in the 1940s and 1950s, jazz drummers such as Max Roach "moved away from their traditional role as strict timekeepers. They developed a more dialogic manner of accompaniment."[86] While Ake is referring to drummers' dialogic relationship with their bandmates, the hypermetric implications of this new rhythm section paradigm as well, as the horn players' individual and collective metric play clearly spoke to, and indeed often with, bebop dancers as well.

In addition to reframing bebop innovation as alternately a dialogue between musicians and dancers or a process of parallel evolution in music and dance, we should also consider the likelihood that many jazz musicians also danced socially to bebop themselves. In his book *Thinking in Jazz*, ethnomusicologist Paul Berliner broadly highlights the importance of Black social dances to jazz musicians' development, claiming that dancing "sensitized them to the subtleties of rhythmic expression, training them to interpret time and to absorb varied rhythms through corresponding dance steps and other patterns of physical motion."[87] While we already know that key bebop players spent their early careers playing in swing bands for crowds of lindy hoppers, the more we learn about the novel syncopations and hypermetric layers to be found in dances like the Jersey bounce, bop lindy, and applejack, the more we might find potential sources of inspiration for the licks and rhythms developed in the 1940s and 1950s that have in many ways formed jazz music's core vocabulary ever since. Furthermore, as Weston's autobiographical account of his youth in Brooklyn

[86] Ake, *Jazz Cultures*, 53.
[87] Paul Berliner, *Thinking in Jazz: The Infinite Art of Improvisation* (Chicago: University of Chicago Press, 1994), 153.

strongly suggests, the generation of jazz musicians who rose to prominence in the 1960s, and who would have been teenagers in the early 1950s, likely danced these dances themselves well before they made their impact as musicians.

Through multi-layered metric play, bebop dancers made, and continue to make, active choices about where and how to experience musical pulse and phrasing, both how to ride them and how to deviate when they so choose, navigating through their own temporal manipulation the "torn riffs" coming from the stage or the record player. DeVeaux describes the rhythmic paradigm Clarke developed with guitarist Charlie Christian at Minton's Playhouse as "a mode of playing that owed little to the 4/4 chugging of dance music."[88] However, understanding the centrality of "off-time" movement in bebop dance helps us see that neither bebop music's fast tempos nor its move away from four-on-the-floor grooves were necessarily emblematic of bebop's ostensible drift away from its role as "dance music," at least not in the eyes of those dancers who found innovative ways to adapt.

## Genre Trouble (or The Problem of Dizzy Gillespie)

When I asked Barbara Sidbury about the ostensible challenges of dancing to bebop, she replied, "there was *never* anything too hard for *me* to dance to. Whether it was bebop, swing, or whatever dance was out there, I was in it."[89] The notion of diving headfirst into "whatever the dance was out there" is an important element of Barbara's approach to music and dance, and she is not attached to the label "bebop dancer" in the same way as Charlie. In contrast to Charlie's enthusiasm for specific bebop recordings, Barbara's more eclectic musical taste, spanning a broad range of popular musical subgenres from the 1940s and 1950s, might suggest a kind of ambivalence when placed against the kind of hip, niche connoisseurship one tends to associate with bebop fandom.[90] Nevertheless, her enthusiastic interest in multiple genres of music—bebop among them—is typical of how many African Americans regarded bebop at the time of its emergence: as one

---

[88] DeVeaux, *Birth of Bebop*, 220.

[89] Sidbury, interview with the author, 2015. Italics by the author to reflect inflection in the recorded interview. My title for this section of course riffs on that of gender theorist Judith Butler's famous book *Gender Trouble: Feminism and the Subversion of Identity* (New York: Routledge, 1990).

[90] There may well be a gendered dimension to this difference in identification and performance of eclecticism vs. connoisseurship as well. As Ramsey notes, bebop fandom was in many ways a "primarily black male youth culture." I do not mean to suggest that young Black women were not enthusiastic fans of bebop music, merely to acknowledge the homosociality that may have defined certain expressions of connoisseurship. Ramsey, *The Amazing Bud Powell*, 35.

Figure 4.5  Advertisement, *Atlanta Daily World,* April 9, 1948, 3.

exciting new style within an expansive, heterogeneous landscape of Black popular music. This attitude toward bebop was not exclusive to audiences, as many musicians openly broadcasted their own musical flexibility across genres, stating proudly that they were well-versed in a range of popular styles, bebop among them. Both in advertisements from ballrooms promoting specific bands and in bands' advertisements offering their services, we see throughout the 1940s a plethora of musicians claiming bebop, or often "rebop," as just one of their many genre competencies. In Atlanta in 1948, for example, r&b singers Savannah Churchill and the Four Tunes joined alto sax player Tab Smith to offer crowds a bill of musical fare spanning "Blues-Boogie Woogie-Swing-Rebop" (figure 4.5).[91] Similarly, Black newspaper advertisements for record stores and radio stations during the 1940s consistently placed bebop among the popular music genres on offer, alongside swing, r&b, blues, and eventually rock 'n' roll. An advertisement

[91] Advertisement, *Atlanta Daily World*, April 9, 1948, 3.

for Cleveland record store Loop Records claimed to celebrate "new 1948 history making Bebop Albums"; on offer under this billing were records from artists more commonly associated with doo wop and r&b: Bobby Caston, Sunny Bridges, Louis Jordan, and Sister Rosetta Tharpe.[92]

Cootie Williams's band, who played the Savoy Ballroom frequently during this period, displays in their recordings a high degree of musical flexibility and eclecticism. As Guthrie P. Ramsey Jr. argues, the band "provides a clear example of the stylistic flux in black popular music during the war years."[93] Ramsey stresses that many bands, like Williams's, are enmeshed in a historiographic predicament woven by critics and scholars who have sought to position bebop as something wholly apart from popular music during precisely this period of tremendous stylistic flux and genre crossover, and he has entreated to jazz historians that "it is important to show that bebop retained powerful connections to black communal values and to the commercial, popular music industry."[94] Like Williams, Lionel Hampton, and others, it seems clear that young Black listeners of the 1940s and 1950s, including avid dancers, have themselves become, in Ramsey's words, "caught between two modernist narratives": one that emphasizes the postwar commercial explosion of Black popular music as Black audiences found themselves economically empowered to engage more substantively as consumers, and another where modern artists of all stripes express a liberated individualism precisely through rejecting commercialism and popular taste.[95] This latter narrative's ubiquitous assemblage of tropes has largely drowned out other framings of bebop musicians.

Jazz historians and critics have long noted Charlie Parker's affinity for popular styles and specifically for blues, r&b, and country music. Yet, Parker's enthusiasm for popular music is often treated as either a mere curiosity or an exceptional trait that marks, along with his noted affinity for Stravinsky, his eidetic musical memory and the savant-like eclecticism that fueled the dense intertextuality within his "busy" sound. While no one would dispute that both Parker's ear and playing were exceptional, I offer that his ecumenical fluency across genres was actually fairly typical for Black musicians and music fans alike. As tenor saxophonist Charles Neville recalled of his youth in New Orleans, "there was no sharp division between bebop and blues players. The best players played both. Both were considered hot music by the hustlers and

[92] Advertisement, *Cleveland Call & Post*, February 7, 1948, 7B.
[93] Guthrie P. Ramsey Jr., *Race Music: Black Cultures from Bebop to Hip-Hop* (Berkeley: University of California Press, 2003), 69.
[94] Ramsey, *The Amazing Bud Powell*, 31.
[95] Ramsey, *Race Music*, 69.

hookers of the underground world of the Dew Drop Inn."[96] In repositioning bebop as a part of, rather than wholly opposed to, the popular music landscape within Black communities, I echo and extend Bruce Boyd Raeburn's desire to reposition New Orleans jazz "broadly as a community-based continuum in which many types of jazz coexist, as opposed to an 'official' jazz canon based on histories celebrating progressive stylistic evolution."[97] For, as Ramsey argues, "the 'commercial' status of a recording did not frustrate the cultural work achieved by its conventions."[98] Indeed the stable materiality of records facilitated for Black teenagers a higher degree of control over sites of musical gathering as they freely transported the sounds of Charlie Parker, Dizzy Gillespie, Tadd Dameron, and others to private basement gatherings and outdoor block parties, which were no less critical sites of bebop dancing than were clubs and ballrooms.

Complicating our notion of genre even further, Dehn indicates that bebop dancing was separable from bebop music. She claims that, at the Savoy Ballroom, applejacking was done principally to boogie woogie music, with the dancers' motions themselves the principal source of "bop" affect.[99] In South Carolina, Dehn interviewed Leotha Meyer, a dance teacher and former Savoy Ballroom regular, who claimed the steps popularized in New York were transmitted to her community in Beaufort, South Carolina, where they took on a life of their own in the church. "They take anything they can catch easy, if not they let it die out. They caught Bop. Everyone does it, even the 5-year-olds. They are crazy about Bop music. Teenagers in sanctified churches do the Huckle Buck."[100] These examples provoke important questions regarding whether music as an expressive form can lay exclusive claim to bebop's aesthetic and whether music necessarily holds primacy in questions of genre. In effect, they ask that we consider whether, just as bebop music clearly can exist without bebop dance, one can dance bebop without bebop music.

To wrestle with the historiographic issues raised by the alternately porous and rigid borders between bebop and contemporaneous popular musics such as boogie woogie and r&b, I would like to revisit and riff on what Ake terms "the problem of Louis Jordan." Alto saxophonist and bandleader Louis

[96] Charles Neville in Art Neville, Aaron Neville, Charles Neville, Cyril Neville, and David Ritz, *The Brothers: An Autobiography* (Cambridge, MA: Da Capo Press, 2000), 38.
[97] Bruce Boyd Raeburn, *New Orleans Style and the Writing of American Jazz History* (Ann Arbor: University of Michigan Press, 2009), 3.
[98] Ramsey, *Race Music*, 48.
[99] Mura Dehn Papers, "The ABC or the Fundamentals of Jazz Dance," 2, Mura Dehn Papers Box 1, Folder 1.
[100] Leotha Meyer, quoted by Mura Dehn in "Bebop Becomes a World Influence," Mura Dehn Papers Box 1, Folder 7. Capitalization in the original.

Jordan's popular appeal, which stemmed both from the popular r&b sound of his music and from his entertaining "clowning" antics, in Ake's words, "flags him as a problematic figure for critics attempting to paint jazz since the 1940s as a serious art form."[101] Ake argues that the specific temporal moment of Jordan's prominence, the 1940s, is principally responsible for his marginalization despite his musical similarities with canonically affirmed jazz musicians who established themselves a decade prior. While he serves as its namesake, Jordan was far from the sole victim of this historiographic trap; Ramsey reaches similar conclusions to Ake through his 1940s case studies of Jordan, trumpeter/bandleader Cootie Williams, and singer Dinah Washington.[102] Jordan's marginalization, Ake argues, is indicative of a broader ideologically driven policing of musical borders between jazz and other popular music genres. As Ake points out in critiquing *Village Voice* critic Nick Tosches's 1992 treatment of Jordan:

> In this view, jazz must, by necessity, be that music enjoyed by only a few navel-gazing, soul-tortured hipsters. Any music that did not exert these angstridden qualities, that inspired audiences to dance or romance or laugh, could be called race music, r&b, rock 'n' roll, soul, pop, in fact almost anything but jazz.[103]

Ake argument makes clear that bebop-centric discourse's restructuring of jazz's borders has specifically foreclosed the possibility of bebop, or any jazz post-"bebop moment," being regarded dance music by foregrounding undanceability—and really the lack of any active engagement beyond a performance of "serious listening"—as an essential marker of rigorous, modern, artistic jazz music.

The innovative embodied practices and nonchalant affect of coolness adopted by bebop dancers, however, further complicate Ake's "problem." That even Ake's apt challenge still dichotomizes "navel-gazing, soul-tortured hipsters" and dancing audience members obfuscates the space in which the Black youth described by Dehn—via their teacher Mr. Bishop—might be located. I therefore suggest that "the problem of Louis Jordan" is a necessary but insufficient piece of the historiographic puzzle. As a potentially useful complement, I offer what I will term, riffing on Ake's formulation, "the problem of Dizzy Gillespie." Gillespie is the one centrally canonic bebop musician who both checks the dominant "bebop moment" narrative's key boxes—a virtuosic

---

[101] Ake, *Jazz Cultures*, 43.
[102] Ramsey, *Race Music*, 44–75.
[103] Ake, *Jazz Cultures*, 49.

**Figure 4.6**  Lobby Card for *Jivin' in Bebop*, 1946. Photo by LMPC via Getty Images.

player, innovative composer, cultural and political rebel—and is also remembered for the same sorts of affective engagement of popular entertainment, including "clowning" antics, which in Ake's formulation are chiefly responsible for Louis Jordan's jazz canonic erasure. Unpacking Gillespie's deft navigation of these dichotomized archetypes helps create needed discursive space for bebop musicians' and bebop dancers' richly nuanced lived experiences and approaches to self-expression.

During the 1940s, Gillespie explicitly and repeatedly promoted bebop as a form of dance music. His band starred in the 1946 film *Jivin' in Bebop* (figure 4.6), which was replete with dance numbers and notably featured an applejack-inflected acrobatic tap routine by the duo Johnny and Henny to a remarkably fast (280 bpm) rendition of the tune "Convulsions" as well as a lindy hop number performed to "Dynamo A."[104] In 1949, Gillespie penned an essay defending his style of music—in Gillespie's words, a piece of "counter-bopaganda"—for the *Los Angeles Sentinel* in which he observed:

---

[104] The Gillespie Big Band's 1946 recording of "Convulsions" is only 210 bpm.

Another argument against bop is that people can't dance to it. Well, I've seen people dancing to our band and to our RCA Victor recordings such as "Swedish Suite" all over the country. As a matter of fact they think the Afro Cuban rhythm affects are especially interesting to a dancer. But very often people don't want to dance, they just want to come up to the bandstand and listen to the music. They pay their money and they take their choice. Is that bad?[105]

With the caution that this column, attributed to Gillespie, may well have been written by an agent or publicist, as was common practice at the time, this passage troubles two pervasive narrative tropes of bebop historiography.[106] First, Gillespie invites dancers' engagement with his music rather than expressing any resentment toward the activity, and neither does he frame bebop's merits in terms of the music's innate hostility toward corporeal audience participation; rather, he offers danceability as one of the music's merits. Second, and highly related, Gillespie enthusiastically frames a bebop performance as a commercial transaction where paying audiences purchase the right to interact with the music however they choose. This is not the attitude of a heroic modernist nobly rejecting engagement with the popular marketplace nor offering antagonism to mass audiences as a path to aesthetic liberation or ascendance into the realm of high art. Here, Gillespie demonstrates that, like generations of jazz musicians before him, he was himself far more comfortable with and invested in the role of "popular entertainer" than were those critics (predominantly white) who positioned him as a serious artist.[107] Indeed, as DeVeaux has argued, even this image of bebop-musician-as-maverick-artist was itself a performative caricature crafted by skillful musician/entertainers such as Gillespie to satisfy the taste of white hipsters who craved the vibe of an authentic, anti-commercial jam session experience and were willing to pay for it.[108]

What then are we to make of Gillespie's own account of this period from his autobiography in which he expresses frustration and enmity toward those audiences whose principle motivation was "to dance close and screw?" Even

[105] Dizzy [John Burks] Gillespie, "Daddy of Bebop Says New Music Is Here to Stay; Gives Reasons," *Los Angeles Sentinel* July 28, 1949, C5.

[106] In an interview with Ronald Welburn, Billy Rowe, formerly an entertainment columnist with the *Pittsburgh Courier,* claimed that guest columns by famous musicians were often penned by those musicians' press agents, but that "they would try to stick to how the person would react to this sort of thing and get his opinion and write the story." See Ronald Garfield Welburn, "American Jazz Criticism, 1914–1940" (PhD diss., New York University, 1983), 234–235.

[107] I discuss the problematics of leftist white male jazz critics' eschewal of popular music and commercial success in depth in Christopher J. Wells, "'A Dreadful Bit of Silliness': Feminine Frivolity and the Early Reception of Ella Fitzgerald," *Women and Music* 21 (2017): 43–65.

[108] DeVeaux, *Birth of Bebop*, 205.

were we to take Gillespie's later remarks at face value, the mere fact of Gillespie's distaste for audiences' corporeal engagement with music—whether vertical or horizontal—does not in and of itself render their embodied experiences a "false" understanding of bebop. In this passage, Gillespie explains his band's struggles in the late 1940s precisely as a disjuncture between what his band prioritized and what dancers cared about:

> Dancers had to hear those four solid beats and could care less about the more esoteric aspects, the beautiful advanced harmonies and rhythms that we played and our virtuosity, as long as they could dance. They didn't care whether we played a flatted fifth or a ruptured 129th.[109]

Gillespie's frustration here is that dancing audiences failed to appreciate those aspects of bebop music that Gillespie himself most prized, in this case its extended harmonic language and layers of asymmetric rhythmic complexity. The hostility toward dancing audiences Gillespie articulates in this oft-quoted passage would seem to affirm the ubiquitous narrative of jazz musicians' ambivalence toward popular audiences as they sought the respect afforded "real" artists. Affirming this perspective, cultural historian David Stowe frames the story of bebop's emergence as one of "big bands betraying their audience by playing undanceable tempos or lacing their charts with the controversial modernisms of what was coming to be called bebop."[110]

Gillespie's big band, however, regularly played dance gigs throughout the 1940s and 1950s. Also, in the same autobiography, Gillespie offers the following passage underscoring dance's centrality to all jazz music:

> Jazz was invented for people to dance. So when you play jazz and people don't feel like dancing or moving the feet, you're getting away from the idea of music. Never lose that feeling of somebody wanting to dance; that's one of the characteristics of our music. You wanna dance when you listen to our music because it transmits that feeling of rhythm.[111]

Furthermore, his lamenting criticism regarding audiences' cochlear inadequacies could also suggest that he may himself have lacked the kinesthetic "chops" to properly appreciate the subtle complexities of bebop dancers' movement. Bebop dancers' penchant for "off-time" dancing yielded a fluid

---

[109] Dizzy Gillespie with Al Fraser, *To Be or Not to Bop* (Garden City, NY: Doubleday, 1979), 356.

[110] David Stowe, *Swing Changes: Big-Band Jazz in New Deal America* (Cambridge, MA: Harvard University Press, 1994), 182.

[111] Gillespie with Fraser, *To Be or Not to Bop*, 484–485.

range of intricate, multi-layered relationships with "those four solid beats" in the music.[112] It may be that the metric and hypermetric subtleties of vir- tuoso social bebop dancers' treatment of pulse were themselves as illegible to Gillespie as his flatted fifths were to them. Then again, Gillespie himself dem- onstrated facility as a dancer on numerous occasions and thus may well have been quite hip to what dancers were doing. Ultimately, however, Gillespie's facility with or understanding of bebop dance is a bit beside the point, as what I am explicitly asking for in raising this possibility is not an assessment of Gillespie's terpsichorean fluency but a broader paradigm shift in how we re- gard rigorous, sensitive listening. It is possible to appreciate music, I argue, in ways that may be illegible to musicians themselves, and any perceptual fissures between bebop dancers' and musicians' approaches to listening should push us toward a robustly heterogeneous concept of "music appreciation," one that moves beyond mere fidelity to the precise epistemologies through which musicians conceptualize and value their own work.

Gillespie, like the Black youth who danced to his and other bebop players' music, certainly fits Ramsey's paradigm as an artist "caught between two mod- ernist narratives."[113] He navigated the same professional conditions of possi- bility as Jordan while simultaneously seeking to advocate for developments in jazz music that challenged musicians and audiences alike. DeVeaux explains Gillespie's deft negotiation of a rapidly shifting, but still highly racialized, commercial landscape:

> In reaching beyond the circumscribed world of the jazz virtuoso to the broader sphere of commercial entertainment, he discovered his own accommodation with audience expectation—what he later called "my own way of 'Tomming.'" Drawing on his experiences in show business, he offered an updated, idiosyn- cratic version of Cab Calloway's urban hipster (it is not very far from "hi-de-ho" to "ooop-bop-sh'bam") or of Louis Armstrong, the original artist-as-entertainer. In short, Gillespie became a "personality," within the bounds allowable to African Americans at midcentury. This strategy put a public face on bebop and un- doubtedly helped to neutralize the impression of racial antagonism that many audiences may have drawn from the sight of black instrumentalists determined not to entertain.[114]

[112] In both *Jivin' in Bebop* and elsewhere, Gillespie proved as a bandleader to be a more than capable dancer. My questioning of his "chops" here is meant more to articulate how Gillespie's criticism highlights divergent fluencies and priorities between musicians and dancers and might be flipped to center danced rather than musicked epistemologies.

[113] Ramsey, *Race Music*, 69.

[114] DeVeaux, *Birth of Bebop*, 435.

The "problem of Dizzy Gillespie," thus, asks us to place bebop, both music and dance, within a dynamic Afro-modernist cultural and aesthetic landscape where—for both musicians and audiences—nonchalant eschewal of both white expectations and the popular culture of previous Black generations, codeswitching to facilitate simultaneous negotiation of popular music's commercial environment and the white modernist critical gatekeeping of "high art," and a genuine investment in jazz as "danceable" music could coexist as elements of a coherent, Afro-modernist whole. It is easy to read Gillespie's navigation of this dynamic cultural landscape as that of an exceptionally skilled public performer and entrepreneur, yet I see Gillespie's movement within this space as more than that. I see his ostensibly conflicting public statements as cohesive and coherent in a manner analogous to his solo on "My Melancholy Baby," which, like the off-time rhythms of bebop dancers, creates the logic of its own cohesion not despite its perpetual motion between grooves but precisely because of it. To Ake's and Ramsey's analyses then, I would offer that considering the "problem of Dizzy Gillespie" alongside the cultural work of Black bebop dancers can help us reframe Gillespie, Jordan, and others not as "caught" between narratives but as bodies in motion, thriving dynamically and coherently within the dialectic groove forged between two narrative streams.

## Conclusion

Eric Porter has written of bebop that it "marked a crucial juncture in African American musicians' critical conversation about jazz, as it ushered in new identities for them and transformed the jazz discourse."[115] Porter is absolutely correct regarding bebop's discursive importance. Whatever one's opinion of bebop's centrality as *the* pivotal moment in jazz music history, it is inarguably central to the fraught yet vibrant discourse of jazz historiography. How one conceptualizes bebop has critical implications for how one lays out jazz historical narratives as a whole. Burns, for example, positions dancing audiences as a kind of bittersweet but necessary human sacrifice on the altar of high modernism as his film both celebrates bebop's innovations and laments: "but those innovations came at a great cost. The jazz audience shrank as young people, both Black and white, found other forms of music to dance to."[116] This idea of a "great cost" is critical to the romanticization of jazz's turn toward an

[115] Porter, *What Is This Thing Called Jazz?*, 55.
[116] Burns, "Risk."

enduring status as a form of art music. The shedding of a popular, dancing audience is the heroic sacrifice jazz music makes to unburden itself of the worldly constraints upon its aesthetic purity and transcend the mortal plane to take its rightful place in the pantheon of truly great art forms.

Safeguarding this transcendent status is a related and fundamentally defensive framing through hypervigilant curation of bebop's periodicity, effectively constricting the music's "true" period exclusively to the early 1940s, before it became broadly popular and was ostensibly corrupted by that popularity. From within this mindset, one might account for and summarily dismiss the history I offer throughout this chapter by noting that most of the evidence upon which I rely comes from the late 1940s and early 1950s: years that some scholars and critics identify not as part of bebop's peak but rather as a sort of corrupted epilogue. The period when bebop seems to have found its strongest popular following among young Black audiences occurs during the years DeVeaux dismisses as a time of decline where bebop was experiencing its inevitable absorption into the machinery of the cultural industry as it "entered well-worn commercial channels" and "followed a familiar pattern of exploitation for a mass consumer audience."[117] Yet, this "late" period was not, for bebop, some kind of kitschy Adornian death rattle but rather a continuation of its existing relationship with Black popular culture more broadly. Indeed, for Black communities, bebop was never so disconnected from mass mediation nor from the engines of commerce as this framing would seem to suggest.

Another means of dismissing the idea of bebop as dance music is to aggressively narrow the aesthetic scope of what music counts as "real bebop" and then to question whether the bulk of the music bebop dancers engaged with meets this purity test. Indeed, the lack of live music in Dehn's films does leave research reliant on her work vulnerable to this very criticism. Oral histories that concord with Dehn's accounts, however, make clear that dancers like Sylvan "Charlie" Charles and Barbara Sidbury danced not only to Cootie Williams and other "in between" bands, but also to those artists canonized as bebop's patron saints—Gillespie, Bird, Monk, Clarke—and to the same recordings now enshrined as the bebop canon's sacred relics. While dancers did find a range of popular music to dance to, bebop was among those popular music genres, often performed in the same spaces and by the same musicians as calypso, r&b, mambo, and what would become rock 'n' roll. Indeed, beyond the evidence from dancer Sylvan Charles and pianist Randy Weston that at least some bebop dancers enjoyed grooving to records now situated within the core of bebop's canon, our historical understanding of bebop and its

---

[117] DeVeaux, *The Birth of Bebop*, 438.

temporal periodization must also account for Black dancers' relatively broad understanding of what constituted the genre "bebop." To even ask whether the music they danced to in the late 1940s and early 1950s is "really bebop" is to advance a hermeneutic of musical style that centers the relationship between Black musicians and audiences of hip, white intellectuals, reproducing a long-standing jazz historical trope of erasing Black audiences' experiences.[118] In considering a period at midcentury where interstate highway construction, it-self the result of ostensibly benevolent planning by educated whites seeking to modernize American cities, gutted the commercial and social centers of Black neighborhoods, the predominantly white jazz critical enterprise has similarly constructed an impregnable discursive median between bebop's modernism and other forms of Black popular music. Like I-10 in New Orleans or I-95 in the South Bronx, this discourse disrupts contiguous Black communities, severing the diverse membership of "everyday" Black audiences from a mean-ingful presence in community theaters and, most notably, in the histories of those forms of expression to which these community theaters gave rise.

In reconsidering bebop's ostensible turn away from "mass audiences," we must also wrestle with the extent to which our historiography centers the experiences and desires of white audiences. Indeed, this is a fundamental his-toriographic problem in discussing the Swing Era, a period many scholars—particularly in the field of American Studies—demarcate as coterminous with swing music's popular ascendance to its briefly held status as a "national" (i.e., popular with white people) "craze." Just as Swing Era historiography marginalizes swing music's origins among Black musicians in dialogue with local Black audiences and scenes, so too does bebop historiography essentially trade one group of white fans for another as it either explicitly or implicitly foregrounds Black musicians' relationships with an elite audience of hip white patrons.[119] While acknowledging that at least some of those relationships were experienced as authentic, genuine, and reciprocal from the perspec-tive of (some) musicians, this historiographic gravity still makes no strong account of those Black audiences whose engagement with bebop music does not necessarily parallel the experiences or perspectives of white audiences, or, for that matter, of Black jazz musicians. Ironically, these dancers may con-form more fully to the mythical archetype of the "bebop hero" than do those

[118] Charles D. Carson poignantly highlights this discursive erasure of Black audiences, and specifi-cally Black middle-class audiences, in his work on smooth jazz. "'Bridging the Gap': Creed Taylor, Grover Washington Jr., and the Crossover Roots of Smooth Jazz," *Black Music Research Journal* 28, no. 1 (April 2008): 1–15; Ramsey, *Race Music*, 34.

[119] Ingrid Monson calls out this dynamic, and explicitly credits Amiri Baraka with having done so decades before her, in "The Problem with White Hipness: Race, Gender, and Cultural Conceptions in Jazz Historical Discourse," *Journal of the American Musicological Society* 48, no. 3 (Autumn 1995): 397–399.

musicians to whom they grooved: most were amateurs who never commer-
cialized their self-expression and jammed socially in small corners, pushing
themselves and each other to greater virtuosic heights—with no promise of
future fame or fortune—through a medium and style whose subtleties few
would understand or genuinely appreciate. Their social milieu thrived in informal basement gatherings, outdoor block parties, and school functions
where tiny videographic fragments hinting at the range of their improvisational creations survive only due to the efforts of a single enthusiastic docu-
mentarian. So long as this romantic version of bebop's affective story exists,
and there is indeed still room for it, it ought to make space for those dancers
in the corner, whether many or few, articulating corporeally a fundamentally
Afro-modern sensibility.

In discussing Afro-modernism's postwar emergence, Ramsey highlights
the centrality of the Black body's shifting relationship with popular culture
and mass media as central to contested discourses of American aesthetic and
sociopolitical values:

> If one of the legacies of nineteenth-century minstrelsy involved the public degra-
> dation of the black body in the American entertainment sphere, then one hundred
> years after minstrelsy's emergence, African Americans used this same signifier to
> upset a racist social order and to affirm in the public entertainment and the private
> spheres their culture and humanity. Although it has some precedent, the new at-
> titude was so prevalent that it represents a huge departure from earlier modes of
> "racial uplift," especially the "politics of respectability" championed by the black
> professional and upper-class citizens, who sought to discipline black bodies into
> bourgeois submission.[120]

Ramsey acknowledges the ubiquity of social dancing but focuses the bulk
of his analysis here on the lyrical and sonic signifiers presented in popular
recordings. As such, my focus on Black audiences' kinetic engagement with
bebop music should only strengthen his emphasis on Black corporeal autonomy as a critical site of Afro-modernist liberation. Dancers' engagement with bebop at house parties, at clubs, at ballrooms, and at school social
functions suggests that the moment of supposed rupture that exemplifies
bebop's transcendent exodus from the realm of popular music and the idea of
bebop/r&b as the fault line where jazz and American popular music part ways
to move along different evolutionary trajectories are discursive constructs
validated only retroactively by subsequent developments and made necessary

---

[120] Ramsey, *Race Music*, 51.

as part of the cultural work to secure jazz's institutional position, categorically, as an art-and-not-pop music properly legible within predominantly white modernist institutional spaces.

As, per Ramsey's analysis, Black embodiment is a central battleground upon which discursive battles over American cultural history are fought, cultures and practices of social bebop dance trouble a central component of canonic treatments of jazz's "bebop moment," exposing the separation of the practices "dancing" and "listening" as a false dichotomy vis-à-vis Black audience engagement. Indeed, even as DeVeaux critiques the prestige culture of the concert and concert hall, he reifies the value judgments of its particular choreography of listening when he claims that even in the Savoy Ballroom, the increasing virtuosity of the music would lead to moments where "dancing would occasionally be supplanted by listening" and also claims that the move toward concertized jazz, and the musical innovations driving it, required listening with undivided, motionless attention.[121] Through multi-layered metric play, however, bebop dancers made active choices about where and how to experience the pulse and phrasing of complex bebop music, both how to ride it and how to deviate from it when they so chose. To this day, Sylvan "Charlie" Charles's favorite moments are when he can dance off-time to fast bebop music. "What I enjoy the most," he told me, "is I get a different feeling if I dance to Charlie Parker or Lou Donaldson, up tempo, when I dance with somebody like Barbara, it puts me on a different level altogether. I get a satisfaction out of that that I don't get from other music."[122] Exploring bebop music through dance also shifts the story of this critical moment of jazz rupture by centering dancers' experiences rather than musicians' desires. This shift in attention offers a counterweight to any clean, ideological narrative of jazz's sonic evolution into a form of complex and challenging artistic expression that can only be properly appreciated, and only properly respected, when audiences listen from a posture that performatively erases their own bodies as participating agents in the event.

Even if one did regard the majority of sweeping claims about bebop-as-art as sufficiently well substantiated and prevailing narratives of the bebop moment as underwritten by real events and perspectives, which is certainly a legitimate perspective, the very existence of bebop dance and dancers, whatever the scale, demands that at minimum there be space for alternative stories. Stories of bebop that emphasize young Black listeners, porous boundaries

---

[121] Scott DeVeaux, "The Emergence of the Jazz Concert, 1935–1945," *American Music* 7, no. 1 (Spring 1989): 9.

[122] Sylvan Charles, interview with the author, January 2015.

with popular music, house party culture, and social dance are no more an existential threat to bebop music than was bebop's emergence to jazz music itself, as numerous "moldy figs" feared at the time. To extend musicologist Robert Walser's use of the phrase "keeping time" as a metaphor for jazz discourse and historiography, the ubiquity of "off-time" dancing and its attendant paradigms for rhythmic innovation among bebop drummers suggest a narrative pathway that meaningfully yields space for bebop dancers: bebop music was forged through the synthesis of multiple time feels and weaved grooves that not only accommodated, but relied upon, the dynamic play among ostensibly incongruent temporal slippages in both sound and movement.[123] Just as unfamiliar chords and sonorities existed alongside the importance of "the changes" as both substitutions for and commentaries upon well-worn tropes and forms, the movements and stories of bebop dancers invite ever more nuanced, ambitious narrative treatments of jazz history's central "cataclysmic" event that deftly and playfully, and at times ambivalently, navigate and signify on the torn riffs of jazz historical discourse.

---

[123] Robert Walser, ed., *Keeping Time: Readings in Jazz History* (New York: Oxford University Press, 1999).

# 5

# "A Fine Art in Danger"

## Marshall Stearns's Jazz Dance Advocacy

In the summer of 1963, Dr. Marshall Stearns, an English professor at Hunter College in New York City, wrote to Glen Wolf, director of the Bureau of Cultural Affairs for the US Department of State, to recommend improvements to the State Department's "jazz diplomacy" tours abroad:

> In the course of twenty or so years lecturing on the subject, I have found one other addition to the music of inestimable value: jazz dancers. They furnish a new and tangible dimension to the music, for certain specific steps go with certain styles of jazz in a most revealing manner. Since dancing is virtually universal, . . . it frequently confers immediate intelligibility upon the music.[1]

A figure well known to jazz music historians, Stearns had, by 1963, long been involved with this type of public advocacy work on behalf of jazz music. His was among the most significant voices in positioning jazz music as a vitally important and fundamentally American form of culture worthy of study in universities and of support from government agencies and nonprofit institutions. The founder of the Institute of Jazz Studies, Stearns was one of a number of influential jazz writers who emerged from the "Hot Club" record collecting movement in the 1930s. Unlike most of his contemporaries, however, Stearns got a PhD and became a college professor, and he spent much of his life working to create a robust space for jazz music within academic institutions and discourses. Multiple scholars—most notably John Gennari and Kenneth Prouty—have credited Stearns with diffusing what Bernard Gendron identifies as the "moldy figs vs. modernists" debates of the 1940s by crafting a "consensus narrative" of jazz history that rooted modernist innovation in rich folk tradition to form a cohesive canon of great artists and styles. Prouty identifies Stearns as "the major force behind the codification of a common historical

---

[1] Marshall Stearns, letter to Glen G. Wolfe, The Marshall Winslow Stearns Collection (MC 030) [hereafter "Marshall Stearns Collection"], Box 10, Folder 29, Institute of Jazz Studies, Rutgers University Libraries.

*Between Beats*. Christi Jay Wells, Oxford University Press (2021). © Oxford University Press.
DOI: 10.1093/oso/9780197559277.003.0005

narrative" and credits him with driving "the development of the modern discipline of jazz history" during the 1950s.[2] Stearns built a platform for this narrative through his *Jazz Goes to College* radio broadcasts, by traveling to give public lectures and workshops, by offering some of the first jazz history courses at the university level, by consulting with the US Department of State on their jazz diplomacy tours throughout the 1950s and 1960s, and through his 1956 book *The Story of Jazz*: a critical source in solidifying this so-called consensus narrative, which has been so influential on subsequent works of jazz music history.

Stearns's efforts to give jazz music and its history substantial academic validation were bolstered by a coterminous explosion of institutional jazz music performance programs. The late 1940s saw the University of North Texas introduce a "dance band" program that would develop into its famous jazz studies program, the Schillinger School in Boston developed a jazz program that would remain a core component when the school restructured as the Berklee College of Music in 1954, and composer Gunther Schuller—as director of the New England Conservatory in the 1960s—also developed a landmark program in jazz studies.[3] Jazz studies has become an accepted, even ubiquitous, part of music school curricula and has influenced the jazz music landscape as a whole such that, as David Ake describes the situation in the United States, "over the past thirty years, college music departments have emerged as among the most powerful forces shaping understandings of jazz in this country."[4] Establishing these initial programs often required convincing boards and administrators that jazz could fit into a conservatory structure and that it belonged in such spaces as a form of fine art both validated by contemporary virtuoso practitioners and underwritten by an established "great tradition" of canonic figures.[5] Stearns's consensus narrative served as the humanistic firmament upon which such claims were made and upon which numerous successful efforts to raise jazz music's credibility as a transcendent form of art music rested.

---

[2] Kenneth Prouty, *Knowing Jazz: Community, Pedagogy, and Canon in the Information Age* (Oxford: University Press of Mississippi, 2012), 71.

[3] Susan Lee Calkins, "A History of Jazz Studies at the New England Conservatory 1969–2009: The Legacy of Gunther Schuller" (DMA diss., Boston University, 2012), 16–17.

[4] David Ake, *Jazz Cultures* (Berkeley: University of California Press, 2002), 112. Indeed, in this chapter I seek to answer Ake's charge that "those writing on jazz must begin to address the ascent, even the centrality, of today's college-level jazz programs." Ake, "Crossing the Street: Rethinking Jazz Education," in *Jazz/Not Jazz: The Music and His Boundaries*, eds. David Ake, Charles Hiroshi Garrett, and Daniel Goldmark (Berkeley: University of California Press, 2012), 258.

[5] Scott DeVeaux, "Constructing the Jazz Tradition: Jazz Historiography," *Black American Literature Forum* 25, no. 3 (Fall 1991): 525–526; Ake, *Jazz Cultures*, 113–122.

Where Stearns is less well known, at least among music historians and jazz music fans, is for his work in the final decade of his life as a scholar of, and fierce advocate for, jazz dance. Throughout the 1950s and until his death in 1966, he amassed massive research files on African American dance forms and practices during the nineteenth and twentieth centuries and conducted over two hundred oral history interviews with dancers. He also collaborated with Black dancers for numerous lecture recitals and television appearances everywhere from the *Today Show* to *Playboy's Penthouse* to the United Nations to the Newport Jazz Festival. His work culminated in the posthumously published 1968 monograph *Jazz Dance: The Story of American Vernacular Dance*, co-authored by his wife Jean Stearns, who completed the monograph after her husband's death. As Stearns and Stearns situated their subject matter in the introduction to *Jazz Dance*:

> This book deals with *American dancing that is performed to and with the rhythms of jazz*—that is, dancing that *swings*. It can, of course, be performed without any ac-companiment, but even then it makes jazz rhythms visible, creating a new dimen-sion. The subtitle, "American Vernacular Dance"—*vernacular* in the sense of native and homegrown—points to a second and no less important characteristic.[6]

Through this work, Marshall Stearns sought to introduce his audiences to a uniquely American, and specifically African American, tradition of move-ment: an authentically American vernacular dance tradition that he claimed was "a thrilling art that deserves study" and that he saw as an indispensable piece of American cultural heritage.[7]

While Stearns's advocacy for jazz dance was as fierce and enthusiastic as his advocacy for jazz music, it failed to achieve comparable results; the jazz dancers Stearns worked with did not take part in State Department jazz di-plomacy tours, his publications and lectures did not inspire new university curricula in jazz dance history and performance, and the vernacular jazz movement practices Stearns promoted barely remained legible as "jazz dance," a designation largely ceded—despite Stearns's considerable efforts to stem this tide—to the theatrical dance practices popularized by white choreographers Jack Cole, Bob Fosse, and Gus Giordano. Stearns recognized and even empha-sized jazz dance's growing precarity. In 1962, he said of rhythm tap dancing that, "unlike jazz [music], with which it runs parallel, tap dance is a fine art

---

[6] Marshall Stearns and Jean Stearns, *Jazz Dance: The Story of American Vernacular Dance* (New York: Macmillan, 1968), xiv.
[7] Stearns and Stearns, *Jazz Dance*, xvi.

in danger of being mislaid and forgotten."[8] The divergent institutional trajectories of jazz music and jazz dance are of course not entirely reducible to the successes and failures in Stearns's advocacy for them, yet Stearns's efforts and their disparate impacts are broadly instructive regarding the terms upon which forms of popular art are made legible to, and accepted into, institutional cultures. This chapter thus focuses on Stearns's collaborations with jazz dancers during the 1950s and early 1960s, both to show the tremendous effort and thoughtful strategy he brought to his mission to institutionalize jazz dance and to highlight several problematic shortcomings in Stearns's dance advocacy from which his music advocacy largely did not suffer. This disparity also illuminates crucial differences in the conditions of possibility, broadbased and outside of Stearns's control, for the institutionalization of jazz music and jazz dance at midcentury.

## American Institutions, the Cold War, and Stearns's "Consensus History"

Stearns came to jazz music, as did many critics of his generation, as a hot record collector, and he gradually began writing for publications such as *Le Jazz Hot* and *Downbeat* during the 1930s. Unlike his contemporaries, such as John Hammond, Leonard Feather, or Hughes Pannasié, however, Stearns was on a pathway toward advanced academic credentials and a career as a university professor. He earned his PhD in medieval literature from Yale University in 1942 and subsequently held positions at New York University, the New School for Social Research, and Hunter College. During the 1950s, Stearns made progress on several fronts toward connecting his passion for jazz music with his position and advanced credentials through his facility navigating the institutional pathways of academia. In 1950, he began teaching the first university-level course in jazz history at the New School, and he founded the Institute of Jazz Studies in 1952, an institution now housed at Rutgers University's Newark campus that remains to this day the world's largest and most significant jazz archive.

He was able to achieve these legitimizing inroads through crafting what Gennari has described as "a consensus history of jazz that conformed to high culture notions of stylistic order and continuity."[9] Where other critics were on

---

[8] Marshall Stearns, "A History of Tap Dance," 1962 Newport Jazz Festival Program, 11, Marshall Stearns Collection Box 10, Folder 28.

[9] John Gennari, *Blowin' Hot and Cool: Jazz and Its Critics* (Chicago: University of Chicago Press, 2006), 208.

either side of a debate between new innovations and old traditions, Stearns was able to establish a single, contiguous narrative of development and progress that validated contemporary aesthetics specifically by grounding them in traditional styles and practices.[10] He articulated this perspective in his 1956 book *The Story of Jazz*, the research for which was funded by a 1950 Guggenheim Fellowship. In this book, Stearns explicitly situates jazz as a music with "an ancient and honorable history" as his work sought to "outline the main currents of a great tradition."[11] Stearns's work also notably positioned African Americans as the central figures within that tradition, and Langston Hughes noted that Stearns's *The Story of Jazz* "gives the Negro full credit for his enormous contributions to America's most popular musical form."[12] Indeed, Stearns had been advocating to position jazz as a form of Black music, rooted in the cultural traditions of West Africa, since the 1930s when the idea that Black people were jazz music's originators and principal exponents was, at least among white intellectuals, far from settled law.

Stearns's jazz music advocacy efforts were coterminous with a period of expansive growth in the development of institutional patronage—both government and private—for music and the performing arts in the United States. Between 1946 and 1976, the three largest granting organizations—the National Endowment for the Arts, the Rockefeller Foundation, and the Ford Foundation—collectively funded music projects to the tune of more than $300 million (over $2 billion in 2018 dollars).[13] Stearns's academic credentials made him legible as an expert able to authenticate jazz music's cultural value within an institutional patronage system where formally recognized expertise played an increasingly strong gatekeeping role. Arts and culture experts' status within and crucial value to these organizations was part of a larger shift in the 1950s toward what research biologist and broadcaster Brian J. Ford has termed the "cult of the expert," where Americans put increasing trust in the opinions of those formally qualified to judge excellence on ostensibly objective criteria. Such paradigms drew from broader American cultural valuing of meritocracy and, in musicologist Michael Uy's astute framing, problematically succeeded in "codifying particular subjectivities and casting them as examples of excellence."[14] On multiple levels, this phenomenon traded upon specific sociocultural and sociopolitical responses to the Cold War. As

[10] Gennari, *Blowin' Hot and Cool*, 208.

[11] Marshall Stearns, *The Story of Jazz* (New York: Oxford University Press, 1956), ix, xii.

[12] Langston Hughes, "Books as Christmas Gifts of a Community Nature," *Chicago Defender*, December 15, 1956, 9.

[13] Michael Sy Uy, "The Big Bang of Musical Patronage in the United States: The National Endowment for the Arts, the Rockefeller Foundation, and the Ford Foundation" (PhD diss., Harvard University, 2017), 1.

[14] Uy, "Big Bang of Musical Patronage," 3.

philosopher Lydia Goehr has argued, the translation of nineteenth-century European romantic notions of musical transcendence to twentieth-century modernist paradigms resulted in the positioning of "high art music" as fundamentally detached from the social and political events of everyday life, such as social and popular dance. This positioning, she argues, has been "sustained by Cold War anxieties" and "fully supported by the complex institution of the concert hall and by the ascendancy and valorization of purely instrumental music."[15]

Jazz music's own "ascendance" to a form of serious art to be taught in universities was itself inextricably linked to these broader intersections between institutional high art patronage and Cold War cultural politics. Where jazz criticism had, throughout the 1930s and 1940s, shared strong intersections and allegiances with the American Communist Party and its "Popular Front" efforts to mobilize popular culture and anti-racism as tools of revolutionary politics, the 1950s saw jazz criticism's redeployment as a tool of the American state on the cultural front of its fight against the Soviet Union and the international spread of communist ideology.[16] Literary scholar Paul Devlin has gone so far as to claim that "jazz was used as a cultural propaganda tool by the United States and its allies against the Soviet Union and its allies in the struggle for global dominance and influence."[17] Toward that end, jazz music was positioned as a fundamentally and uniquely American—and indeed specifically African American—symbol of individualism, diversity, and virtuosity. Thus, the "consensus history" Stearns so effectively solidified both fueled and was fueled by American exceptionalism as it centered African American culture and performers in a manner readily exploitable by the state as an instrument to counteract the Soviet Union's tactic of highlighting the hypocrisy inherent in the United States' official and unofficial systems of racial segregation.

Much of this work occurred with little regard for Black audiences, whose move toward popular culture formations such as r&b and rock 'n' roll that centered blues more than jazz became a rationalization for disavowing the importance of meaningfully including Black listeners in newly institutionalized conceptions of jazz as a serious art form. Where white critics and intellectuals, and even some Black critics and intellectuals, saw participation

---

[15] Lydia Goehr, "Political Music and the Politics of Music," *Journal of Aesthetics and Art Criticism* 52, no. 1 (Winter 1994): 105, 103–104.

[16] For more on jazz diplomacy and the Cold War, see Jonathon Bakan, "Jazz and the 'Popular Front': 'Swing Musicians' and the Left-Wing Movements of the 1930s and 1940s," *Jazz Perspectives* 3, no. 1 (April 2009): 35–56; Danielle Fosler-Lussier, *Music in America's Cold War Diplomacy* (Berkeley: University of California Press, 2015); and Lisa E. Davenport, *Jazz Diplomacy: Promoting America in the Cold War Era* (Jackson: University of Mississippi Press, 2009).

[17] Paul Devlin, "Jazz Autobiography and the Cold War," *Popular Music and Society* 38 (2015): 140.

in the sphere of commercial popular culture as a lamentable bastardization of folk/vernacular forms, Black audiences more broadly turned increasingly toward commercial popular culture as an arena to express both social and economic autonomy. As Guthrie P. Ramsey Jr. argues, postwar blues and r&b developments "marked a new beginning, a second Reconstruction, and a new cultural politics in African American history."[18] In Ramsey's analysis, social dance practices in house parties and commercial dance halls, rooted in jazz dances but now done principally to other forms of Black popular music (as Thomas F. DeFrantz also observes), represented an Afro-modernist flipping of representational politics that was shaped by Black working class control over Black embodiment in the sphere of commercial popular culture.[19]

> If one of the legacies of nineteenth century minstrelsy involved the public degradation of the black body in the American entertainment sphere, then one hundred years after minstrelsy's emergence, African Americans used this same signifier to upset a racist social order and to affirm in the public entertainment and the private spheres their culture and humanity. Although it has some precedent, the new attitude was so prevalent that it represents a huge departure from earlier modes of "racial uplift," especially the "politics of respectability" championed by the black professional and upper-class citizens, who sought to discipline black bodies into bourgeois submission.[20]

Broadly empowering though this relationship with popular culture may have been, it is also a reason Black audiences, and especially their house parties and social dance practices, were increasingly bracketed out of new positionings of "jazz" as a serious and universally American art form during the 1950s. Even as jazz criticism and jazz advocacy became ever more detached from their leftist American Communist Party roots, they still retained a disdain for the corrupting influence of popular culture, an enmity that only grew as the Popular Front strategy of the 1930s faded and as jazz's newly won institutional allies saw the political emboldening that popular culture increasingly offered African Americans as a liability rather than an asset. Just as the end of World War II saw a period of rapidly shifting allegiances and oppositions, so too was jazz music's alignment with Black vernacular dance and with popular culture severely strained by the interests and agendas of the music's newfound institutional allies.

[18] Ramsey, *Race Music*, 51.
[19] Ramsey, *Race Music*, 51; DeFrantz, *Dancing Revelations*, 101.
[20] Ramsey, *Race Music*, 51.

Jazz music's growing relationship with institutional formations of "seriousness" and "Americanness" also necessarily meant a closer relationship with whiteness. As Eric Porter has argued of jazz in the 1950s, the emergent popularity of Dave Brubeck and of the Newport Jazz Festival yielded a simultaneity of validation and erasure for Black jazz musicians and audiences. In Porter's words,

> The popularity of jazz with white audiences validated the work of African American musicians and aestheticians and eventually called into question the distance between elite and popular culture. Yet this visibility was a mixed blessing. . . . The culture industry played a contradictory role by sometimes making jazz visible as a black cultural form, while at other moments erasing black contributions to the genre.[21]

In his role as an institutional advocate for jazz music, and certainly in his advocacy work for jazz dance, Stearns explicitly centered and credited Black practitioners both past and present, yet in doing so, his institutional negotiations and the folkloric curatorial strategies underwriting them reinforced a series of erasures nevertheless.

## "Colorfully Conceived Steps": Minns and James at Newport

During the 1950s, Stearns collaborated principally with two lindy hop dancers: Al Minns and Leon James. Both Minns and James were former Harvest Moon Ball champions and members of Whitey's Lindy Hoppers, the internationally touring professional group during the 1930s composed of elite-level dancers from Harlem's Savoy Ballroom (discussed extensively in chapter 3). Stearns likely became acquainted with the pair through Mura Dehn, who worked with Minns and James during the 1950s on her documentary film project *The Spirit Moves* and at public presentations in and around New York City. Dehn began working with Minns and James in the mid-1940s and featured the pair in November 1950 for a jazz dance lecture demonstration at Cooper Union, a program on which Stearns also appeared giving introductory remarks.[22] In 1951, Stearns invited Minns and James to participate

---

[21] Porter, *What Is This Thing Called Jazz?*, 10.

[22] "Lecture Demonstration Dance Program—Friday Evening, November 17th Mura Dehn and Group. At Cooper Union, 17 November 1950," unpublished typescript. Mura Dehn Papers, Box 20, Folder 229. The 1950 Cooper Union performance is the first documented account of a concert organized by Dehn with Minns and James where they are mentioned by name, but a handwritten list of concerts includes several in

in one of his roundtable retreats at the Music Inn in Lenox, Massachusetts. The Music Inn, a rural property in the Berkshire mountains, aspired to be "a Tanglewood for American vernacular music."[23] Minns and James participated in Stearns's first Music Inn roundtable along with Asadata Dafora, the dancer and choreographer from Sierra Leone, and Trinidadian dancer Geoffrey Holder. Stearns's engagement with Minns and James provided him a basis to make the same connections regarding jazz dance's African routes that he emphasized in his writing on jazz music. In Stearns and Stearns's *Jazz Dance*, the chapter on "Africa and the West Indies" (within the section "prehistory") opens with a description of an informal Music Inn "experiment" where Minns, James, Dafora, and Holder engaged in collective improvisation and exchange. The exercise reflected Music Inn owner Philip Barber's philosophy of "instantaneous talent combustion," where simply assembling talented performers from diverse traditions for an informal jam session would lead organically to new discoveries.[24] By Stearns's account, the four dancers continually exclaimed in joyful discovery as they made connections between their traditions, which Stearns framed as confirmation of anthropologist Melville Herskovitz's theories regarding African retentions.[25]

Minns and James appeared multiple times at the Music Inn during the 1950s, and their dance presentations helped persuade skeptical intellectuals of jazz's value as a form of art music. Herman Schloss offered these "reflections of a non-jazz enthusiast" after seeing a Minns and James presentation in August 1958:

I cannot in all honesty unequivocally declare here and now that after having seen this aforementioned performance I have become a jazz convert in the same manner people declare for Christ at a Billy Graham revival meeting. However, the historical development of the jazz dance developed on the stage of the Music Barn has erased the thick layer of anti-jazz prejudice in my mind and has enabled me to at least admit that jazz is a bona fide subdivision of the art form—music—borne of joy and sadness, satire and deep reflection and all other human emotions which existed in Africa before the slaves were forcibly brought to this country which were rampant in the Reconstruction era, and were present in a New Orleans gin mill at

the 1940s, as early as 1946, featuring the "Savoy group," which likely would have included the pair. Mura Dehn, handwritten concert list on Traditional Jazz Dance Company letterhead, n.d., likely 1970s, Mura Dehn Papers, Box 20, Folder 2.

[23] Mark Burford, "Mahalia Jackson Meets the Wise Men: Defining Jazz at the Music Inn," *Musical Quarterly* 97, no. 3 (Fall 2014): 440.
[24] Stearns and Stearns, *Jazz Dance*, 11.
[25] Burford, "Mahalia Jackson Meets the Wise Men," 443.

the turn of the century, in a Chicago speakeasy in the twenties and at a Harlem rent party during the economic depression of the thirties.[26]

These Music Inn events led Stearns to begin integrating jazz dance into a series of jazz history lectures, which he designed in collaboration with pianist and composer Randy Weston. According to Weston, upon hearing him play Thelonious Monk's music, Stearns made the following proposition: "Let's do the history of jazz together, you put together a quartet, we'll get the two dancers from the Savoy Ballroom to deal with the dance aspect of the music, and we'll tour the universities."[27] Taking him up on a version of this proposal, Weston accompanied Stearns's Music Inn lectures beginning in 1953 and also provided music for Stearns's lectures with Minns and James on a number of lecture/presentation gigs during the 1950s.[28]

Minns and James were subsequently featured in Stearns's jazz dance program at the Newport Jazz Festival in 1958. A first for the festival, Stearns presented a lecture accompanied by demonstrations from Minns and James, who danced to recorded music.[29] According to John S. Wilson's account for the *New York Times*:

> Starting with the Cake Walk, Minns and James succinctly pointed up the derivations and associations of each dance step as they strutted, kicked, shuffled, leaped, shook and writhed their way through the Camel Walk, Slow Drag, Shimmy, Black Bottom, Charleston, Snake Hips, Lindy, Shim Sham, Shorty George, Shag, Sand, Applejack, and several other colorfully named, colorfully conceived steps.[30]

According to Wilson's review, the capacity crowd of 400 in attendance "responded with clamorous enthusiasm to the dancers' high spirited and witty demonstrations of a neglected area of American popular culture."[31] Musical selections for the lecture demonstration ran the gamut from "a 1907 Cakewalk by John Philip Sousa to a relatively recent bop disk by Dizzy Gillespie."[32] Wilson noted that, while the dance program "stole the spotlight," it was "the

[26] Herman Schloss, "Reaction of a Non Jazz Enthusiast to the Jazz Dance Performance of Leon James and Al Mines [*sic*]," 1958, Marshall Stearns Collection Box 10, Folder 16.
[27] Randy Weston with Willard Jenkins, *African Rhythms: The Autobiography of Randy Weston* (Durham, NC: Duke University Press, 2010), 52.
[28] Weston and Jenkins, *African Rhythms*, 52.
[29] "Lecture-Recitals for the General Public at Newport July 4th and 5th, 1958," printed flyer, Marshall Stearns Collection Box 10, Folder 4.
[30] *New York Times*, as quoted in Philadelphia Art Alliance, "Newport Jazz Dancers Here February 27," *Art Alliance Bulletin*, February 1959, Stearns Collection Box 23, Folder 2.
[31] John S. Wilson, "Lecture on Dance Steals Jazz Fete," *New York Times*, July 6, 1958, 50.
[32] Wilson, "Lecture on Dance," 50.

least publicized aspect of the Newport Jazz Festival."[33] A *Variety* review hailed the program as "the best of the Festival, and probably its most concrete contribution to the art of jazz."[34] In addition, the largely well-received program garnered particular praise from Langston Hughes, who remarked in a letter to poet and novelist Arna Bontemps that he considered the presentation a highlight of the festival.[35] While accounts of the 1958 festival lecture demonstration itself are somewhat limited, surviving records of the trio's subsequent lecture demonstrations offer further insight into the Newport performance. Writing for *Dance Magazine*, Selma Jeanne Cohen offered a fairly robust account of a December 1958 performance at Manhattan's 92nd Street Y:

> Messrs. Minns and James danced with skilled assurance and versatility, effortlessly adapting themselves to the panorama of historic styles. Their flair for comedy gave their satires the proper bite, and their feeling for characterization enhanced all their numbers. . . . Professor Stearns kept the continuity smooth and provided valuable background information, including, whenever possible, precise dates for the dances. He also added to the authenticity of the program by using contemporary recordings to accompany the dancers.[36]

According to Cohen, Stearns's commentary affirmed an Afrocentric narrative of jazz dance's origins that traced the dance "from Africa, by way of Cuba, from Mississippi levees and Manhattan house rent parties (25 cents admission to help pay the monthly bill), to swing at the Savoy, mambo at the Palladium, and rock 'n' roll at teen-age gatherings."[37]

The success of the 1958 Newport program led to multiple appearances on Dave Garroway's *Today Show* for NBC. On the *Today Show*, Stearns framed vernacular jazz dance as the result of slow, gradual evolution over the course of several hundred years, likening it to great literary traditions and other forms of art among great civilizations. He described Minns and James as "the

---

[33] Wilson, "Lecture on Dance," 50.

[34] *Variety*, as quoted in Philadelphia Art Alliance, "Newport Jazz Dancers Here February 27," *Art Alliance Bulletin*, February 1959, Stearns Collection Box 23, Folder 2.

[35] Langston Hughes to Arna Bontemps, July 9, 1948, in *Arna Bontemps–Langston Hughes Letters, 1925–1967*, ed. Charles H. Nichols (New York: Paragon House, 1990), 374, cited in Gennari, *Blowin' Hot and Cool*, 231.

[36] Selma Jeanne Cohen, "An American Jazz Dance Concert," *Dance Magazine*, December 28, 1958. Clipping in Marshall Stearns Collection Box 23, Folder 2.

[37] Cohen, "American Jazz Dance Concert." This language bears striking resemblance to the African Academy of Arts Research's founder Kingsley Ozuomba Mbadiwe's description of his organization's 1945 African Dances and Modern Rhythms Festival: "the march of African music from Africa to the American continents." David F. García, *Listening for Africa: Freedom, Modernity, and the Logic of Black Music's African Origins* (Durham, NC: Duke University Press, 2017), 129.

**Figure 5.1** Jazz critic and musicologist Marshall Stearns; folk, gospel, and jazz singer and activist Barbara Dane; and poet and playwright Langston Hughes backstage at the Newport Folk Festival in June 1959 in Newport, Rhode Island. Photo by David Gahr/ Getty Images.

only true professional exponents of the jazz dance."[38] Also notable from the surviving transcript of this appearance are Stearns's pains to emphasize individual dances' African American or West African origins as well as the specific interventions, lamentable in Stearns's view, that white performers made in modifying and popularizing these dances. As Minns and James demonstrated the camel walk, Stearns pointed out that the family of "animal dances" to which it belonged had West African roots and that the "Castle walk" was white ballroom dancers Vernon and Irene Castle's attempt to "make it more genteel." Stearns also claimed that the shimmy, African American in origin, became broadly known only once employed by white actress and dancer Gilda Gray and that it was "cleaned up a little, and it became popular among white people."[39] Within these high-profile forums, Stearns used his role as an expert to emphasize jazz dance's African American roots, as he had done for jazz music twenty years prior.

[38] Typed Transcript, "Development of the Jazz Dance Is Demonstrated," Transcript of Marshall Stearns with Al Minns and Leon James on *The Today Show* with Dave Garroway, Transcript, July 16, 1958, transcribed by Radio Reports, Inc. Marshall Stearns Collection Box 14, Folder 1.
[39] Marshall Stearns, 1958 *Today Show* transcript. Marshall Stearns Collection Box 14, Folder 1.

In presenting these jazz dance lectures both at Newport and elsewhere, Stearns both leveraged and expanded upon his existing credibility as a scholar of jazz music. He built his platform as both a music and dance scholar in part through his ongoing relationship with the Newport Jazz Festival, where he had served as an authenticating expert from the very first festival in 1954. There, he appeared alongside other university professors—ethnomusicologist Allan Merriam of Northwestern University, composer Henry Cowell of the Peabody Conservatory, and composer and folklorist Willis James of Spelman College— on a panel entitled "The Place of Jazz in American Culture."[40] Stearns himself seemed highly aware of his role as an authenticating force, having penned a tongue-in-cheek poem for the festival that closed with the lines "So come on down to Newport, if you wanna be confused/A panel of professors will authenticate the blues."[41] Stearns shared in festival founder George Wein's goal of growing jazz music's audience as well as its institutional capital by positioning it as both rigorously intellectual and universal in its appeal, an aspirational framing he sought to map onto jazz dance as well.[42] As Stearns would later tell Hugh Hefner on the television show *Playboy's Penthouse*, "although most people don't realize it, the jazz dance has an ancient and honorable tradition, it has a complete vocabulary of steps through which almost any human emotion can be communicated."[43] Here, we see Stearns step into his role as a credentialed authenticator of folk traditions, highlighting jazz dance's depth and cohesiveness as an "honorable" expressive tradition as well as its ability to communicate "almost any human emotion": a clear nod to the idea that "great" art is necessarily able to transcend cultural and historical specificities to reflect ostensibly universal human experiences. Jazz scholar Tony Whyton outlines this paradigm's potency as a tool that helped jazz music punch its ticket to universities and other institutional spaces:

> Indeed, the construction and celebration of a jazz canon has placed many jazz artists into the mythologised world of autonomous art, where music is deemed to transcend the social. This ideology of autonomous art creates a romanticised narrative where the iconic genius figure (typically male) transcends time and context;

[40] John Gennari, "Hipsters, Bluebloods, Rebels, and Hooligans: The Cultural Politics of the Newport Jazz Festival: 1954–1960," in *Uptown Conversation: The New Jazz Studies*, eds. Robert O'Meally, Brent Hayes Edwards, and Farah Jasmine Griffin (New York: Columbia University Press, 2004), 130.
[41] Quoted in Gennari, "Hipsters, Bluebloods, Rebels, and Hooligans," 126.
[42] Gennari, *Blowin' Hot and Cool*, 228–233.
[43] Marshall Stearns, in conversation with Hugh Hefner on *Playboy's Penthouse*, syndicated television program, December 31, 1959.

his work is treated in isolation and his music is regarded as conveying universal appeal.[44]

Operating within (or perhaps self-consciously exploiting) this paradigm, Stearns strove to position jazz dance—like jazz music, classical music, and all truly "great" forms of art—as a transcendent, universal language.

## "Like Artistic Colonials": The Nationalist Politics of *Jazz Ballet No. 1*

Stearns's efforts to position jazz dance as both authentic folk culture and transcendent art would lead to experimentation with bringing jazz dance to concert stages by fusing it with recognized forms of European concert dance, specifically ballet. His approach took a page from the philosophy of W. E. B. Du Bois, who had long argued that all great artistic traditions arose from the conscious development of folk practices indigenous to a particular race or cultural group.[45] As Stearns wrote in *Dance Magazine*, "we need a return to folk roots, a process which has characterized fine art from time immemorial—in this case, a return to the folk roots of the jazz dance."[46] During his first *Today Show* appearance with Minns and James, Stearns impressed upon Garroway that his goal in promoting American vernacular dances—jazz dances—was to motivate American choreographers to make more and better use of these traditions:

> Nowhere yet in our musical comedies have we used the authentic jazz dance. We've been influenced by it—all our dances show some understanding of it—but they haven't used the pure thing yet, and here it is right in our own back yard. . . . I'm just hoping some day somebody will compose a great jazz ballet, an American ballet, using these dance steps which have never been used.[47]

Stearns would attempt to realize this vision himself the following year, commissioning *Jazz Ballet No. 1* for the 1959 Newport Jazz Festival (figures

---

[44] Tony Whyton, "Birth of the School: Discursive Methodologies in Jazz Education," *Music Education Research* 8, no. 1 (2006): 70.

[45] Du Bois outlines this paradigm in his famous essay *The Conservation of Races* (Washington, DC: American Negro Academy, 1897), available online at The Gutenberg Project, accessed June 19, 2019, https://www.gutenberg.org/files/31254/31254-h/31254-h.htm.

[46] Marshall Stearns, "Is Modern Jazz Hopelessly Square?," *Dance Magazine*, May 1959, reprinted in Gus Giordano, ed., *Anthology of American Jazz Dance* (Evanston, IL: Orion, 1975), 44.

[47] Marshall Stearns, 1958 *Today Show* transcript. Marshall Stearns Collection Box 14, Folder 1.

**Figure 5.2**  Still photographs from a rehearsal of *Jazz Ballet No. 1*, 1959. Marshall Stearns Collection, unprocessed materials.

5.1 and 5.2). He hired Willy Sandberg of the Swedish National Ballet to choreograph the piece, with input from Minns and James.[48] Their collaboration yielded a work for four dancers—the trio was joined by Jacqueline Walcott, a former member of Katherine Dunham's dance company—that adapted characters and plots from the Italian *commedia dell'arte* tradition.[49] In *Jazz Ballet No. 1*, four archetypal *commedia* characters were reimagined as a

---

[48] This may be more appropriately described as a co-choreographic effort between the three of them as Black jazz dancers in the early and mid-twentieth century were regularly denied choreographic credit for their original creative work.

[49] 1959 Newport Jazz Festival Program, 33, Newport Jazz Festival Records [hereafter "Newport Collection"], Institute of Jazz Studies, Rutgers University Libraries, Box 3.

group of roadside hitchhikers. Each character emphasized a different vernacular dance style: Harlequin (Sandberg) performed Latin American movement and Columbine (Walcott) rock 'n' roll steps, while Pierrot and Pantalon (Minns and James) performed blues and bebop dance respectively.[50] The Festival program's brief plot synopsis reveals troubling details about the dancers' roles: "Harlequin the trickster outwitted the aging cuckold Pantalon and won Columbine while poor Perrot [sic] looked on moonstruck."[51] This plot would suggest that Minns and James, the two vernacular dancers, each played witless comic relief foils, the antagonist and buffoon respectively, to the love story playing out between the ballet and modern dancers. According to James Wilson of the *New York Times*, the dancers

> mixed the ingredients of dance, pantimime [sic], and music with great wit and imagination. Mr. Sandberg, as Harlequin, was inclined to depend to some extent on his formal ballet background, but Miss Walcott, Mr. Minns as Pierrot, and Mr. James as Pantaloon stayed completely within the idiom of jazz movements and showed that they could be extremely useful in building and developing a dance sequence.
>
> Miss Walcott danced Columbine with a loose, sinuous grace that conveyed the spirit of her provocative role brilliantly and Mr. Minns danced a brief solo that had an almost Chaplinesque quality of jaunty pathos. The ballet is a delightful little cameo in itself and should provide a mine of suggestions for future works.[52]

Stearns would have been particularly validated by Wilson's claim that the piece "should provide a mine of suggestions for future works," as his explicit goal in commissioning the piece was not so much to present a single work but to realize on stage the paradigm for which he advocated in his lecture demonstrations, in hopes that others would be inspired to develop it further.

Further exemplifying Stearns's commitment to the fusion of jazz with European concert forms, the piece was performed to the Modern Jazz Quartet's (MJQ) 1956 recording "Fontessa." Setting the dance to a piece by the MJQ is notable in evoking that group's own preference for tuxedos and concert hall performances as a means to syncretize jazz performance with high art concert culture. Indeed, the 1959 Newport program book clarified that the performance would use recorded music "so that the MJQ cannot distract attention from the dance itself."[53] Still, the connection runs deeper as "Fontessa"

[50] "The Jazz Ballet: Jazz and the commedia dell'arte," Newport Jazz Festival Program 1959, 65, Newport Collection Box 3.

[51] "The Jazz Ballet," 65, Newport Collection Box 3.

[52] John S. Wilson, "'Jazz Ballet No. 1' Given in Newport," *New York Times* July 5, 1959, 60.

[53] "The Jazz Ballet," 65, Newport Collection Box 3.

itself was, according to MJQ pianist John Lewis, who composed the piece, inspired by the same set of *commedia dell'arte* characters, renderings of whom appear on the album cover. As Lewis explains the piece,

> Fontessa is a little suite inspired by the Renaissance Commedia dell'Arte. I had particularly in mind their plays which consisted of a very sketchy plot and in which the details, the lines, etc. were improvised. This suite consists first of a short Prelude to raise the curtain and provide the theme. The first piece after the Prelude has the character of older jazz and improvised parts are by the vibraphone. This piece could perhaps be the character of Harlequin. The second piece has the character of less older jazz and the improvised parts are played by the piano. The character here could perhaps be Pierrot. The third piece is of a still later jazz character and develops the main motif. The improvised parts are by the drums. This character could perhaps be Pantaloon [*sic*]. The opening Prelude closes the suite. Fontessa is the three-note main motif of the suite and is perhaps a substitute for the character of Colombine.[54]

In the sparse opening bars of "Fontessa," the vibraphone evokes the same music box affect as iconic ballet music such as Tchaikovsky's "Dance of the Sugar Plum Fairy" before it is joined by a swinging groove that anticipates Ellington and Strayhorn's subsequent take on Tchaikovsky's iconic work in their 1960 album *The Nutcracker Suite*. On the whole, the work's tone poem-like design, featuring elements of repetition, implied leitmotif, and distinct affective sections within a through-composed structure, invites the kind of narrative choreography to which the *commedia* subject matter would have lent itself.

Evoking recognizable elements of ballet music and dance while still grounded in "authentic" jazz practices, *Jazz Ballet No. 1* aligned with Stearns's larger aspirations for jazz dance. He hoped by legitimizing vernacular jazz movement and promoting it as a serious art form rooted in uniquely American traditions to encourage the emergence of a new form of concertized jazz dance less "tainted" by formal European traditions than other forms concert dance that either called themselves "jazz" or claimed jazz influences. Toward that end, Stearns boasted that this performance would be the "first

---

[54] John Lewis, "Fontessa." Liner notes for *Fontessa*, Atlantic Records, 1956, LP, 1. Quoted in Christopher Coady, *John Lewis and the Challenge of "Real" Black Music* (Ann Arbor: University of Michigan Press, 2016), 129–130. Coady discusses "Fontessa" and Lewis's navigation of jazz idioms and *commedia dell'arte* tropes on 129–131. It certainly seems reasonable to assume that Lewis's piece and his use of these tropes and characters was the basis for the choice to make them the focal point of *Jazz Ballet No. 1*, I have not seen documents from Stearns or anyone else involved with the ballet that explicitly credit Lewis as a generative source in this way.

ballet done with completely authentic jazz steps."[55] The 1959 Newport program explicates his perspective:

Past attempts at jazz ballet, he [Stearns] pointed out, have usually involved a pastiche of styles, involving, at times, movements of European ballet with American popular dance steps and, most incongruous of all, Hindu dance movements. But the new ballet at Newport is a distinct departure in that it is based entirely on American steps and permits the free expression of the dancers, just as jazz permits it for instrumentalists—and the *comedia* [*sic*] permitted it to actors.[56]

The festival's program took pains to explicate the *commedia dell'arte*'s connection with jazz music and jazz dance, as "all three are based on the idea of letting the individual performer express himself within a framework of tradition."[57] Stearns's impulse to link jazz with *commedia dell'arte* reflected his "double life" as a jazz historian and scholar of medieval English literature, and specifically of Chaucer. When interviewed, Stearns consistently sought to identify his interests in jazz and Chaucer as a cohesive interest in largely compatible aesthetic traditions.

In addition to likening jazz dance to great literature, Stearns also sought validation by infusing his perspective on jazz dance with healthy doses of American exceptionalism as he maligned American choreographers for relying too heavily on foreign material. He articulated this perspective in a presentation he gave earlier that year with Minns and James for Jazz at the Phoenix. In his lecture notes, Stearns espouses his dissatisfaction with contemporary American concert and musical theater dance:

Incidentally, the jazz dance--the REAL jazz dance--has YET TO BE USED at our concerts, in our musicals (West Side Story, for example, makes little use of it), or in our ballets. Dance-wise, we seem to be ARTISTIC COLONIALS, more impressed by European arts than our own, and employing ballet, Hindu, and modern dance movements which are imported.[58]

In a return appearance to the *Today Show* in November 1959, Stearns referred to the lindy hop as "our national dance" and commented to host Garroway that "most choreographers do not draw sufficiently on American

---

[55] "The Jazz Ballet," 65, Newport Collection Box 3.

[56] "The Jazz Ballet," 65, Newport Collection Box 3.

[57] "The Jazz Ballet," 65, Newport Collection Box 3.

[58] Marshall Stearns, lecture notes for "Jazz at the Phoenix," May 1959, Marshall Stearns Collection Box 10, Folder 19. Capitalization and underlining in the original.

dance patterns."[59] While he acknowledged that a number of contemporary choreographers' work displayed jazz influences, he insisted none of them had yet made use of "pure jazz [dance]," of which he considered Minns and James master exponents.

Stearns's repeated use of the term "artistic colonials" in his writings and lectures expresses less a genuinely anti-colonialist stance than an isolationist nativism emblematic of how Stearns's rhetoric fit within a larger current of American exceptionalism during the 1950s. Broadly, American aesthetic discourse in the 1950s reflected a push away from Orientalism that, while it may have initially expressed anti-colonialist impulses, was co-opted by an exceptionalist project to promote uniquely, and ostensibly "natively," American aesthetic paradigms. The articulation of a distinctly American aesthetic system and a guiding ideology for that system served not only to distinguish American art practices from those of the Soviet Union, but also to divorce them both from Francophone exoticism and from the Germanic paradigms that had become associated with the Third Reich and from whose logics German and Austrian refugees now prominent in American arts institutions were particularly eager to distance themselves. As a key figure in repackaging jazz criticism—a discourse with strong roots in anti-racist activism with ties to the American Communist Party—as a cultural weapon in the US Department of State's Cold War arsenal, Stearns skillfully deflected McCarthy Era charges of "un-Americanism" onto those forms of art he saw as competitors or threats to his project of advancing vernacular jazz dance.

That Stearns's derision of foreign influences refers specifically to "Hindu" movements is almost certainly a targeted critique of Jack Cole, who is widely credited as the pioneer of what is now referred to as "theatrical jazz dance."[60] Trained as a modern dancer, Cole was also an active lindy hopper at the Savoy Ballroom during the 1930s and 1940s. His 1943 choreography to Benny Goodman's "Sing, Sing, Sing" notably incorporated his training in classical Indian Bharata Natyam movement, causing some critics to give his style the moniker "Hindu Swing."[61] Stearns singled out Cole in his 1959 *Dance Magazine* essay "Is Modern Jazz Hopelessly Square?," charging that Cole "had much to do with the present popularity of pseudo-Oriental movements. As far as the jazz dance is concerned, the result is suicidal."[62] Labeling "theatrical

[59] Typescript for segment "Jazz Dance #2," *Today Show*. Taped 11/18/59, aired 11/19/59. Marshall Stearns Collection Box 14, Folder 1.

[60] Teal Darkenwald, "Jack Cole and Theatrical Jazz Dance," in *Jazz Dance: A History of Roots and Branches*, eds. Lindsay Guarino and Wendy Oliver (Gainesville: University Press of Florida, 2014): 82.

[61] Constance Valis Hill, "From Bharata Natyam to Bop: Jack Cole's 'Modern Jazz Dance,'" *Dance Research Journal* 33, no. 2 (Winter 2001/02): 30.

[62] Stearns, "Is Modern Jazz Hopelessly Square?," 44.

jazz" choreographers "artistic colonials" was thus a strategic move to align Stearns's jazz dance advocacy with the American exceptionalist rhetoric of contemporaneous discourse in modern dance. At mid-century, American modern dance was driven in large part by a discursive confluence of individualism, abstract expressionism, and "high art" concert rhetoric that served to frame the genre as a uniquely American cultural product. One core aspect was the idea that American modern dancers were entirely disentangling their work from European concert traditions. Stearns, however, charged that American choreographers—and specifically Cole, George Balanchine, Agnes de Mille, and Jerome Robbins—had proven themselves "ashamed of our own indigenous creations and incapable of using them."[63] Stearns's repeated claims that artists such as de Mille and Balanchine had failed to make use of "our own indigenous creations" were likely meant to strike a particular Cold War chord and to position vernacular jazz dance as uniquely capable of fulfilling the American concert dance community's strong desire for an entirely American form of dance that modern dance choreographers, in Stearns's estimation, had failed to create.

Stearns's perception that Black dance was being increasingly diluted was related to specific postwar developments in the world of American concert dance. As Susan Manning has shown, the racialized spheres of "Negro dance" and "Modern dance," which while operating separately from one another had for decades each defined themselves as oppositional to popular and vernacular movement, drew closer together, owing to increasing movement toward racial integration nationally as well as the solidification of a "unified patronage system." This patronage system resulted from the same elements that had begun supporting jazz music's own institutional turn: an explosion in college and university programs, private foundation support, and federal funding, most notably in the 1950s and early 1960s from the US Department of State.[64] In addition, the increased presence of modern dance-influenced choreography on the Broadway stage was a reaction to the "red scare" and McCarthyism as many dancers from the 1930s–1940s world of "Leftist dance" found themselves blacklisted from concert dance opportunities but still able to work on Broadway.[65] Considered in this context, Stearns's critiques of choreographers in the realms of "modern dance" and "theatrical jazz" certainly carry overtones of McCarthy Era red-baiting.

[63] Stearns, "Is Modern Jazz Hopelessly Square?," 42.

[64] Susan Manning, *Modern Dance, Negro Dance: Race in Motion* (Minneapolis: University of Minnesota Press, 2006), 184–186.

[65] Manning, *Modern Dance, Negro Dance*, 184–185.

The frequent shots Stearns took at Agnes de Mille in particular were likely tied to her role as a member of the American National Theater Association's (ANTA) dance panel. ANTA was a private organization contracted by the State Department to evaluate potential cultural ambassadors to send on international cultural diplomacy tours. While Stearns himself served as a jazz consultant to ANTA's music panel, he had no such role for dance, and the dance panel was notably insular in its promotion of New York City's concert dance scene and its consistent support for Martha Graham as an ideal choreographic representative of American freedom.[66] Hoping to capitalize on their successful 1958 Newport performance, Stearns, Minns, and James held a private lecture-demonstration performance in Stearns's home for the ANTA dance panel in the fall of that year. While the event received qualified support from the panel itself, it was ultimately rejected by the State Department. Considered in light of this rejection, it becomes even clearer that commissioning *Jazz Ballet No. 1* for Newport 1959 was an attempt on Stearns's part to bring his dancers' work more in line with the ANTA panel's established standards and preferences. First, in having the work choreographed to a specific composition by a respected composer in the world of jazz, "Fontessa" by John Lewis, Stearns's commission was in concordance with the ANTA dance panel's strong preference for concert pieces set to musical works by American composers.[67] Second, placing the dancers into the roles of *commedia dell'arte* stock characters neatly fits the mid-century modernist choreographic paradigm Susan Manning has labeled "mythic abstraction." Mythic abstraction emphasized characterizations that revived archetypes from European and Euro-American cultural traditions—Hellenic mythology, Shakespearean plays, the folkloric American West—in ways that centered whiteness as neutral and universal.[68] The panel, whose makeup overwhelmingly represented dominant voices in modern dance, consistently favored works of mythic abstraction over those by Black choreographers such as Katherine Dunham and Pearl Primus, whose works emphasized, in Manning's words, "black self representation."[69]

---

[66] Fosler-Lussier, *Music in America's Cold War Diplomacy*, 118–119. Clare Croft, *Dancers as Diplomats: American Choreography in Cultural Exchange* (New York: Oxford University Press, 2015), 40.

[67] Croft, *Dancers as Diplomats*, 51.

[68] Hannah Ziessel Mackenzie-Margulies, "Where's Leon (or) That Extraordinary Drama: Dancing Jazz, Negotiating Historiography, and Performing Americanism on the Cold War Cultural Tours" (BA thesis, Reed College, 2016), 48. My understanding of this connection between *Jazz Ballet No. 1* and Manning's notion of mythic abstraction comes from the thesis research of Mackenzie-Margulies, who was an undergraduate student during my time teaching at Reed College. I thank her for her blessing to present and elaborate upon this pivotal insight here.

[69] Manning, *Modern Dance, Negro Dance*, 188. Clare Croft further discusses this dynamic, explaining that when featuring Black dancers and choreographers, "State Department officials and members of the

Considered in this context, Stearns's claim that *commedia* stock characters provide an open formal structure analogous to a twelve-bar blues chorus is a particularly savvy rhetorical move, and one certainly in keeping with Stearns's practice of drawing parallels between jazz music and Chaucer, to resituate mythic abstraction firmly within an Afrological improvisatory paradigm.[70] As the 1959 Newport program explains Stearns's thinking:

> The dancers will build their individual performances on the basic framework of the story, just as musicians build solos on the chords of the 12 bars in the blues—and just as in the *comedia* [sic], the actors put the flesh and blood of characterization on the thin skeleton of the plot. Hence the parallel, hence the modeling of this ballet on the *comedia dell'arte* tale.[71]

Throughout the 1960s, Stearns would consistently return to the vision he sought to realize in this ballet as he advocated for the direction in which he hoped to see jazz dance develop. Stearns wrote in 1962, by way of explaining the decline of tap dancing, that

> Ballet and other styles from abroad became the craze and, like artistic colonials, we threw away the wonderful swinging rhythms of tap for a lot of agonized swooping sliding, posing, and gliding. You can see what went wrong by watching television. Look at any big production number: the dancers come slithering out and throw themselves around.[72]

In *Jazz Dance*, Stearns is particularly critical of Jerome Robbins's *N.Y. Export: Opus Jazz*, offering that

> The truth is that Robbins, who has been acclaimed "the first jazz choreographer," employs movements that are *derived* from the vernacular, changed and molded— quite properly—to fit his own notions. That they are not particularly authentic is

---

ANTA Dance Panel considered race and formal innovation together, seeking African American representation, while also stripping African American artists of their identities." Croft, *Dancers as Diplomats*, 83–84.

[70] My use of the term "Afrological" here follows George Lewis, who introduces the term alongside its counterpart "Eurological" as terms that "refer metaphorically to musical and behavior which, in my view, exemplify particular 'logic.' At the same time, these terms are intended to historicize the particularity of perspective characteristic of two systems in such divergent cultural environments." George Lewis, "Improvised Music after 1950: Afrological and Eurological Perspectives," *Black Music Research Journal* 22, supplement (2002): 217.

[71] "The Jazz Ballet," 65, Newport Collection Box 3.

[72] Marshall Stearns, "A History of the Tap Dance," 1962 *Newport Jazz Festival Program*, 11, Marshall Stearns Collection Box 10, Folder 28.

of little importance; that they lack the rhythmic propulsion which is at the heart of jazz is less fortunate, since it could create additional force and flavor.[73]

Stearns's critique of Robbins's work, though it includes a fairly extensive review of commentary from dance critics, relies principally on Leon James's appraisal. According to Stearns, James "could find little or no jazz movement in it." Echoing, and perhaps a direct source for, Stearns's feminizing dismissal of ballet as a genre is James's description of this work as "just a bunch of girl-boys doing stretches, bumps, slides, and calisthenics."[74]

That Stearns would choose to quote and underscore this characterization of "girl-boys doing stretches" aligns with one of his central dance advocacy strategies: to position authentic jazz dance as a thoroughly masculine, and thus robustly American, solution to the broad femininity of concert and theatrical dance. In response to claims from Agnes de Mille that concert dance's gravity toward a feminine aesthetic resulted from the imbalance of high-level female performers to male ones, Stearns offered that, "although this is unfortunately true of much of the ballet, as well as the contemporary dance, it is patently false when applied to the jazz dance or to African dancing, to which the jazz dance owes so much."[75] Stearns's lecture notes and interview transcripts make frequent reference to the problem in modern dance that "the girls look stronger than the boys" and expands his masculine framing of vernacular jazz dance in his book, where he claims:

Dancers and dance critics—especially of ballet—seem to be concerned about one aspect of the dance: Is dancing for sissies? . . . Perhaps it is enough to add that the question of whether or not dancers were sissies *never arose in the native American tradition of vernacular dance.*[76]

Beyond such rhetoric, Stearns's masculine-centric strategy is structural as well; the book *Jazz Dance,* Stearns's lectures, and his choice of collaborating partners all support a historical narrative and a jazz dance canon that consistently center virtuosic male practitioners.

---

[73] Stearns and Stearns, *Jazz Dance*, 357. Italics in the original. Stearns and Stearns's citation for the "the first jazz choreographer" quotation is Robert Kotlowitz, "Corsets, Corned Beef, and Choreography," *Show* (December 1964), 91.

[74] James, quoted by Stearns and Stearns, *Jazz Dance*, 357.

[75] Stearns, "Is Modern Jazz Hopelessly Square?," 42.

[76] Stearns and Stearns, *Jazz Dance,* 354–355. Italics in the original.

For Stearns, critiques of modern dance as unmasculine and un-American were inextricably linked. His notes for a 1964 television presentation on rhythm tap dance pair these concerns:

[6] CONCLUDING REMARKS

    A. TAP DANCE is a masculine art, it is strong.

    B. TAP DANCE grew up in the United States and flourished, but now shows signs of disappearing, because of the increased interest in modern dance, Hindu, and ballet.[77]

Stearns's feminization of ballet and theatrical jazz dance as well as his "great man" approach to constructing a jazz dance historical canon reproduce a common strategy among white male jazz music critics: the positioning of jazz music as a form of counter-masculinity meant to marginalize a competing aesthetic or cultural formation through pejorative feminization. I have argued elsewhere that white male jazz music critics in the 1930s, the tradition in which Stearns's work is rooted, frequently positioned Black masculinity as a potent source of folk authenticity and as a counterweight to the feminized aesthetics of mainstream commercial popular music.[78] Keeping in mind that Stearns and other jazz critics in the 1950s repackaged the discursive instruments of 1930s leftist jazz criticism as cultural weapons conscripted to serve pro-American, anti-Soviet propaganda, we see how easily Black male bodies and Black masculinity become fungible signifiers for a range of aspirational white male social, political, and stylistic formations. Whatever the needs of the political moment, jazz dance and jazz music critics' aestheto-political contorting of Black male bodies underscores writer and activist James Baldwin's observation that "to be an American Negro is also to be a kind of walking phallic symbol: which means that one pays, in one's own personality, for the sexual insecurity of others."[79] In this case, emphasizing Black masculinity as a vehicle to display American culture brought long-standing fetishized tropes of Black masculinity into the service of American foreign policy goals, framing the Soviet Union as weak and effeminate while simultaneously assuaging charges of American racism.

---

[77] Series of six index cards of typed notes [presumable Stearns's], 6th card, Marshall Stearns Collection Box 14, Folder 9. Capitalization as in the original.

[78] Christopher J. Wells, "'A Dreadful Bit of Silliness': Feminine Frivolity and Ella Fitzgerald's Early Critical Reception," *Women & Music* 21 (2017): 44–47.

[79] James Baldwin, "The Black Boy Looks at the White Boy," in *The Price of the Ticket: Collected Nonfiction, 1948–1985* (New York: St. Martin's/Marek, 1985), 290. As quoted in Ingrid Monson, "The Problem with White Hipness: Race, Gender, and Cultural Conceptions in Jazz Historical Discourse," *Journal of the American Musicological Society* 48, no. 3 (Fall 1995): 402.

This transparently raced and gendered framing was one piece of Stearns's broader strategy, via the concert dance stage, to help jazz dancers share in the types of institutional patronage that jazz musicians were increasingly able to access. Emphasizing the concert stage rather than the popular dance hall was arguably a necessary move toward this end, as the legitimization process for jazz music, particularly in the eyes of the US Department of State, meant distancing the music from its associations with dance. The State Department's guidance for cultural presentations drew an explicit line between "jazz as an art form," which could be part of cultural diplomacy programs, and "popular dance bands," which could not.[80] Stearns thus attempted, through *Jazz Ballet No. 1* and through his rhetorical assaults on American modern and theatrical dance, to legitimize the jazz dance of Minns and James as not only a viable addition but a preferable, more authentically American alternative to the modern dance favored by ANTA on behalf of the State Department. If included in cultural diplomacy efforts, Stearns sought to argue, Minns and James's jazz dancing would simultaneously bolster broader positionings of American art as robustly masculine and, just as jazz music was meant to do in this context, provide a counternarrative to Soviet critiques of American racial injustice.

Where *Jazz Ballet No. 1* was the fullest realization of Stearns's attempt to situate jazz dance as concert dance, a January 1960 appearance with Minns and James on Hugh Hefner's television program *Playboy's Penthouse* exemplifies Stearns's broader efforts to legitimize jazz dance by highlighting its roots as a form of authentic American folk art.[81] After chatting with Hefner about the importance and rich history of jazz dance, Stearns calls Minns and James over from their conversations with Hefner's otherwise all-white guests to help Stearns illustrate jazz dance history. Stearns narrates a series of jazz steps and their history to Hefner, punctuated with demonstrations from Minns and James (figure 5.3). Following a compressed version of their long-established format, the trio begin with the cakewalk in the 1890s, followed by the Charleston and the lindy hop in the 1920s and 1930s, and the big apple in the late 1930s. Stearns's treatment of the big apple in particular speaks to the often problematically romanticized folkloric perspective present throughout Stearns's work on jazz dance. Stearns presents the big apple as a

---

[80] Christian Herter, Department of State Instruction CA 265 "Cultural Presentations: President's Program: Program Guide," Central Decimal File 55–59 032/7-959, National Archives College Park, as quoted in Fosler-Lussier, *Music in America's Cold War Diplomacy*, 116.

[81] The air date found in "News from Playboy's Penthouse," typescript on Playboy letterhead, December 31, 1959. Marshall Stearns Collection Box 14, Folder 7. As Fosler-Lussier explains, one means of legitimating jazz was by framing it as a form of high art that evolved from folkloric practices, a narrative common in framings of European high art. Fosler-Lussier, *Music in America's Cold War Diplomacy*, 124.

**Figure 5.3** Al Minns (*center*) and Leon James (*right*) demonstrating the "stomp off" per Marshall Stearns's (*left*) narration for Hugh Hefner (*offscreen*) and his guests on *Playboy's Penthouse*, December 31, 1959.

jazz-infused folk dance derived from the Virginia reel and explicates its roots in the American south, yet the version Minns and James demonstrate is in fact a fully choreographed dance routine conceived by Frankie Manning, a fellow member of Whitey's Lindy Hoppers, who created this routine based solely on a written description of the southern big apple he received from his boss Herbert White. Yet, this professional routine is re-framed to fit Stearns's broader narrative that jazz dance represents a uniquely American heritage of Euro-African folk syncretisms.[82] In his work on Mahalia Jackson's time with Stearns at the Music Inn, Musicologist Mark Burford has argued that Stearns and the other scholars present were not focused on the gospel singer as a contemporary professional, but rather that to them, she was only "legible as a living embodiment of origin myths."[83] The same could certainly be said of Minns and James here.

---

[82] The intellectual history and ethical pitfalls of the American musical folklorism upon which Stearns drew are discussed in depth in Benjamin Filine, *Romancing the Folk: Public Memory and American Roots Music* (Chapel Hill: University of North Carolina Press, 2001) and Karl Hagstrom Miller, *Segregating Sound: Inventing Folk and Pop Music in the Age of Jim Crow* (Durham, NC: Duke University Press, 2010).

[83] Burford, "Mahalia Jackson Meets the Three Wise Men," 438.

## "Exponents of Jazz-Based Dances": Minns and James after Stearns

Minns and James were not, however, merely passive agents fleshing out Stearns's narrative, and their agency as performers is apparent in their work throughout the 1960s after their collaboration with Stearns came to an end. The pair continued performing with Stearns through 1960 but thereafter struck out on their own, forging tighter connections with jazz musicians active in the emergent Black Arts Movement.[84] The pair returned to Newport in 1961, without Stearns, on an evening concert that also featured Art Blakey & The Jazz Messengers, Stan Getz, Sarah Vaughan, and Oscar Peterson.[85] While it is unclear whether there was some specific falling out, it is likely, or at least possible, that Stearns ran into similar conflicts with the duo that Mura Dehn had had a decade prior. Dehn claimed there was a disconnect in mindset that led to the end of her collaborative relationship with the duo as Minns, James, and other Black dancers were, in her view, more concerned with getting paid and with becoming famous stars than they were with supporting her efforts to present and preserve Black vernacular dances as forms of art.[86] Moving between more entrepreneurial and high cultural approaches, Minns and James remained active in presenting vernacular jazz dance in different formats throughout the 1960s (figure 5.4).

While their "History of Jazz Dance" presentations retained the basic format and content from their work with Stearns, Minns and James seemed much more inclined to frame their movements as part of a contiguous living tradition of Black popular dance than as part of a dying tradition of "jazz dance" specifically. The pair were featured in a 1961 story in *Ebony* magazine that includes a short writeup with several pages of dance photography and descriptions of chronologically ordered steps tracing the development of Black vernacular dance, here notably referred to simply as "American social dancing" (figure 5.5).[87] The article, which notably makes no mention of Stearns, does identify Minns and James as "talented exponents of jazz-based dances" yet frames the pair's lecture demonstrations principally as an exposition of the contiguous history of "jazz dances from the Cakewalk of 1907 to the Watusi of today."[88] The progression of photographs and descriptions

---

[84] There is a *New York Times* report of the three performing together at the New School in November 1960. *New York Times*, November 14, 1960, 36.

[85] "Newport Festival Ends with Top Stars Aboard," *Chicago Defender*, July 6, 1961, 16.

[86] Typed transcript of interview with Mura Dehn by Maria Kandilakis, Mura Dehn Papers, Box 20, Folder 216.

[87] "Popular Dances from the Cakewalk to the Watusi: Famous Dance Team Traces Fascinating History of American Social Dancing," *Ebony* 16, no. 10 (August 1961): 32–38.

[88] "Popular Dances," 33.

**Figure 5.4** Al Minns and Leon James dancing on stage to "Come Back Baby," with Muddy Waters and band at the Newport Jazz Festival, 1960.

moves from what we might still, and what Stearns would have, identified as "jazz dances" such as the Charleston, black bottom, and lindy hop through Black popular dance forms not necessarily associated principally with jazz music such as the watusi, hucklebuck, and twist as well as Latin dances in-cluding the mambo, "cha cha cha," and Pachanga. The perspective offered by this *Ebony* article notably anticipates DeFrantz's later framing of jazz dance as at one point coterminous with "black vernacular social dance": a contiguous tradition whose assemblages of movement practice share aesthetic impulses and ideologies across generations and live in dynamic conversation with pop-ular culture and popular music.

Notably, the aesthetic structures surrounding black social dances and their music outlast any historical moment or movement/musical genre. Certain specific dance movements recur in different historical eras, as in the swiveling and swinging step of the Charleston in the 1920s that resurfaced as the mashed potatoes in the 1960s. In this case, the style of the music that accompanied the social dance changed, but the movements and their aesthetic imperatives—the importance of angularity in the positioning of the elbows and knees, the use of isolated rhythmic markers in

(a)

Figure 5.5a  Al Minns and Leon James demonstrating "jazz dances" beginning with the Cakewalk. "Popular dances from the Cakewalk to the Watusi: Famous Dance Team Traces Fascinating History of American Social Dancing," *Ebony* 16, no. 10 (August 1961): 32.

the movements of shoulders and arms, the propulsive energy driving the motion—revealed a continuity of movement ideology.[89]

DeFrantz has also noted that "jazz dance," during the period of Stearns's interest in it, "implied a nostalgic memory of a time when contemporary black social dances inevitably landed on Broadway stages and Hollywood screens."[90] While Minns and James were among those dancers who graced Broadway stages and Hollywood screens during the 1930s and 1940s, their work as self-advocates evidences far more interest in engaging the popular culture of the present than in invoking nostalgia for days gone by. In *Ebony*—in a publication that centers its Black audience—Minns and James are presented not as practitioners of a jazz-based art form tragically subsumed by dances associated with r&b, rock, and other contemporaneous popular musics but as practitioners able to position all of these dances as part of a contiguous history

[89] DeFrantz, *Dancing Revelations*, 101–102.
[90] DeFrantz, *Dancing Revelations*, 102.

**Figure 5.5b** Al Minns, Leon James, and Adele [last name unknown] demonstrate popular dance forms of the 1940s through the early 1960s. "Popular Dances from the Cakewalk to the Watusi: Famous Dance Team Traces Fascinating History of American Social Dancing," *Ebony* 16, no. 10 (August 1961): 38.

of American social dance credited explicitly to Black innovation across generations. The history Minns and James present celebrates rather than laments this dance tradition's thriving development as a part of popular culture—rather than "folk" or "vernacular" culture—and aligns with popular music outside the boundaries of jazz, a sphere of cultural production and of commerce in which the pair clearly had long wanted to re-establish a professional presence even as Dehn and Stearns had sought to foreclose that possibility. In addition to reframing jazz dance's relationship with contemporary Black popular culture, Minns and James's engagement in cultural and educational programming during the 1960s also took a decidedly Afro-centric turn. In December 1961, they were among thirty-three African Americans invited to Nigeria by the American Society of African Culture (AMSAC) to celebrate the opening of its new center in Lagos. Among the participants were writer Langston Hughes and singer Nina Simone as well as dancer Geoffrey Holder and scholar Willis James; recall that both (Willis) James and Holder had worked with Minns and (Leon) James a decade earlier at the Music Inn. The duo participated in a two-day conference and series of evening performances designed to emphasize the common roots of and linkages between African and African American cultures. This approach pleased and resonated with the Nigerian press, one member of whom described the pair as "a picture of precision and perfection."[91] During these performances, Minns and James would dance on one side of the stage and Nigerian dancers would dance on the other to illustrate the concordances and contrasts between African and African American dance.[92] This scenario's similarity to Minns and James's Music Inn exchange with Holder a decade earlier makes clear that at least to some extent, Stearns's approach and format remained present even in his absence.

Minns and James followed up their Nigerian excursion with a performance at lower Manhattan's Village Gate sharing a bill with the South African singer Miriam Makeba and the Randy Weston Quartet.[93] Indeed, the pair worked regularly with Weston throughout the 1960s. They performed alongside Weston's group again in 1962 for a presentation titled "the Jazz Story," offered without Stearns, that would present "the story of the birth and development of American jazz, our only authentic native American music."[94] Their continued collaboration with Weston further underscores Stearns's absent presence. Weston met Minns and James in the early 1950s while working as a breakfast cook at the Music Inn as he was also becoming acquainted with Stearns. Stearns's influence on Weston was significant as, according to Weston, Stearns's jazz history lectures at the Music Inn were his first exposure to an Africanist framing of jazz music's history and development. Weston would subsequently spend his career aligned with the Pan-African threads of the Black Arts Movement, exploring jazz as, fundamentally, a form of African music. In turn, Weston exposed Stearns to contemporaneous innovations by musicians such as Thelonious Monk and Bud Powell, which proved vital to the "consensus history" Stearns put forward in 1956 with the release of *The Story of Jazz*.[95] Through years of working together with Stearns, his former

---

[91] "33 US Negroes Off for 2-Day Cultural Program in Nigeria," *Chicago Daily Defender*, December 12, 1961, 4. "American Society of African Culture (AMSAC) Presents a Stupendous Display," *Africa*, February 1962, 11, quoted in Lonneke Geerlings, "Performances in the Theatre of the Cold War: The American Society of African Culture and the 1961 Lagos Festival," *Journal of Transatlantic Studies* 16, no. 1 (March 2018): 9.

[92] Weston and Jenkins, *African Rhythms*, 105.

[93] Ad, *New York Amsterdam News*, December 23, 1961, 17.

[94] "Concerts Will Benefit Center," *New Journal and Guide*, October 13, 1962, 16.

[95] Weston and Jenkins, *African Rhythms*, 48–50.

interlocutors Minns, James, and Weston were able to adapt the format of Stearns's academic presentations such that they could offer similar events without his direct involvement and could at times do so for predominantly Black audiences.

Minns and James's focus on engaging Black communities extended beyond lecture demonstrations. Throughout 1962, the pair worked to reunite social jazz dancing with contemporary jazz music, seeking to adapt the ballroom culture of their youths to modern jazz performances in small venues. They held a regular engagement at the Woodstock Hotel offering "an informal, relaxed evening of jazz for people who like to listen or dance," which the *New York Amsterdam News* reported "has been highly successful in reversing the current trend toward non-participating night club jazz."[96] Together with a band led by trumpeter Clark Terry and tenor saxophonist Al Cohn, Minns and James sought to encourage audience dancing in an attempt to reverse the unsettling trend that, in Minns's words, "people have gotten the idea that it's square to dance to jazz."[97] John S. Wilson of the *New York Times* was optimistic about the weekly event, observing that it "should appeal to many people who find passive attendance at jazz clubs uninviting."[98] While these optimistic reports in the *Amsterdam News* and the *New York Times* may have overestimated the impact Minns and James's event would have, the attempt to create spaces for social dance in collaboration with contemporary jazz musicians does illustrate a significant departure both from Stearns's more folkloric framing and from his concert hall aspirations.

While Dehn complained about Minns and James's entrepreneurial ambitions, the pair was clearly driven to carve a place for jazz dance within modern jazz music's commercial mainstream rather than frame their work as either a dying folk art in need of institutional intervention or a form of transcendent modern art to be appreciated exclusively in concert halls. Minns and James likely saw their work as part of a living tradition that could thrive within a new commercial and aesthetic landscape. The pair adapted their dance practices and presentation styles to the range of contexts that had supplanted ballrooms as jazz's principal venues: the concert stage, the academic lecture presentation, the summer jazz festival, and the small nightclub. Minns and James's work in the 1960s was also part of a broader shift among Black jazz artists away from white curatorial interventions that presented jazz as an expression of democracy or of the American cultural mainstream and toward

---

[96] "Second Jazz Dance Showcase Friday Night," *New York Amsterdam News*, June 16, 1962, 20.

[97] Al Minns quoted by John S. Wilson, "Jazz Dancers Gets New Support," *New York Times* May 22, 1962, 30.

[98] John S. Wilson, "Jazz Dancers Gets New Support," *New York Times*, May 22, 1962, 30.

alignment with emergent Afro-centric discourses shaping the Black freedom struggle. Thomas F. DeFrantz chronicles the emergence of "black dance" as a conceptual and aesthetic category in the 1960s as a part of the broader Black Arts Movement, and he argues that Black dance intersected with the Black Arts and Black Power movements' push for "a cohesive 'black aesthetic,' inspired by, for, and about black people."[99] Minns and James's collaborations with Max Roach, Miriam Makeba, and Randy Weston are particularly notable in this regard as these musicians all consistently made African diasporic solidarity a central theme in their work.[100]

Though Minns and James—while serving as physical narrators of Stearns's narration, as "the living embodiment of origin myths"—may have failed during the 1950s to penetrate the predominantly white institutional infrastructure for American concert dance, in the 1960s they found new opportunities to innovate in collaboration with other Black performing artists, opportunities that better reflected their own goals and interests. Eric Porter has said of Black musicians with complex, and at times ambivalent, relationships with the identity "jazz musician" that, "at a basic level, the ways musicians have interrogated the word 'jazz' and wondered about its relevance to their projects provide a guide for rethinking the idea of a coherent jazz tradition."[101] Minns and James's variegated projects during the 1960s point to similar potentials for Black dancers to consider in what ways and in what places the identity of "jazz dancer" did or did not serve them. Those "jazz dancers" whose movement work centered the production of percussive sound—I refer here specifically to rhythm tap dancers—approached this process with a particular set of emergent options available to them, including opportunities to foreground their status as sounding artists and embrace the status afforded those able to claim the mantle of "musician."

## (Re)Staging the Hoofer's Club: Rhythm Tap at Newport

As Minns and James forged their own path, Stearns shifted his focus in the early 1960s to a specific subgenre of jazz dance: rhythm tap. In tap dancing, Stearns found a mode of Black vernacular dance more readily translatable to

---

[99] DeFrantz, "African American Dance," 5. Ingrid Monson highlights Roach and Weston as two jazz musicians who, in the early 1960s, made African diasporic solidarity.

[100] Ingrid Monson, *Freedom Sounds: Civil Rights Call Out to Jazz and Africa* (New York: Oxford University Press, 2007), 142–143.

[101] Porter, *What Is This Thing Called Jazz?*, xiii.

(a)

**Figure 5.6a**  Cholly Atkins, Honi Coles, and Marshall Stearns appear on *Camera Three* with James Macandrew.

high art patronage systems because of its hybrid status as a dance practice that produces percussive rhythms legible as musical sound. He undertook a sustained partnership with tap dancers Honi Coles and Cholly Atkins, who had long worked together as a duo (figure 5.6). Coles and Atkins formed a two-man act in 1946 that they performed well into the 1950s before a substantial decline in available work for tap dancers prompted the pair to seek other employment. By the time they began working with Stearns, Coles was a floor manager at the Apollo Theater and Atkins a movement coach and choreographer for Motown Records.[102] Coles and Atkins's style complemented Stearns's hope to render vernacular dance legible in high art contexts. As a "Class Act," the pair notably had a history of blending ballet and modern dance movements into their routines, in some ways already embodying the aesthetic Stearns had sought to engineer with Minns and James in 1959. Stearns notes in *Jazz Dance* that Coles and Atkins, who had long been interested in ballet and modern dance, had spent the 1950s working in various capacities to integrate aspects of concert dance styles into their act and that Atkins had served as a coach at Katherine Dunham's dance school in the early 1950s.[103]

[102] Constance Valis Hill, *Tap Dancing America: A Cultural History* (New York: Oxford University Press, 2010), 160–163.
[103] Stearns and Stearns, *Jazz Dance*, 307–310.

**Figure 5.6b**  Coles and Atkins perform a soft shoe routine to "Taking a Chance on Love."
December 10, 1964.

This new trio's first major program together took place at the 1962 Newport
Jazz Festival. In the festival program, George Wein remarked that he had
been encouraged by the success of Stearns's dance programming at previous
festivals and expressed his continued enthusiasm for dance programming at
Newport.[104] Stearns's presentation that year, titled "The History of the Tap
Dance and Its Relationship to Jazz," was held on Saturday afternoon and featured five tap dancers—Coles, Atkins, Pete Nugent, Bunny Briggs, and Baby
Laurence—along with a quartet led by trumpeter Roy Eldridge and drummer
Jo Jones (figure 5.7).[105] Tap dance historian Constance Valis Hill has described
the 1962 performance as a "momentous day for tap dance" that helped reverse
the 1950s lull and "marked the beginning of the return of (black) rhythm
dancers to the stage."[106] In narrating the program, Stearns offered extensive
information on tap dancing's development in the nineteenth century before
discussing the emergence of various twentieth-century styles and famous

---

[104] George Wein, "Thoughts on Producing a Jazz Festival," in *George Wein Presents Newport '62* [1962
Newport Jazz Festival Program], 2. Marshall Stearns Collection Box 10, Folder 28. Wein's description in the
festival program does not mention Atkins, but the other accounts in the Stearns collection indicate Atkins
was a prominent part of the proceedings.
[105] Wein, "Thoughts on Producing a Jazz Festival."
[106] Valis Hill, *Tap Dance America*, 202–203. Parentheses in the original.

**Figure 5.7** Baby Laurence, Pete Nugent, Honi Coles, Cholly Atkins, and Bunny Briggs at the 1962 Newport Jazz Festival. Joe Alper Photo Collection, LLC.

performers. The dancers onstage were weaved into Stearns's historical narrative as premier exponents of the various styles that developed after the 1920s. Nugent, Coles, and Atkins were all "class acts," Briggs one of the main exponents of "paddle & roll," and Laurence a modernist whose innovations were closely tied to bebop.[107] The dancers also played an active role in designing and shaping the program, and they built in staged challenges and collective improvisations that drew directly from their experiences at the famed Hoofer's Club exchanging two-, four-, and eight-bar phrases in a circle.[108] Throughout, they called upon Pete Nugent to demonstrate older steps and routines; Nugent demonstrated excerpts from Bill Robinson's routines, Jack Wiggins's "Tango Twist" step, Eddie Rector's "Bambalina" routine, and Leonard Ruffin's contributions to soft shoe dancing.[109] Throughout, Stearns espoused a history that largely paralleled the same racialized, miscegenated

[107] Marshall Stearns, "Narration for the '62 Newport Program," unpublished typescript, Marshall Stearns Collection Box 10, Folder 28.

[108] "Pete, Honi, Charlie *** Plans for Newport," unpublished typescript, Marshall Stearns Collection Box 10, Folder 28.

[109] Stearns, "Narration for the '62 Newport Program," Marshall Stearns Collection Box 10, Folder 28.

aesthetic narrative—a fusion of European forms with African rhythms and style—through which he had championed jazz music in decades prior.

The program, however, did not shy away from discussing racial prejudice. Especially when discussing both the class acts and the reasons for tap dance's decline, Stearns and his interlocutors were explicit in highlighting the racism that had constrained great Black dancers' careers. Stearns attributed the class acts' failure to thrive professionally to "a sort of racial bottleneck through which the <u>colored</u> class acts never passed."[110] In discussing tap's class acts, Stearns was sure to position Black dancers as the core innovators as he had done in the 1930s and 1940s with Black jazz musicians. Specifically, he claimed that Fred Astaire was not a significant factor in the development of class acts. Stearns argued, contrary to popular belief and opinion, both that Astaire was not principally a tap dancer and that many class acts were already well established by the time Astaire and Ginger Rogers filmed *Flying Down to Rio* in 1933.

The "Hoofer's Club" elements of this Newport presentation recall the stylized "jam session" performance format employed by promoter Milt Gabler in the 1930s. Attempting to reproduce the ostensibly non-commercial authenticity of backroom jam sessions, Gabler, along with Norman Granz and other impresarios, sought to wed the jam session atmosphere (or at least their understanding of it) to a concert format, including "informal jam sessions" as a presentational subgenre within jazz music concerts.[111] As a prominent leader in the United Hot Clubs of America, Stearns would certainly have been familiar both with these concerts and with the cultural ethos guiding them. Those who subscribed to this ethos sought access to experiences of Black vulnerability and intimacy by reproducing those performance circumstances—a Minton's jam session, a Hoofer's Club cutting contest—marked romantically as spaces in which Black artists performed for each other and for themselves.[112] This impulse to reproduce in public those ostensibly authentic experiences of Black culture-making to which white audiences would ordinarily not have access was an extension of the entitled "slumming" impulse that drove white patronage of Harlem nightlife in the 1920s through the 1940s. Thus, for the tap dancers with whom Stearns collaborated, accommodating a predominantly white audience's demands and desires by offering them a facsimile of insider

[110] Stearns, "Narration for the '62 Newport Program," Marshall Stearns Collection Box 10, Folder 28. Underline in the original.

[111] Scott DeVeaux, "Emergence of the Jazz Concert, 1935–1945," *American Music* 7, no. 1 (Spring 1989): 13, 20.

[112] DeVeaux, *The Birth of Bebop*, 202–207.

access was nothing new. These dancers built their careers in the 1930s and 1940s during an explosion of popularity and public visibility for tap dancing, but one in which Black tap dancers were repeatedly asked not only to fulfill white expectations of Black bodies' spectacular athleticism, but also to do so while performing character archetypes rooted in blackface minstrelsy.[113] Though the white impresarios and audiences who supported these dancers in the early 1960s were in many ways explicitly ambivalent toward these types of caricatures, they nonetheless exacted specific demands upon Black tap dancers in a manner that reproduced exploitive logics of white patronage of Black popular culture that date to nineteenth-century blackface minstrel performance (if not earlier). Ironically, the specific forms these demands took were shaped through white intellectuals' own performances of ostensibly anti-racist sentiment and self-positionings as supporters of Black dancers and musicians.

Stearns and his tap dancer collaborators returned to Newport for another program in 1963. The lineup was similar with Coles, Atkins, and Nugent now joined by Charles "Cookie" Cook, Ernest Brown, and Chuck Green.[114] They were accompanied by a quartet made up of pianist Gildo Mahones, trumpeter Clark Terry, drummer Sam Woodyard, and bassist Wendell Marshall. Photographer and filmmaker Burt Goldblatt filmed the event and offers a vivid description:

> It was a marvelous afternoon. Dancers Cholly Atkins, Ernest Brown, Honi Cole, Charlie Cook, Chuck Green, and Pete Nugent delighted the audience. Gildo Mahones, piano and bass, Sam Woodyard, Duke Ellington's drummer, and the lyrical trumpet of Clark Terry provided a beautiful backdrop for the array of talented feet that moved across that stage. Chuck Green explained and demonstrated different steps and rhythms, moving from waltzes to rock and roll. The showmanship was dazzling. Marshall Stearns had captivated Freebody Park once again with another great dance program.[115]

The 1963 program also featured more explicit language designed to situate tap dancing as a form of high art. This rhetoric focused specifically on emphasizing tap dancing's close relationship to musicality and musicianship. Aided by his jazz musician collaborators, Stearns positioned rhythm tap as possessing the sort of highly intricate, improvised musicality already legible

[113] Valis Hill, *Tap Dance America*, 98–99; Brenda Dixon Gottschild, "Between Two Eras: 'Norton and Margot' in the Afro-American Entertainment World," in *Dancing Many Drums*, 267–269.
[114] "Newport Dance Program 1963 July 6," typescript, Marshall Stearns Collection Box 10, Folder 31.
[115] Burt Goldblatt, *Newport Jazz Festival: The Illustrated History* (New York: Dial Press, 1977), 103–106.

as worthy artistic expression in the realm of jazz music. Stearns also felt it necessary to emphasize themes of musicianship in articulating tap's superiority to forms of European and Euro-American concert dance. His rehearsal notes for the 1963 performance continue in the line of his writing from the late 1950s with criticism of choreographers including Pete Genarro, Jerome Robbins, and Bob Fosse.[116] In this case, Stearns's critique of ballet, modern, and theatrical dance emphasized the superior musical acumen of tap dancers as his proposed narration for the 1963 program offers that, while modern dancers merely "follow" or reflect the music, tap dancers "can superimpose counterpoint on the music" in highly individual ways.[117]

In validating rhythm tap dancers through the same rhetoric he successfully applied to jazz musicians, Stearns's tap dance lectures reveal broader efforts to form for jazz dances the sort of consensus history he successfully formed for jazz music by emphasizing their intertwined histories. As Stearns explains, "buck dancing came before jazz music, but they both went to school with African rhythms and, by the twenties, were wedded and developed together from there on."[118] As a sounding art form, tap could be presented as itself a form of musical expression. Stearns could thus credit rhythm tap dancers with informing the development of jazz music and specifically jazz drumming. As he wrote in 1962, "until the explosion within jazz called Bop in the mid-forties, the great tap dancers were showing the way to jazz drummers."[119] He again turned to ballet and modern dance as foils, highlighting tap's virtuosity and expressive merits by underscoring his framing of tap dancers as producers of musical sound. His 1963 Newport rehearsal notes make this position clear:

> With modern dance the music is doing the same thing as the dancer. Tap dancers can superimpose counterpoint on the music—--in modern dance all the movements are musically described. The rhythmic patterns are the same as the music. There are guys who dance alone who have interpretation and there is some individuality in the choreography but it's so minor that only good dancers can see it. To most people looking at it it's the same--everybody is doing the same thing. . . . Tap is far more difficult than ballet because you have to be conscious of both movement and sound . . . in ballet you're only conscious of the movement. Tap

[116] "Misc. notes at rehearsal," typescript, July 4, 1963, Marshall Stearns Collection Box 10, Folder 31.

[117] Stearns, "Misc. notes," Marshall Stearns Collection Box 10, Folder 31.

[118] Stearns, "A History of the Tap Dance," Newport 1962 program, 11, Marshall Stearns Collection Box 10, Folder 28.

[119] Stearns, "A History of the Tap Dance," Marshall Stearns Collection Box 10, Folder 28. Capitalization in the original.

has to look good and sound good. And in ballet the steps and movements are all set--there's no improvisation.[120]

Here, Stearns establishes rhythm tap and jazz music as "married" art forms whose developments were inextricably linked. If jazz music was to be considered a form of high modern art, then so too, it follows, must tap dance.

The 1963 Newport Jazz Festival included multiple events that sought to cement the idea that tap dancing was a form of music-making. Most notably, the festival featured a battle of rhythm between several tap dancers and drummer Sam Woodyard. Rehearsal notes indicate a carefully crafted plan to feature tap dancers and jazz drummers as rhythmic musicians of equal stature. The dancers were to start with a series of simple eight-bar patterns designed specifically to make apparent to the audience that Woodyard was able to reproduce the dancers' rhythms precisely. Then, after moving to "trading fours," the dancers would begin to outshine Woodyard as, per the notes, "as it progresses we'll kid with Sam. . . We'll say 'You're catching everything.' Then we'll throw a curve to him later on. Honi will give him one of his centipede steps and Chuck will do things he never can catch."[121] Woodyard would then respond with figures that drummers can do and tap dancers cannot, the goal being to position each medium as having its own unique rhythmic capabilities and to position practitioners of neither expressive medium as necessarily possessing superior musicianship to the other. Placing these tap dancers on par with jazz drummers as virtuoso percussionists helped make available to tap dancers an identity far more welcome within jazz's institutional mainstreaming than "popular entertainer": that of "serious jazz musician."

## Baby Laurence: Dance Master

Stearns's efforts to position tap dancers as serious jazz musicians likely took a page from the discourse that had long surrounded tap dancer Baby Laurence, who took part in Stearns's 1962 Newport lecture demonstration. In 1942, dance critic Edwin Denby described Laurence as "a man who did a tap dance as purely acoustic as a drum solo. It was interesting how he ignored the 'elegant' style in shoulders and hips, sacrificing this Broadway convention to the sounds he made."[122] Indeed, Stearns's rhythm tap lecture demonstrations followed, and

---

[120]  Stearns, "Misc. notes," Marshall Stearns Collection Box 10, Folder 31.

[121]  Stearns, "Misc. notes," Marshall Stearns Collection Box 10, Folder 31.

[122]  Edwin Denby, review reprinted in *Looking at the Dance* (New York: Pellegrini & Cudahy, 1949), 360. Quoted in Stearns and Stearns, *Jazz Dance*, 338.

were likely inspired by, Laurence's own well-received presentation at Newport in 1960. As a dancer, Laurence associated himself principally with bebop music, and he managed to carve a unique niche in the late 1950s and early 1960s principally by regarding and presenting himself as a musician. As Stearns wrote of Laurence in *Jazz Dance*, "from the first, Baby was primarily interested in the sounds he could make."[123] Exemplifying his self-presentation as a musician, documentary footage from a Baltimore street fair performance shows Laurence effectively fronting a four-piece combo from the stage, announcing bebop standard "Billie's Bounce" as the band's next tune (tellingly, his exact words are: "our next tune"). Throughout the performance, Laurence positions himself as a sounding instrumentalist and member of the band rather than as a dancer performing in front of them. Laurence begins by performing the "head" of "Billie's Bounce," doubled by the organ, before launching into a multi-chorus solo and ultimately returning to the head along with the ensemble.[124] The performance stemmed from Laurence's practice of reproducing the rhythms of bebop solos from memory while practicing alongside iconic recordings.[125] Laurence also recorded an album in 1959, *Baby Laurence: Dancemaster*, that tap dancer and critic Jane Goldberg would later describe as "the first album ever to treat jazz dance as music."[126] At the beginning of a solo piece entitled "Concerto in Taps," Laurence offers the sort of spoken preamble that became increasingly popular among jazz musicians in the late 1950s:[127]

> Here, ladies and gentlemen, I'd like to do a dance that I have had the pleasure of doing at the Museum of Modern Art, downtown New York, and at the Cass Theatre, downtown Detroit, and at the Civic Opera House, downtown Chicago. I have also had the pleasure of doing this dance before some of the crowned heads of Europe and America, such as the great Duke of Ellington and for the Count of Basie, for the Earl of Hines, the King of Cole, oh I could go on for hours. Seriously though, this dance is one of my own and original creations. It's a conglomeration of different rhythms in varied tempos. So, in unity with the new school of music, I have added a tinge to the dance. I call this "Concerto in Taps," it is done without the music, I sincerely hope you will like it.[128]

[123] Stearns and Stearns, *Jazz Dance*, 339.
[124] This footage appears in the documentary film Bill Hancock, *Jazz Hoofer the Story of the Legendary Baby Laurence* (New York: Rhapsody Films, 1981). Jennifer Dunning, "Film: Old Dance on Tap," *New York Times*, July 4, 1981, 36.
[125] Stearns and Stearns, *Jazz Dance*, 340.
[126] Jane Goldberg, "Top of the Taps," *Soho News* 4, no. 28 (April 14–20, 1977).
[127] Darren Mueller discusses this trend with specific attention to the performative sociality and aesthetic codeswitching of Cannonball Adderley's opening stage announcement on a 1959 recording in "Capturing the Scene: *The Cannonball Adderley Quartet in San Francisco*," a chapter of his monograph currently in progress. I am grateful to Darren for an advance copy of this chapter.
[128] Baby Laurence, preamble to "Concerto in Taps," *Baby Laurence: Dance Master*, 1961.

In this preamble, which both mentions prestigious venues and playfully riffs on jazz "royalty," Laurence offers the same investment in and ironic play with conventions of concert seriousness that Duke Ellington employed throughout his career to introduce his concert-length suites, and this preamble specifically feels reminiscent of Ellington's remarks during the 1943 premiere of *Black, Brown, & Beige* at Carnegie Hall. In addition, *Dancemaster*'s original liner notes were written by jazz critic and impresario Nat Hentoff, who framed Laurence thus: "In the consistency and fluidity of his beat, the bending melodic lines of his phrasing, and his overall instrumentalized conception, Baby is a jazz musician."[129]

Following Hentoff in treating Laurence as a significant jazz musician, Stearns, as he had done with so many jazz greats in decades prior, invited Laurence to lecture for a jazz history class at the New School in the fall of 1961, a year that also saw Laurence perform regularly with Charles Mingus's band.[130] After offering a history of tap dancing and explicating its concordances with jazz music, Laurence performed for the class a five-minute, improvised "Concerto of Percussion," which featured, by Stearns's account, "a variety of alternately light and heavy taps, scraps, and stamps, in the course of a series of hops, jumps and spins. They were all executed on an area of about three square feet, and the emphasis was upon footwork—plus new and complex rhythms."[131] That Laurence would perform in a relatively small space where "the emphasis was upon footwork" is well in line with his self-positioning as more sounding artist than performing entertainer. Laurence identified firmly as a "jazz hoofer," who was not, in Stearns's words, "concerned with presenting a pretty picture. He stays in one spot, concentrates on his footwork, and builds up a cascading complexity of sound."[132] As Laurence himself recounted to Stearns, "I think my style of dancing was influenced more by Tatum and Parker than by other dancers. While I danced, I hummed Parker's solos to myself and tried to fit rhythmic patterns to them with my feet—those solos have subtle new accents that some musicians haven't heard."[133]

At Newport '62, following their roles in Stearns's Saturday afternoon presentation, Laurence and fellow tap dancer Bunny Briggs also performed that evening on the main stage with the Duke Ellington Orchestra.[134] Briggs would go on to develop a lasting relationship with the Ellington orchestra, most

[129] Nat Hentoff, liner notes for *Baby Laurence: Dance Master*, 1961.
[130] Goldberg, "Top of the Taps."
[131] Stearns and Stearns, *Jazz Dance*, 337.
[132] Stearns and Stearns, *Jazz Dance*, 341.
[133] Laurence, quoted in Stearns and Stearns, *Jazz Dance*, 340.
[134] Valis Hill, *Tap Dance America*, 202.

notably appearing as a featured soloist in the closing number of Ellington's first *Concert of Sacred Music,* "David Danced before the Lord." As Stearns wrote of the pair in the '62 Newport program:

> Until the explosion within jazz called Bop in the mid-forties, the great tap dancers were showing the way to jazz drummers. The complicated and eccentric rhythms of bop drummers changed all that, and tap dancers ran feet-first into a real hurdle. Two who survived and flourished, Bunny Briggs and Baby Lawrence [sic], broke up the old steps to fit the new rhythms and perfected a style called "paddle and roll." Briggs and Lawrence are the favorite dancers, respectively of Duke Ellington and Count Basie.[135]

By underscoring the musicianship of Briggs, Laurence, and other tap dancers, Stearns leveraged discourses from the third-stream movement, emergent academic formulations of jazz music theory and pedagogy, and state-funded cultural diplomacy efforts that made "serious jazz musician" a viable, even lucrative, identity for jazz performers. Affixed to Stearns's broader "Hoofer's Club" presentation, this tactic in many ways mirrored the discursive strategy DeVeaux identifies as central to bebop musicians' self-positioning in the 1940s: offering white critics and cultural brokers a fetishistic window into an authentic "back room" Black jam session space while also making their music legible as a form of modernist high art.[136]

## The Folkloric Precarity of Stearns's "Dying Breed"

Though Stearns deployed the language of sound and musicianship to help tap dancers access cultural capital, his positioning of both rhythm tap and jazz dance more broadly diverged in crucial ways from the largely successful consensus narrative he built for jazz music. Rather than emphasize a contiguous link between rich history and contemporary innovation, Stearns followed the path of contemporaneous folklorists such as Alan Lomax in positioning jazz dance as a precarious and rapidly dying tradition in need of archiving and preservation. Nowhere is this more apparent than in Stearns and Stearns's *Jazz Dance,* where the last section is titled "Requiem," and that section's final chapter labels the generation of dancers with whom Stearns worked in the

---

[135] Stearns, "A History of the Tap Dance," Marshall Stearns Collection Box 10, Folder 28.
[136] Scott DeVeaux, *The Birth of Bebop: A Social and Musical History* (Berkeley: University of California Press, 1997), 204–205.

1960s "the dying breed."[137] According to Stearns's "dying breed" narrative, there were several comorbidities to blame for jazz dance's lamentable status as a "dying art." Along with Stearns's usual suspects—Agnes de Mille for bringing ballet to Broadway, Jack Cole for diluting American heritage, popular audiences for drifting to rock 'n' roll, etc.—Stearns also charged bebop musicians with starving rhythm tap of the conditions in which it had thrived. In the 1940s, he argues, jazz drummers' rhythms became sufficiently complicated that dancers could no longer inspire or innovate alongside them but rather were pushed into a subordinate role as dependent followers who, in Stearns's estimation, blindly followed both the musical style of Charlie Parker and his self-destructive substance abuse.[138] Understanding and valuing them principally as living archives, Stearns framed jazz dancers as tragic characters and as precarious surviving artifacts from a bygone era.

Nowhere was this framing more apparent than in Stearns's work with, and discussion of, the tap dancer Earl "Groundhog" Basie. Basie had enjoyed a long career as a touring dancer, initially apprenticing under and performing with the Whitman Sisters on the T.O.B.A. circuit before ultimately working with Chuck Green as the tap duo "Chuck and Chuckles" and appearing in several Hollywood films in the 1950s.[139] Stearns collaborated with Max Roach and Art D'Lugoff to feature Groundhog Basie at D'Lugoff's iconic Lower Manhattan venue the Village Gate along with several other tap dancers and a combo featuring both Roach and Jo Jones on drums. In promoting the event, Stearns emphasized that Basie was a rare find and in his opening remarks at the event identified him as a "lost dancer."[140] As Stearns cautioned a reporter from the *New Yorker*, "don't be late. Groundhog may disappear tomorrow."[141] In *Jazz Dance*, Stearns emphasizes Basie's elusiveness as much as his expertise, beginning the chapter featuring Basie by narrating his own adventure trying unsuccessfully to track down the dancer in Cincinnati. Stearns laments that "this trip, too, was a failure, and we had not located the man behind a puzzling legend. Groundhog had disappeared."[142] Stearns closes the chapter with a story of Basie missing a planned meeting between the two, offering a classically romantic "vanished just as quickly as he appeared" bookend to a framing already replete with "magical Negro" tropes.[143]

---

[137] Stearns and Stearns, *Jazz Dance*, 348–362.
[138] Stearns and Stearns, *Jazz Dance*, 348.
[139] Stearns and Stearns, *Jazz Dance*, 343–345.
[140] "Ground Hog," *The New Yorker*, December 12, 1964, 47.
[141] "Ground Hog," *The New Yorker*, December 12, 1964, 48.
[142] Stearns and Stearns, *Jazz Dance*, 342.
[143] The concept of a "magical Negro," or a magic-imbued Black supporting character who acts as a companion to a white protagonist, has gained significant traction in recent years and is discussed at length by

In his framing of Groundhog Basie and other dancers, Stearns reproduces romanticized tropes of precarity common in folkloric writings authored by white cultural brokers of Black American folk art. Stearns's decades of work highlighting jazz's roots in Black folk traditions functioned within a larger wave of folkloric study of Black American music led by scholars such as Alan Lomax, Willis James, Alan Merriam, and the dancer/choreographer Katherine Dunham. Among its features as an intellectual discourse, folklorism prizes the concept that the "authentic" music of the "folk," closer to genuine cultural truth than popular music, exists principally outside of the commercial sphere. This belief is predicated on a longing for musical and cultural spaces untainted by capitalism and industrialization within whose soundscapes one can find unmediated expressions of, in the words of Karl Hagstrom Miller, "essential racial characteristics, capacities, and stages of evolution."[144] In his book *Segregating Sound*, Miller startlingly though quite convincingly implicates the roots of academic folklore in the United States as intimately bound with the logics of blackface minstrelsy, a connection that both highlights the colonialist anthropological logics that informed the early development of ethnomusicology as a discipline and that, by the very nature of minstrelized performance, fundamentally destabilizes the already performative boundary between truth and artifice.[145]

Aligning himself with this folkloric tradition, Stearns's focus on precarity and preservation is one important way in which his framing of jazz dance differs from his work on jazz music. As he himself wrote in the '62 Newport program: "unlike jazz, with which it runs parallel, tap dance is a fine art in danger of being mislaid and forgotten."[146] Where his jazz music narrative established a contiguous throughline from folkloric heritage to current innovations, his jazz dance narrative leaned harder toward the fetishization of older performers and an attendant insistence that jazz dance was a precarious, dying art form deeply in need if not of active rescue then at least of rigorous documentation and preservation: for in Stearns's words, "vernacular dance died hard as one dancer after another quit, got sick, or simply disappeared."[147] That said, Stearns's dance narrative did share many of his music narrative's

Krin Gabbard, who refers to such characters as "black angels," in *Black Magic: White Hollywood and African American Culture* (New Brunswick, NJ: Rutgers University Press, 2004), 143–178.

[144] Karl Hagstrom Miller, *Segregating Sound: Inventing Folk and Pop Music in the Age of Jim Crow* (Durham, NC: Duke University Press, 2010), 5.
[145] Miller, Segregating Sound, 5–6.
[146] Stearns, "A History of Tap Dance," 1962 Newport Festival Program, Marshall Stearns Collection Box 10, Folder 28.
[147] Stearns and Stearns, *Jazz Dance*, 352.

critical features, most notably an explicit acknowledgment that both jazz dance and jazz music's roots lay in West African practices and that their most significant innovators were African American. However, Stearns did not, ultimately, prize contemporary Black innovation in dance and movement as he did in jazz music, especially when this dance innovation occurred on the concert stage. Rather than make connections between his thorough historical study of vernacular dance and existing contemporaneous developments among Black concert dancers, Stearns made attempts to craft a new "pure jazz"–based concert art form whole cloth, an effort that largely failed. His inability to see the continuities between Black vernacular practices and the work of contemporary Black concert dancers and choreographers prevented him from forging a compelling consensus narrative, as concert works did not fit within his rigorously policed, aggressively folkloric formulation of "jazz dance."

In seeking to distance vernacular or "authentic" jazz dance from contemporaneous concert dance innovations, Stearns consciously or unconsciously dismissed the work of important Black choreographers. For example, Alvin Ailey's highly innovative integration of Black vernacular movement into his concert works has contributed to his well-deserved status as one of the twentieth century's most significant choreographers. While Stearns does, on *Jazz Dance*'s very last page, mention Ailey in passing as one of the choreographers crafting "increasingly successful borrowings and blends from both the art and the vernacular dance traditions," it is the only time Ailey is mentioned in the book.[148] Given Stearns's close ties with the State Department, he would have certainly been aware of Ailey's ability to achieve what Stearns himself could not: inclusion on State Department diplomacy tours, a feat Ailey first accomplished in 1962.[149] Furthermore, given Stearns's ample opportunity for exposure to Ailey's work, including his signature piece *Revelations*, Stearns's failure throughout *Jazz Dance* to address Ailey's efforts to, in DeFrantz's words, "stage African American culture as a paradigm capable of representing high modernity" underscores Stearns's myopic commitment to jazz dance as a strictly folkloric and popular offering rather than a contiguous living tradition informing contemporary Black concert dance.[150] In another glaring omission, Stearns discusses Katherine Dunham principally as a fellow folklorist of vernacular movement rather than as an innovative choreographer in her own right and one who was creating innovative art that drew upon movement

148 Stearns and Stearns, *Jazz Dance*, 362.
149 Croft, *Dancers as Diplomats*, 94.
150 DeFrantz, *Dancing Revelations*, xvi.

styles across the African diaspora including notable uses of American vernacular jazz steps and numerous collaborations with jazz musicians.[151] Perhaps
more problematic still is Stearns's relative inattention to the concert jazz dance
work of Pepsi Bethel. Bethel was a Savoy Ballroom dancer of the generation
just after Minns and James, and he competed successfully in 400 Club contests
and at multiple Harvest Moon Balls in the 1940s. He worked closely with
Mura Dehn on the *Spirit Moves*, even appearing along with Minns and James
as a trio performing the social "Tranky Doo" routine in the film. During the
1950s, Bethel sought training in modern dance and began developing his own
concert dance style that integrated the vernacular jazz movements of which
he was a master practitioner.[152] His innovations throughout the 1950s and
1960s were distinct from those of the white choreographers Stearns criticized
as Bethel was, in Karen Hubbard's words, "crafting U.S. vernacular dance
from the first part of the twentieth century (authentic jazz) into narrative concert dance about black culture."[153] On face, Bethel's work seems ideal for a
Stearnsian consensus narrative treatment, yet Bethel receives brief mention
in Stearns's book as a member of the "young generation" of Savoy Ballroom
dancers but, notably, not as a choreographer.[154]

## Conclusion

Though Stearns did concede, and even hope, that jazz dance would see more
fusions with "art dance" in the future, his prognostication carried the deeply
problematic, and demonstrably incorrect, implication that such work had not
long been happening already. DeFrantz notes that while Stearns and Stearns's
work was an important, even pioneering, piece of research, their book's exclusively "vernacular" framing of jazz dance fell short because of their "critical assumption that jazz dance can only be considered a 'vernacular' form."[155]
The entire field of "Negro dance," which Susan Manning articulates as a
contiguous African American concert dance tradition that grew up alongside Black social dances, is entirely absent from Stearns's definition of jazz
dance. Ironically, even as Stearns sharply criticized the predominantly white

---

[151] Stearns and Stearns, 17; Saroya Corbett, "Katherine Dunham's Mark on Jazz," in *Jazz Dance: A History of the Roots and Branches*, eds. Lindsay Guarino and Wendy Oliver (Gainesville: University Press of Florida, 2014), 92, 95.

[152] Karen Hubbard, "The Authentic Jazz Dance Legacy of Pepsi Bethel," in *Jazz Dance: Roots and Branches*, eds. Lindsay Guarino and Wendy Oliver (Gainesville: University Press of Florida), 80.

[153] Hubbard, "Authentic Jazz Dance Legacy," 80.

[154] Stearns and Stearns, *Jazz Dance*, 326.

[155] DeFrantz, "African American Dance," 13.

modern dance community, their work performed similar erasures. For many white choreographers, both at the time and to this day, the strong influence of Afrological movements and aesthetics remain largely erased in histories of modern and contemporary dance. As musicologist and composer George Lewis has argued in his work on Afrological and Eurological paradigms for musical improvisation, the exclusively Eurological historicizations of American experimentalism exclude clear Afrological influences on this repertoire, and Stearns's efforts to cast American concert and theatrical dance as principally or exclusively white and European similarly reaffirms a series of problematic erasures where the Afrological movements and aesthetics of jazz dancers like Minns and James exist, in music and dance scholar Hannah Mackenzie Margulies's words, "as an absent presence that continues to haunt much of American concert dance."[156]

The assignment of restrictive nomenclature to African American dance and dancers is, of course, a problem that extends far beyond Stearns and his projects. Even the term "Black dance" has long been polarizing given the danger it poses of centering whiteness as an unmarked hegemon, as Brenda Dixon Gottschild explains:

> Many African American choreographers regarded this label as a restrictive lens that made so-called black dance the designated alien or outsider that was obliged to contrast and measure up to the unnamed, "normal" standard—white dance. And this is why, to this day, a crop of vintage African American choreographers detest this term. Therein lies one pitfall of institutionalized racism: the belief that whites, white endeavors, and white institutions are the norm and that white American culture is not, in itself, an ethnic category. What this perspective does is to circumscribe variations from the norm as Other, under rubrics like black dance. Once the category has been established, there is little room for free movement and self-definition.[157]

The discursive constrictions Gottschild outlines also underscore the pitfalls of Stearns's rigorous, albeit well-intentioned, gatekeeping of "jazz dance." Stearns's narrowly curated authenticity discourse resists both popular dances that move to musics outside the genre label "jazz" (r&b, rock 'n' roll, etc.) and concertized styles that are not, by Stearns's measure, sufficiently fidelitous to folk cultural forms as practiced by those specific jazz dancers with whom he

---

[156] Mackenzie-Margulies, "Where's Leon?," 10.

[157] Brenda Dixon Gottschild, *The Black Dancing Body: A Geography from Coon to Cool* (New York: Palgrave Macmillan, 2003), 16.

collaborated and with whose specific perspectives and interests he aligned himself and his work. Furthermore, any implication that jazz dances either could not or should not evolve into or become fused with concert dance also, ironically, forecloses one of Stearns's own central advocacy goals: to see so-called vernacular jazz dances regarded as art in and of themselves. DeFrantz argues convincingly that Stearns's folkloric, vernacular framing fundamentally erases the "transcendent mastery" of the many artists whose contributions he chronicled, effectively consigning jazz dance to the margins by categorically defining it outside the realm of artistry. DeFrantz asks of Stearns and Stearns's work the necessary and provocative question: "why was it not possible to consider the dances of the African diaspora they chronicled in their book as art?"[158]

Even had Stearns himself gotten to a place where he could have positioned jazz dance as art, the mid-century institutional conditions of possibility for dance and music were broadly different such that it seems obvious in retrospect that even employing the same advocacy strategies could not produce identical results. Institutional dispositions toward ostensibly "serious" musics, informed by an anxious stance toward bodies Susan Cook has astutely termed "enculturated somatophobia," necessarily impacted Stearns's ability to advocate for jazz dance.[159] The State Department's own formulation, for example, explicitly defined jazz as an "art form" by excluding "popular dance." In discussing university adoption of jazz curricula, Ake situates the reinforcement of a "mind/body" split in academic jazz spaces as critical to translating the music into a Eurocentric intellectual and aesthetic system that fetishizes notions of transcendence and universalism as necessarily disembodied ideals.[160] While central to American modernism during the Cold War, such themes of universalism and transcendence were not, and arguably could not be, available to African Americans engaging in embodied practices as the primitivist colonial gaze upon Black bodies constructed and maintained the alterity upon which whiteness could exist as an unmarked hegemonic construct. As DeFrantz explains:

> Although the actions and artistry of black Americans may indeed express "universal" truths, the black body itself never achieves this transcendence in any discourse of the West. Marked even before it can be seen, before it can even exist, the black body carries its web of work and sexual potentials, athletic and creative

---

[158] DeFrantz, "African American Dance," 13.

[159] Gottschild, *The Black Dancing Body*, 44. Gottschild attributes the term to Cook but provides no specific citation.

[160] Ake, *Jazz Cultures*, 118.

resources, and stratified social locations onto the stages of the modern. Black bodies offer a cipher of "not-ness" that enabled whites to articulate modernity in the first part of the twentieth century.[161]

As dance necessarily and unavoidably centers bodies, DeFrantz's formulation reveals the problematic racialization that motivated the institutional severance of Black music from Black dance: Black sounds could be modern, Black bodies could not.

To say that Stearns's institutionalization efforts largely failed is not to say, however, that jazz dance entirely failed to achieve institutional validation. Rather, recognizing its validation requires a more expansive understanding both of Black dance than Stearns's limited "authentic jazz dance" formulation offered and of what "institutional validation" can look like. In 1945, Katherine Dunham opened the Katherine Dunham School of Arts and Research, combining high-level dance and social science training and featuring a credit transfer relationship with Columbia University.[162] Alongside notable anthropologists, Dunham employed Marie Bryant, who had danced with the Duke Ellington Orchestra and taught Black social dance.[163] Among its many notable students were theatrical jazz dance pioneer Pete Gennaro and Geoffrey Holder, the Trinidadian dancer who collaborated with Minns and James at Stearns's Music Inn demonstrations and again on their AMSAC-sponsored presentations in Nigeria. Though her school closed in 1955, Dunham continued doing the work of institution building throughout her life. In the late 1960s, she collaborated with Southern Illinois University to found the Performing Arts Training Center (PATC) in East St. Louis, an institution at the center of the Black Arts Movement in the St. Louis area during the 1970s. Dunham's work with the PATC displays an adept ability to skillfully negotiate the competing demands of SIU's institutional interests, Johnson-era community development policy, the goals and expectations of the Rockefeller Foundation and other private funders, and the community needs and cultural norms of East St. Louis's Black population.[164]

The Pan-Africanist movements of the 1960s also informed the introduction of West African dance, paired with West African dance drumming, at multiple universities including UCLA and Wesleyan, the groundwork for which had

[161] DeFrantz, *Dancing Revelations*, 19–20.
[162] Corbett, "Katherine Dunham's Mark," 93. The school was originally called the Dunham School of Dance and Theater.
[163] Joanna Dee Das, *Katherine Dunham: Dance and the African Diaspora* (New York: Oxford University Press, 2017), 110.
[164] Dee Das, *Katherine Dunham*, 175–194.

been laid by the anthropological engagement of scholar/choreographers such as Dunham, Pearl Primus, and Assadata Dafora.[165] Regarding Pearl Primus, Farah Jasmine Griffin has notably said that for her, "traditional African dance and contemporary black vernacular dance were more than mere inspirations for modernist choreography; they were equal participants in helping to create a modern dance vocabulary."[166] Alvin Ailey's dance company, founded in 1958, has, according to DeFrantz, "grown from a small pick-up company to a large, carefully managed, internationally renowned enterprise including several ensembles of dancers and a thriving school."[167] Pepsi Bethel, who ultimately settled into a regular teaching position with the Alvin Ailey Dance Theater, did participate in State Department tours in the 1960s, launched his own dance company in 1972, and published his own manuscript on authentic jazz dance with support from the National Endowment for the Arts.[168] In critiquing the advocacy work of jazz impresario John Hammond during the 1930s and 1940s, John Gennari argues that Hammond's narrative centered those artists whom he felt needed, and who welcomed, his assistance. Hammond's rebukes, however, fell upon musicians like Bessie Smith and Duke Ellington, who neither needed nor particularly wanted his support and the curatorial meddling that came with it.[169] While I would stop short of making precisely this critique of Stearns, it is clear that his narrative does tend to bracket out those Black artists who, perfectly capable of institution building on their own, did not need "saving." Stearns's "requiem" perhaps mourns only a relatively narrow conception of Black dance practices, one of far less relevance to African American and African diasporic dance practitioners broadly than to himself and to the relatively small subset of dancers with whom he collaborated professionally and connected personally.

Those Black musicians and dancers with whom Stearns did connect, however, found his influence tangible and meaningful; to discount their voices would itself be an act of erasure. Randy Weston credits Stearns with helping him form the Afrocentric perspective that would shape the rest of his life and career.[170] As Weston once said to me in the green room when we served on a jazz history panel together, "Thank God for Marshall." Honi Coles wrote

[165] George Worlasi Kwasi Dor, *West African Drumming and Dance in North American Universities* (Jackson: University of Mississippi Press, 2014), 30–34. Farah Jasmine Griffin discusses Primus's career extensively in *Harlem Nocturne*, 19–78.

[166] Griffin, *Harlem Nocturne*, 25.

[167] DeFrantz, *Dancing Revelations*, xiii.

[168] Hubbard, "Authentic Jazz Dance Legacy," 78–81.

[169] Gennari, *Blowin' Hot and Cool*, 24–25.

[170] Weston and Jenkins, *African Rhythms*, 52.

to Marshall and Jean Stearns after their 1962 Hoofers Club performance at Newport, thanking them profusely for the opportunity:

> I'd like again to express my extreme pleasure, for the way things went over, for all partys [*sic*] concerned, at the Festival. I didn't get a chance to compliment you on a wonderful job of research + presentation. I'm sure all of the rest of the fellows join me in thanking you for the opportunity. It was a ball!![171]

The Stearnses maintained a close relationship with Coles and Atkins, visiting with them and their families frequently and engaging in multiple interviews over a number of years. In his autobiography, Cholly Atkins explicitly credits Stearns with helping position tap dancing as a form of high art in a way that helped spark a genuine resurgence of interest in rhythm tap in the decades after Stearns's death:

> Marshall Stearns was really the one who generated respect for [tap] as an art form and created a situation where serious music critics could see it in the right context. Marshall was trying to preserve tap, to show the connection between real Jazz music and tap dancing from an artistic standpoint.[172]

Minns and James also honored Stearns after his death. The pair reunited in 1969 to present a memorial show in Stearns's honor at New York City's Town Hall. The program, entitled "Jazz as Dance," played to a sold-out crowd as Minns and James performed an array of jazz dances paired with lecture-style descriptions adapted from their years of work with Stearns.[173] Stearns's work has also influenced contemporary jazz dance scholars; Takiyah Nur Amin calls the Stearns and Stearns's book "the seminal text on jazz dance," and, along with his critiques, DeFrantz describes the work as "authoritative," claiming that "the achievement of their volume lies in the subtle way that they align personal testimony with scholarly research to construct a layered and compelling history of dance practice."[174] In a similar vein, Jacqui Malone in the acknowledgments to *Steppin' the Blues* singles out the Stearnses, writing that, "To Marshall and Jean Stearns I owe a special debt. Their fundamental

---

[171] Honi Coles to Mr. and Mrs. Marshall Stearns, July 15, 1962, Marshall Stearns Collection Box 10, Folder 28. Capitalization in the original.

[172] Cholly Atkins and Jacqui Malone, *Class Act: The Jazz Life of Choreographer Cholly Atkins* (New York: Columbia University Press, 2003), 139.

[173] John S. Wilson, "Two Jazz Dancers Re-create the Past," *New York Times*, January 20, 1969, 30.

[174] Takiyah Nur Amin, "The African Origins of an American Art Form," in *Jazz Dance: A History of the Roots and Branches*, eds. Lindsay Guarino and Wendy Oliver (Gainesville: University Press of Florida, 2014), 42. DeFrantz, "African American Dance," 12.

contributions to the field of American Vernacular Dance have smoothed my path and have been an ongoing source of inspiration."[175] Malone's perspective was no doubt informed by her own close collaborative relationship with Cholly Atkins and by Atkins's positive experience working with the Stearnses including their efforts, successful in his view, to position rhythm tap dance "as an art form" meriting serious consideration and respect.

Certainly, Stearns's efforts to distance vernacular or authentic jazz dance from concert and theatrical jazz dance were driven by his genuine desire to foreground Black innovation and to resist its uncredited absorption into what he saw as a Eurocentric or "white" form of dance. Stearns had, after all, done that very thing far more successfully with jazz music as early the 1930s when the idea that jazz music even was African American in origin was far less universally accepted than it is today. In addition, Stearns advocated fiercely for the specific dancers he worked with who felt their own professional careers had been injured by emergent concert dance fusions that were—from their perspectives—unrecognizable as forms of jazz dance. Finally, Stearns's health declined rapidly in the 1960s—the book was completed by his wife Jean Stearns and published posthumously—and I often wonder whether his perspective on jazz dance would have grown to more fully embrace innovations in Black concert dance had he lived longer.

Nevertheless, Stearns's myopic romanticization did cause real harm as it helped sever jazz dance history's connections with contemporary innovations by Black artists on the concert stage. Ironically, this is precisely the opposite of what *The Story of Jazz* accomplished for jazz music history and a significant factor in his jazz dance advocacy's failure to help produce a robust environment for institutional patronage of Black dance beyond the specific opportunities he afforded those artists with whom he worked personally. The focus of his advocacy was oriented toward the folkloric impulses that clearly influenced Stearns's framing and that infuse long-standing colonialist tropes of racial primitivism with an American exceptionalist emphasis on the ethnicized romanticization of miscegenated "roots." As Karl Hagstrom Miller observes, "the folkloric paradigm is the air that we breathe, it provides the basis for most of our music histories and analyses, even many of those that are critical of folkloric authenticity."[176] As it remains a central text in American dance history, Stearns's narrative continues to perform work in the world. For example, within the predominantly white lindy hop "revival" community, where Stearns's work is ubiquitously referenced and indeed where I first

175 Malone, *Steppin' on the Blues*, xi.
176 Miller, *Segregating Sound*, 6.

became familiar with it, his "dying breed" narrative has bred a justification for centering white people and white values as white lindy hop dancers' sense of entitlement and ownership is often justified through a ubiquitous false narrative that the lindy hop "died" and was "revived" by white people. As dancer and lecturer Odysseus Bailer explains:

> Another popular statement made by mostly white dancers in the scene is, "If it wasn't for the white dancers and musicians, the music and dance would die." And since we have preserved the music and the dance, I don't have or see an issue with the dance scene being majority white. . . Remember, the majority of writers that were commenting on jazz and blues music and dance were white, and their focus wasn't about going into black communities to accurately document the origin and history of the craft, but to buttress the idea or notion of white Americans being the "preserver" of the music and the dance.[177]

This centering of white "preservers" and white values often leads to the exclusion of Black dancers, cultural norms, and aesthetics, especially when Black dancers' own practices and forms of jazz dancing do not precisely mirror the specific generation whose dancing Stearns identified as "authentic." In my many years as a lindy hop dancer and member of this community, I have observed multiple instances where Black dancers with concert dance backgrounds are dismissed by or excluded from the contemporary lindy hop scene because the forms of movement they've learned in studying the work of Ailey, Dunham, and other jazz-informed Black concert dance idioms are dismissed as too stylized and "inauthentic" to be considered "genuine" jazz movement.

Given both its historical context and contemporary resonances, Stearns's work also offers a necessary cautionary tale for any of us in academia who advocate for curricular reform and the inclusion of marginalized musical genres. Personally, as a white scholar who was recently involved in designing an undergraduate major in popular music and who currently participates in an interdisciplinary research cluster exploring hip hop in academia, the negotiations through which jazz music punched its ticket to the ivory tower, largely jettisoning jazz dance, are ever present in my mind. When working as a credentialed academic advocate for hip hop, a fundamentally multidisciplinary mode of expression, I observe emergent modes of patronage that should be strikingly familiar to jazz historians: a canonizing Smithsonian anthology of

---

[177] Odysseus Bailer, "White People Did Not Save Blues and Jazz Music and the Dance," document posted to Facebook and OneDrive. May 2019.

great recordings, multimillion-dollar State Department cultural diplomacy funding, and diverse albeit highly negotiated integration into academic curricula.[178] As this negotiation moves forward, who gets to decide which aspects of hip hop are part of a great tradition and which are bastardizations to be scrubbed away to reveal the genre's ostensibly "pure" form? Is it, as Stearns once regarded jazz dance, a "fine art in danger," and, if so, from whom?

[178] For further discussion on the ethics and power dynamics of hip hop in State Department diplomacy and in academic classrooms respectively, see Mark Katz, "The Case for Hip-Hop Diplomacy," *American Music Review* 46, no. 2 (Spring 2017): 1–5; Felicia M. Miyakawa and Richard Mook, "Avoiding the 'Culture Vulture' Paradigm: Constructing an Ethical Hip-Hop Curriculum," *Journal of Music History Pedagogy* 5, no. 1 (2014): 41–58.

# 6

# Dancing *Every* Note

## Community Theater and Kinetic Memory at Jazz 966

I went to New York City in January 2015 to interview Sylvan Charles and
Barbara Sidbury—whom we met in chapter 4—for my research on bebop
dance. The interviews were arranged by my friend Judy Pritchett, Frankie
Manning's longtime manager and now president of the Frankie Manning
Foundation. Judy suggested that we meet the pair the night before the
interviews at a jazz club in Brooklyn; this jazz club, she explained to me, was
also a senior center. Emerging from the C train and walking a few blocks
down Fulton Street, I pass a series of upscale cocktail bars and hipster eateries
of the kind that have come to dominate much of Central Brooklyn's landscape
and come to a large, green metal door (figure 6.1). I follow the sound up the
stairs to a rec room that has been transformed into what *Our Time Press* has
referred to as "Bed Stuy's Best Kept Secret": Jazz 966.[1] As the band plays in the
bebop-informed style we have come to call "straight ahead jazz," a floor full
of dancers are on the floor moving to this music, realizing, in many ways, the
vision Al Minns, Leon James, and Clark Terry set out over fifty years ago with
their attempt at a modern jazz-based dance club.

Jazz 966 is a weekly jazz night held in a recreational room within the Grace
Agard Harewood Neighborhood Senior Center in Brooklyn's Clinton Hill
neighborhood. For nearly thirty years, Jazz 966 has run weekly on Friday
nights featuring jazz musicians with strong local, national, and international reputations. Among those artists who have performed at Jazz 966 are
Lou Donaldson, Houston Person, Gloria Lynn, and Wynton Marsalis as well
as a broad array other top-flight New York City jazz musicians. Jazz 966 is
unusual, and possibly unique, in the relationship it actively promotes between social dancing and modern/contemporary forms of jazz music. At Jazz
966, performers play music rooted in a broad array of post–Swing Era jazz
styles rooted in bebop, hard bop, and various forms of fusion from across

---

[1] "Jazz 966—Bed Stuy's Best Kept Secret—October Schedule," *Our Time Press* n/d, https://www.
ourtimepress.com/jazz-966-bedstuys-best-kept-secret-october-schedule/, Accessed January 29, 2020. *Our
Time Press* is an African American–owned newspaper based in Brooklyn.

*Between Beats*. Christi Jay Wells, Oxford University Press (2021). © Oxford University Press.
DOI: 10.1093/oso/9780197559277.003.0006

**Figure 6.1** The Front Entrance to the Grace Agar Harewood Senior Center. Fulton Street, Brooklyn, NY. From "Save Our Building," posted by "Dr Mambo," March 19, 2015, https://www.youtube.com/watch?v=8zFM-WFkFy8.

the African diaspora while the club has an active dance floor with audience members dancing socially to nearly every song.

Like the venue that houses it, Jazz 966 is integrated into the neighborhood's local, community-based nonprofit infrastructure. The jazz club's founder, Dr. Samuel Pinn Jr., was also a founding member of the Fort Greene Council, which runs the Harewood Center as part of its broader mission "to provide services at several stages of the life cycle, at the beginning with our early childhood programs, and through the conclusion [of life] with our programs for the elderly."[2] Established by Pinn in 1973, the Fort Greene Council works to empower the Central Brooklyn community, and its seniors in particular, through an expansive range of programs well beyond Jazz 966.[3] Jazz 966 was, however, clearly a passion project for the "serious jazz enthusiast" Pinn, described by the *Our Time Press* as a "community activist and culture keeper," who started the weekly venue in November 1990 as a "cultural arts program for the agency's senior population."[4] As Jazz 966's current website explains their mission and format:

[2] Fort Greene Council, "About Us," https://www.fortgreenecouncil.org/jazz966.
[3] "Mourning the death of Dr. Sam Pinn Jr. co-Founder and Chairman of Fort Greene Council, Inc., and co-Founder and Director of Jazz966," New York State Senate, J3667, https://www.nysenate.gov/legislation/resolutions/2017/j3667.
[4] Fort Greene Council, "About Us."

Every Friday night, September through June, JAZZ966 presents a wide range of musical formats including straight-ahead jazz, big band jazz, hard bop, cool jazz, the blues, classic soul, R&B, Afro-Caribbean and Afro-Latin jazz.

One of the foremost jazz venues in the city, jazz966 attracts people of all ages who come to enjoy the city's most talented musicians in an affordable and enjoyable setting.[5]

Notably, this messaging does not emphasize dance but does emphasize the eclectic array of music one is likely to hear, including genres both central to and on the margins of contemporary understandings of "jazz." Dance at Jazz 966 functions as part of a broader assemblage of practices that build and maintain a "community theater" in Guthrie P. Ramsey Jr.'s sense of the term, often facing the headwinds of New York City's Manhattan-centric jazz economy and the ever-present specter of gentrification threatening neighborhood cohesiveness in Central Brooklyn.

## "They Don't Dance at the Blue Note, They Don't Dance at the Vanguard"

Jazz 966 offers a vital resource to seniors for whom nightlife and jazz have long been important parts of their life but who might otherwise lose touch with their neighborhood and community. As longtime Jazz 966 host Harold Valle has remarked, "contrary to popular belief, seniors do venture out after dark, we need a place to go."[6] Jazz 966 provides such a place for Delrosa Marshall and her husband Ted Harvin, who have been regulars at the venue since 2008 (figure 6.2). When the pair were profiled for NPR's *Jazz Night in America*, Harvin recalled:

> I was dancing with this young lady, she asked me how old I was, and [when] I told her she said "you're too old to be out clubbing!" I said, "you know, you're right. I'm too old to be out clubbing," and I went home. That was it. I'm still too old to go clubbing, but I think of 966 as a club for senior citizens. . . . That's something I need because I can't get out anymore. It's my chance to meet people and say hello.[7]

[5] Fort Greene Council, "About Us."

[6] Harold Valle quoted in Matthew Perlman, "Fort Greene Daycare, Senior Centers in Peril as City Dawdles in Lease Talks," *Brooklyn Paper*, March 9, 2015, https://www.brooklynpaper.com/stories/38/11/dtg-fort-greene-council-center-danger-2015-03-13-bk_38_11.html.

[7] Niki Walker, "Jazz, Love and Letting Loose: Brooklyn's Surprising Senior Jazz Scene," *Jazz Night in America: Video Episodes and Shorts*, National Public Radio, December 10, 2018, https://www.npr.org/2018/12/07/674573861/jazz-love-and-letting-loose-brooklyns-surprising-senior-jazz-scene.

**Figure 6.2** Ted Harvin and Delrosa Marshall dancing at Jazz 966. "Jazz, Love, and Letting Loose," *Jazz Night in America*, NPR. Posted by "Jazz Night in America," December 10, 2018, https://www.npr.org/2018/12/07/674573861/ jazz-love-and-letting-loose-brooklyns-surprising-senior-jazz-scene.

As Marshall said of the venue, "this place keeps the mind young."

The weekly jazz venue was founded in 1990 by community activist and Ramapo College professor Dr. Samuel Pinn Jr. along with a group of compatriots under the auspices of the Fort Greene Council. They were looking for a means to keep Central Brooklyn's abundant jazz fans and musicians within their own neighborhood rather than simply contribute talent and treasure to a Manhattan-centric scene that was growing increasingly financially inaccessible to their community. They were confident they could attract artists of the caliber performing at Manhattan clubs like the Blue Note, Village Vanguard, and Village Gate to perform on Fulton Street in Brooklyn within a community center space that then housed a day care and senior citizen programs (and still does to this day). Among Jazz 966's first program facilitators were the late Torrie McCartney and her husband Mike Howard, and Howard recounted to me that the club's founding resulted from a community need that Pinn and his close friend Arnold Freeman felt was not being met by major Manhattan jazz clubs: "They visited the Blue Note, the Vanguard, I guess the Village Gate back in the day, and saw no dancing and high prices. World class acts, no doubt, and said 'damn, we've got a place, we've got a room, and we can make this happen.'"[8] The initial vision was for, in Howard's words, a grand "entertainment emporium," and that "unlike those staid Manhattan establishments, Dr. Pinn's emporium would include a dance floor, dining, local announcements, poetry and most significant, affordable admission."[9] Pinn and the event's other co-founders were not only community activists, but also had strong ties to the jazz industry and were able to leverage those connections to book top flight acts from the very beginning. Musicians who appeared at Jazz 966 in the 1990s, helping grow the venue's reputation, included Bob Cunningham, Hamiet Bluiett, Irene Reid, Lou Donaldson, Randy Weston, and Gloria Lynn. Gloria Lynn's first appearance in particular, Howard recalls, was a major boost to the venue's public visibility.

In addition to affordability and a steady supply of top-flight jazz musicians, central to Pinn's vision for this "entertainment emporium" was the presence of popular and social dance. As Howard explained in our interview, "Dance was there. Dance captured the mood and the atmosphere. It did it, no matter who played there.... That was the thing, the addition of dance to jazz, because usually you're sitting and watching jazz. So that was key, very important... they don't dance at the Blue Note, they don't dance at the Vanguard."[10] During the mid-1990s when Jazz 966 moved to its current location (it was previously housed in a smaller space in the same building), the event's founders rigorously debated how the space would be designed and, most notably, where the dance floor would be placed: in front of the band before the seated tables or in the back of the room behind them.[11] Those on both sides of this apparently "heated" argument were concerned about the specific types of sociality their design choices might facilitate or foreclose. While for certain marquee acts the dance floor is filled with seating, patrons still find ways to creatively refigure the space. During Wynton Marsalis's 2014 appearance, despite a packed house, patrons still danced in the hallway and in the space near the kitchen.[12] Dance was thus a formative element of the space at both the levels of design and of praxis and has remained so even in those moments where the planned dance floor is temporarily removed; through embodied practice, dancers make their own dance floor, reaffirming both Michel de Certeau's notions of space-as-planned vs. space-as-lived and the long-standing Black community practice of making a way out of no way.[13]

[8] Mike Howard, interview with the author, December 20, 2019.

[9] Mike Howard, unpublished typescript given to the author, n.d. (2019?).

[10] Mike Howard, interview with author.

[11] Mike Howard, interview with author.

[12] Nikita White, public Facebook comment on video posted by Wynton Marsalis, January 11, 2014. Accessed January 2020.

[13] Michel de Certeau, *The Practice of Everyday Life*, trans. Steven Randall (Berkeley: University of California Press, 1983), 93.

One regular attendee at Jazz 966 during the mid-2000s was musicologist Guthrie P. Ramsey Jr., whose scholarship I have referred to and quoted throughout this book, as I will continue to do throughout this chapter (as he remarked to me during our phone interview, "you're ethnographizing me"). During a period where Ramsey and his wife (art historian Kellie Jones) were based in Central Brooklyn, the pair became regular Jazz 966 attendees. In Ramsey's words, "that was our Friday night thing that we would do. Go there and mostly watch, and we would dance a little but mostly just sit there and enjoy these people."[14] Ramsey first heard about Jazz 966 from a developer named Arthur Square, whom he met at the Bedford-Stuyvesant YMCA. As Ramsey recalls, Square entreated to him that "if I don't go by 966, I don't know what jazz is." Upon attending for the first time, Ramsey immediately connected the social practices at the venue, including but not limited to the dancing, with Black social dance spaces he was familiar with from his Chicago upbringing:

> My wife and I finally went to it, and we had a blast. Because, people were our age and older, I think we were in our fifties then, and it reminded me of the stepper sets or bop sets in Chicago where dancers would once a week rent out a space and dance their dances. It reminded me of that because it was nice tables and people were drinking their own things that they brought with them. There was, of course, food available, a nice soul food dinner, and a live band, which I had never seen that before with one of those sets, to have a live band every single week. So of course, now I'm fascinated.[15]

True to Pinn's vision, Ramsey was impressed from the outset with the caliber of musician Jazz 966 brought in, observing that "I know I've heard some class A keynote musicians that you would be happy to pay a $60 cover to hear." Unlike most New York City jazz clubs, however, Ramsey described Jazz 966 as a "traditional party." When I asked him what that meant, he clarified that, "for that generation of people, it means that dance is gonna be the centerpiece. You're not gonna invite people to party and there's no dancing."[16]

The "traditional party" emphasis on dancing that Ramsey experienced has always been central to Jazz 966's design. From early on, the presence of dance was central to Pinn's thinking, and he remarked in a 1998 interview with the *New York Daily News* that the venue's crowd trended older in part

---

[14] Guthrie P. Ramsey Jr., interview with the author, March 2020.
[15] Ramsey, interview with author.
[16] Ramsey, interview with author.

because "they have a kinetic memory of the jazz of the '50s and the '60s."[17] The kinetic memory Pinn describes invites some productive corporeal riffing on Ramsey's conceptualization of cultural memory. Indeed, in laying out his notion of "community theaters," Ramsey offers that these spaces themselves might better be described as "sites of cultural memory," and he identifies "the social dance" as one such site in Black communities.[18] As Ramsey explicates the complex, dynamic interactions between history, memory, and music, "the meaning of music lies somewhere in the mix and jumble of the past: in the nexus of the biases, quirks, and individual rhythms of memory and the material evidence of history."[19] To Ramsey's articulation of this "mix and jumble" I would add that movement itself, the kinetic memory to which Pinn refers, collapses the dichotomy of memorial and historical ways of knowing; as the body expresses the individual rhythms of memory, it enacts the material evidence of history.[20] For some of Jazz 966's patrons, that kinetic memory runs back to Black ballrooms of the swing and bebop eras. As Bedford-Stuyvesant resident Coleridge Cumberbatch remarked of the venue, "It reminds you of the old Savoy Ballroom." He and his wife Alma identify as "old Savoy fans," and have said that Jazz 966 provided them a "nice, comfortable place."[21]

While an eclectic mix of jazz music helps patrons access kinetic memories of decades past, also central to the event's dance-focused design is the presence of non-jazz popular music during DJ'd band breaks, including healthy doses of funk and hip hop. During my visits in 2015, while younger people were not always as eager as their elders to get on the dance floor for "Billy's Bounce" or "Moanin'," they definitely got up during band breaks for "the Wobble" and the "Cha Cha Slide," as did I and as did elder attendees. The focus on a broader range of Black popular music during the band breaks is a long-standing practice at the event and one specifically included to help facilitate social dancing. Over the years, the organizers have found that non-jazz popular music during the band breaks helps maintain the dance party atmosphere and facilitates its continuance during the live jazz music, which attendees may be less entrained to understand as music for dancing.[22] Ramsey also recalls

[17] Samuel Pinn, quoted in Joyce Shelby, "Hip Seniors Jazz It Up: Fort Greene Center Is a Club on Fridays," *New York Daily News*, December 11, 1998, 2.

[18] Guthrie P. Ramsey Jr., *Race Music: Black Cultures from Bebop to Hip-Hop* (Berkeley: University of California Press, 2003), 4.

[19] Ramsey, *Race Music*, 27.

[20] In making this claim, I am aware of the dangerous ground I tread as I brush against the well-worn and deeply pernicious trope of white dance scholars reducing Black people's bodies to living archives of "authentic" historical movement material. Rather, what I mean to express is that the materiality of Black embodiment both carries history and disrupts the privileging of documentary "objectivity" that would epistemologically bifurcate history and memory in the first place.

[21] Quoted in Shelby, "Hip Seniors Jazz It Up," 2.

[22] Mike Howard, interview with author.

this as a staple during his years as a regular attendee, recalling that, "in between the live sets, they had a cycle of about four or five songs that they always played. And people would do their line dances, and they would do their Latin dances, and I liked the setup, it was just a marvelous setup that was just so culturally specific to *them* that it was a success every weekend."[23] Despite this emphasis on musical diversity and intergenerational community building, however, Jazz 966 has for its entire history battled the stigma of being housed in a senior center. Even current regulars, Barbara Sidbury included, were initially hesitant to attend for this reason. Over the last few years, organizers have booked a greater diversity of music acts, some of whom are not "jazz-as-such," to draw more younger listeners to the venue even as featuring jazz remains central to Jazz 966's mission.[24]

This musical eclecticism's relationship to intergenerational transfer has also long been an explicit piece of Pinn's vision for Jazz 966 and the cultural work it performs. In 1998, he remarked that "our young people are more into world beat and hip hop. That's their jazz. They want to dance. But I think there can be a blending of traditional jazz and hip hop."[25] Indeed, the presence of contemporary line dances absolutely reflects a contiguous Black tradition with clear connections various forms of social choreography including the Savoy Ballroom's Tranky Doo and Frankie Manning's choreographed Big Apple routine during the 1930s. As with other Black expressive practices whose lineages intertwine with jazz, line dances currently thrive principally outside of jazz as the genre is conceived today. Black urban line dances' presence as part of such spaces in no way marks the jazz dances from which they emerged as "dead" traditions, but rather affirms their status as living traditions that continue to grow and change outside of jazz's spatial and sonic borderlands. In the case of Jazz 966, however, line dance traditions *do* exist as part of a jazz space and as offer a critical pathway for intergenerational community on the dance floor. The line dance anthems present during band breaks thus underscore the porous boundary between contemporary jazz and other forms of Black popular music that run against the grain of dominant narratives in both jazz and popular music historiography, rearticulating the fluid borders between these spheres that have long existed in predominantly African American spaces.[26]

---

[23] Ramsey, interview with the author, March 2020. Italics reflect Ramsey's emphasis and inflection.
[24] Mike Howard, interview with author.
[25] Samuel Pinn, quoted in Shelby, "Hip Seniors Jazz It Up," 2.
[26] Ramsey, interview with author.

# Dancing *Every* Note

In formal interviews and informal conversations, the club's dancing patrons have expressed to me the significance of dancing as an active form of rigorous, participatory, and sensitive musical listening through which those regarded as the best dancers—most of whom are Black men and women in their sixties through eighties—express in their movement a subtle yet virtuosic musicality legible to other attendees, who advise me to carefully watch those dancers who "feel *every* note." This embodied relationship with styles of jazz not typically associated with dancing is far from a novel phenomenon specific to this venue. Rather, it maintains and reflects a broader history of audience kinship with jazz as a form of dance music that has long been normalized among African American jazz listeners.

As I watch the dance floor together with Sylvan "Charlie" Charles, he grabs my shoulder and tells me "look how he's attacking the time! [pointing to different dancers on the floor] He do it his way, he do it his way, and he do it a different way. Each attack it different!"[27] Charlie makes clear to me that my own dancing on Jazz 966's dance floor earns me an introduction to, and his deep analysis of, this aesthetic system as he trusts he can talk with me seriously about the dancing once he's seen me move myself: "I seen you out there, so I know you'll get what I'm trying to tell you." This is not, at least overtly, an act of cultural gatekeeping but rather one of mutual legibility. Charlie's assessment of my own embodied knowledge gives him sufficient confidence that I'll be able to understand the things he's telling and showing me and that explaining them is thus worth the time and effort. When talking with them in interviews or hanging out at a dance event, Charlie and other older male dancers impart to me that their dancing isn't about flash or large expressive gestures but rather a nuanced musical sensibility expressed through each movement choice. Watching couples dancing on the floor at Jazz 966, they help me understand that the best dancers, in their simple movements, communicate the depth of their virtuosity as listeners. The highest praise they express is that someone "dances *every* note."

The growth over the past several years of video footage of Jazz 966 on YouTube affords an opportunity to discuss the music and dancing that happens there in greater depth than my experiences alone would allow. Footage from the Danny Mixon Quartet's October 2016

---

[27] I should note that Charlie is a not a regular at Jazz 966 but rather, as a Harlem resident, a regular at the Cotton Club. He attends Jazz 966 sporadically principally to dance with Barbara Sidbury, though he does enthusiastically appreciate the music played there as well.

**Figure 6.3** Jazz 966 regulars Barbara and Donald dancing to "This I Dig of You," Danny Mixon Sextet, Jazz 966, October 8, 2016. Posted by "George A. Grey," https://www.youtube.com/watch?v=gLhYeQU9JcY.

performance—posted to YouTube by drummer George Gray—encapsulates how dancers can, in Charlie's sense, "dance every note."[28] To begin their second set, the quartet performs a nine-minute 225 bpm rendition of Hank Mobley's hard bop staple "This I Dig of You," precisely the sort of tune we might expect to interrupt jazz social jazz dancing. The dance floor, however, remains active the whole time, and the dance practices present exemplify those I have observed in person at the venue. After the band plays the head, Barbara Sidbury and Donald, another Jazz 966 regular, take to the floor together (figure 6.3). This itself is in keeping with an unspoken point of etiquette at Jazz 966: dancers listen from their seats through at least the head of a tune, and often the first solo as well, before taking to the dance floor. The etiquette at this place, as Charlie explained to me, was not to get up and dance right away but to let the band play for a bit both out of respect for the musicians and to affirm that one's motivation to dance to that song is genuine, effectively an accommodation between older and newer jazz listening practices.[29] Both Donald and Barbara operate from a "six count" basic

---

[28] Danny Mixon Quartet, Jazz 966, October 8, 2016, "Danny Mixon Quartet Live at Jazz 966 10 8 16 Beginning Second Set," posted by "George Gray," https://www.youtube.com/watch?v=gLhYeQU9JcY.

[29] Ramsey affirmed in our interview both that he recognized this convention as well and that it was legible to the musicians.

pattern of two full steps with weight transfer and two iterations of a tap-step pattern where the "taps" involve no weight transfer:

```
1     2     3   4   5   6
[Step-Step]-[Tap Step]-[Tap-Step]
```

Their use of this basic framework in practice, however, is quite fluid. Just as lindy hoppers did in the 1930s and still do to this day, the pair freely modifies this footwork, extending or omitting chunks of it to create "figures" of varying length. They will, for example, omit a "step-step" to create a ten-count figure:

```
1     2     3   4   5   6   7   8   9   10
[Step-Step]-[Tap-Step]-[Tap-Step]-[Tap-Step]-[Tap-Step]
```

At one point, after a series of several six-count patterns, Barbara varies her pattern with a hesitation, and Donald responds with a brief excursion into half-time movement, performing a "tap step" at half speed by swinging his leg around, and thus extending his pattern to eight counts, while articulating a half-time pulse in his torso:

```
1     2     3   4   5   6   7   8
[Step-Step]-[Tap-Step]-[Swings Leg—Step     ]
```

This brief half-time articulation from Donald responds both to Barbara and to the music, as his half-time adjustment momentarily aligns precisely with Mixon's comping. Perhaps sensing he's still a bit off from Barbara, who did not join him in this moment of half-time temporal extension, Donald pauses for two beats before his next figure, which is also in eight counts as he adds an extra "step-step" pattern.

```
1     2     3   4   5   6   7   8
[Step-Step]-[Step-Step]-[Tap-Step]-[Tap-Step]
```

Barbara does not join Donald in his variations here, opting instead to remain in her basic six-count pattern. She does, however, ultimately meet back up with Donald by extending her own pattern with additional tap-steps—effectively vamping—until the pair sync back up. One common aphorism about partnered social jazz dancing is that it is a "three-way dance" involving oneself, one's dance partner, and the music. In this brief piece of temporal play, Barbara and Donald exemplify this dynamic and extend it into the jazz world of "inside" and "outside" playing, shifting the relationship they share with each other and with the music, phasing in and out of various kinds of "alignment" at will, crafting multi-layered flows of give-and-take.

Following "This I Dig of You," the quartet begins an up-tempo (185 bpm) rendition of "Autumn Leaves," and two somewhat younger dancers take the floor and lock right in with Gray's drumming. As these dancers perform a sim-ilar "six count with hops" pattern to Barbara and Donald, they attune to Gray's rhythms and specifically with his fills and the bebop-era "bombs" he's drop-ping. Their pattern allows them, without shifting their footwork, to move with the drummer's shifting syncopations as their embodied pulse can shift seam-lessly between steps and hops. The woman from this pairing notably uses her hops to trace and respond to the affective contours of James Stewart's tenor saxophone solo, making subtle changes to her footfalls within a spectrum we could call "taps to kicks" where her foot height and expressive microtiming express a subtle kinship with, and response to, the melody line. Their dancing drifts into sections of "breakaway" solo movement of the type Mura Dehn identified among bop lindy dancers in the 1950s, and their movement be-tween haptically connected and breakaway sections demonstrates an aural interaction with musical form. The most sustained breakaway period of this type begins at the start of the bridge during the final chorus of Stewart's solo. Here, the dancers display another common rhythmic feature of this dancing: a form of syncopation we might still call "off-time" despite its alignment more or less with the rhythm section's tactus. The "more or less" is crucial, however, as these dancers maintains a framework of six-count patterns throughout, yet occasionally dance slightly under tempo to the point that they phase one full beat "off" from their previous relationship with the musical phrasing. This ef-fectively creates an interchangeability between dancing on beat and dancing on the backbeat, and it is, notably, something I have also experienced as a regular feature of Chicago Steppin'.[30]

At roughly five minutes into this song, and midway through Mixon's three-chorus piano solo, Donald returns to the floor with another dance partner and

---

[30] Chicago Steppin' is a partnered dance, rooted in Swing Era Black social dances, that is done primarily to contemporary r&b and soul music as well as to hip hop. It is currently practiced across the United States, predominantly in Black communities, as one style under the umbrella of "contemporary urban ballroom" dances. In our interview, Ramsey drew connections between the dancing at Jazz 966 and not only Chicago Steppin' but also Philadelphia-style Bop, and other Jazz 966 regulars have also described their style to me as "Bop." Chicago Steppin' is also discussed at length by Black Hawk Hancock, a sociologist whose ethno-graphic study of Chicago's Steppin' community appears in his book *American Allegory: Lindy Hop and the Racial Imagination* (Chicago: University of Chicago Press, 2013): 161–194.

offers another take on "attacking the time." This pair dances an eight-beat pattern, essentially eight-count lindy hop footwork, dancing both half-time and on the backbeat. After Mixon's solo, the band begins the final statement of the head, and drummer George Gray stops articulating the tactus on the ride symbol and instead articulates the melody along with Mixon and tenor saxophonist James Stewart, bassist Lisle Atkinson shifts his walking pattern to half-time, a brief departure before the band reintroduces its up-tempo groove at the bridge. Throughout this whimsical sixteen-bar departure, Donald and his partner maintain their backbeat, half-time pattern, a groove that makes just as much sense throughout this section as it does when the 185 bpm tactus ultimately returns. Essentially, for this final chorus of "Autumn Leaves," the pattern of this dancing couple becomes the most stable rhythmic element in the room.

This analysis of two couples dancing to two songs during one set of one evening's performance far from covers the full expanse of dance practices at Jazz 966. Even within this snapshot, there is much more to say about the other couples dancing during these songs, who express their groove relationship with the band through different patterns and time feels, and about the numerous additional filmed instances of these dancers and other Jazz 966 regulars. Broadly, the embodied, participatory listening at Jazz 966 upends multiple assumptions about modern jazz's supposed hostility toward dancing. For example, the idea that modern tunes last too long for dancing is troubled by an occasion captured on film in August 2012, where the floor stayed packed full of dancers through the Kenyatta Beasley Septet's fourteen-minute, 180 bpm rendition of Frank Foster's "Hip Shakin'" (figure 6.4).[31] Dancers also create as dynamic a relationship with tunes at the intersection of jazz and early r&b as they do to so-called straight-ahead jazz. At the September 2019 "Sam Pin-a-Thon," Barbara Sidbury offers a nuanced palette of rhythmic movements to a rendition of Louis Jordan's "Let the Good Times Roll" as the sax player shouts to her, "don't hurt 'em!"[32] The dancing and listening practices at Jazz 966—their etiquette, their metric play, their nuanced footfalls and knee lifts—both form and are formed by a deep sensitivity to the expressive microtiming of sound, space, and place. The patrons who dance and listen in this space summon kinetic memories of dances and places past, speaking community to and through movement in the present for those willing, and able, to listen.

[31] KBeaswax, "Hip Shakin'," posted August 11, 2019. Description: "Hip Shakin' from The Frank Foster Songbook by The Kenyatta Beasley Septet. (Sony/Orchard) Recorded Live at Jazz 966. Brooklyn, NY 8/10/12," https://www.youtube.com/watch?v=td7hKphMqYo.

[32] Jazz Corner, "9-20-19 'Let the Good Time Roll'—by Louis Jordan and his Tympany 5 (1946)," September 21, 2019, https://www.youtube.com/watch?v=iROKbWzTp_o.

**Figure 6.4** The Kenyatta Beasley Septet performs "Hip Shakin'" at Jazz 966, August 10, 2012. Posted by "KBeaswax," https://www.youtube.com/watch?v=td7hKphMqYo.

## "We Can't Lose This": Gentrification and Precarity

When I last attended Jazz 966 in December 2019, I noticed smaller crowds than in previous years, a phenomenon multiple people affirmed to me had become the new normal as they expressed concern about the event's dwindling attendance and its aging population of regulars. As Mike Howard lamented nostalgically to me in our interview, "It ain't like it was."[33] There is a palpable sense among regulars that Jazz 966's apex or heyday is in the past as the event searches for its next chapter and for an identity that remains both true to its original vision and adaptable to changing times and changing tastes. The subtext of much of this anxiety is the event's identity and its future after the deaths of founder Samuel Pinn Jr. and emcee Harold Valle within a few months of each other in late 2017 and early 2018 respectively. At a 2018 memorial celebration for Pinn, just a few months after his passing, New York City Public Advocate Letitia James (now New York State Attorney General at time of writing) affirmed Pinn's legacy as a steward of Black community institutions, health, and culture. As she promised the attendees, "his legacy must continue, and we children of dreamers must protect these institutions . . . and [protect] Central Brooklyn against the forces that threaten to destroy us."[34]

---

[33] Howard, interview with author.
[34] Letitia James, quoted in Priscilla Mensah, "A Life Well-Lived: Politicians and Community Members Gather to Honor Community Culture-Keeper Dr. Sam Pinn," *Our Time Press*, n.d. (Feb/Mar 2018?),

James's comments evoke a specific struggle as several years ago, Jazz 966 faced a tangible, existential threat: the potential loss of its venue. Owing in part to the dynamics of rapid, aggressive gentrification in Central Brooklyn, the Harewood Senior Center that houses Jazz 966 was under threat of closure in 2015 when New York City failed to reach a new lease agreement with the building's owner, and the owner threatened to begin taking other offers on the property. During a community meeting, Pinn explained that the center was in a "crisis situation," as the city government resisted the landlord's proposed rent increase, even as the offer did remain at below half of the going market rate.[35] In response, seventy-five local residents, including the seniors and children who benefit from the Fort Greene Council programming the building houses as well as the jazz musicians and enthusiasts who frequent Jazz 966, staged a protest at City Hall in lower Manhattan to demand the city address its "moral obligation" to resolve the leasing issue and save the senior center, even confronting New York City Mayor Bill de Blasio as he passed by to make their case directly (figure 6.5). Jazz 966's cachet among the city's jazz elite helped frame the important work done by the Fort Greene Council and Harewood Senior Center more broadly. As jazz singer Steve Cromity remarked, "we can't lose this."[36]

Though the venue continues to thrive, the vulnerability that necessitates such advocacy on Jazz 966's behalf also reflects a legacy of precarity for jazz venues in New York City, and especially for those that invite and encourage dancing. Since the 1920s, the city's "cabaret laws," finally repealed in 2017, had imposed significant financial penalties on clubs that encourage or even permit audience members to dance. Furthermore, from the broad-based segregation of Jim Crow laws to the racialized implementation of the Interstate Highway System following the Federal-Aid Highway Act of 1956, African Americans have long fought against a range of explicit and implicit legal engines threatening to eviscerate culturally rich spaces essential to community life in Black neighborhoods.[37]

https://www.ourtimepress.com/a-life-well-lived-politicians-and-community-members-gather-to-honor-community-culture-keeper-dr-sam-pinn/, accessed June 23, 2020.

[35] Perlman, "Fort Greene Daycare, Senior Centers in Peril."

[36] James Crugnale, "Refuge on the Market: Fort Greene Community Center's Days Numbered, Officials Say," *Brooklyn Paper*, March 17, 2015, https://www.brooklynpaper.com/stories/38/12/dtg-fort-greene-council-update-2015-03-20-bk_38_12.html.

[37] Michael E. Crutcher Jr. discusses this history both nationally and specifically regarding Claiborne avenue in New Orleans's Tremé neighborhood in *Tremé: Race and Place in a New Orleans Neighborhood* (Athens: University of Georgia Press, 2010), 50–65.

**Figure 6.5** "Save Our Building" protest advocating for the Grace Agar Harewood Senior Center at City Hall in Lower Manhattan, 2015. From "Save Our Building," posted by "Dr Mambo," March 19, 2015, https://www.youtube.com/watch?v=8zFM-WFkFy8.

Jazz 966 and the Harewood Center's recent battles for survival amid rising housing costs reflect broader threats to long-standing Black communities in Central Brooklyn. Concentrated for a time within neighborhoods along the L train corridor—principally Williamsburg and later Bushwick—Brooklyn's rapidly spreading gentrification is increasingly impacting Central Brooklyn neighborhoods including Bedford-Stuyvesant and Clinton Hill. A wave of gentrification has been sweeping through Central Brooklyn for the past decade as young white residents seeking refuge from Manhattan prices (as well as those in already thoroughly gentrified Williamsburg) and to access Brooklyn's current reputation for a specific flavor of "hipness." This swell of demand for limited housing stock has caused rents to rise and is pushing out long-standing Black residents as well as the community institutions they have built. As the area's Black population has declined sharply over the past several years, residents are concerned not only about housing costs but also about these neighborhoods' livability for Black seniors. As a 2015 debate over supermarkets and new commercial development makes clear, conflicts over the future uses of space in the neighborhood necessarily entangle issues of culture, age/generation, and race.[38] Ramsey observed this change a few

---

[38] Matthew Perlman, "Black Pol's Gentrification Claim: White People Don't Eat the Way We Do," *The Brooklyn Paper*, February 24, 2015, http://www.brooklynpaper.com/stories/38/9/dtg-key-food-outrage-racism-2015-02-27-bk_38_9.html.

years ago both broadly in his neighborhood and among Jazz 966 regulars specifically:

> What was going on in my Brooklyn life was that some of the Black neighbors I had were losing their houses. Maybe one generation had bought it, the generation of the 966ers, but the children were having problems holding on to the homes or didn't want to hold onto the homes as prices started raising. The neighborhood that I moved into was very, very different within the period of a decade. That preceded the changes in 966 the last time I went there. . . . People [at Jazz 966] were talking about how the changes were affecting them personally. The neighborhood went from a Black neighborhood, where you rarely saw any white people, to one where if you get off the train, you would question if any Black people lived there.[39]

Ramsey is certainly not alone in seeing changing faces on the train as a harbinger of gentrification. In her ethnographic neighborhood memoir, *East of Flatbush, North of Home*, ethnomusicologist Danielle Brown also recounts the changing racial landscape of New York City subway cars as one of several warning signs:

> I thought East Flatbush wouldn't be touched, at least not for a while, but slowly the signs of gentrification were becoming evident—white people; I saw them. They weren't everywhere; it's not like Bed-Stuy. But once you see a few white folks riding down your block on bikes or even pass one on the street, you prepare for the inevitable. Remember the subways and how the ride from Flatbush would teem with black and brown faces? Now, some white ones were sprinkled in.[40]

Brown notes that Black and brown people are particularly attuned to, and may have hypervigilant responses to, these warning signs given intergenerational histories of displacement.

The displacement gentrification brings involves not only the physical displacement of longtime residents, but also the de-centering of the community norms and cultural traditions that over time come to define a neighborhood. While Brooklyn's Black residents often explicitly welcome new arrivals—even young, white, and wealthy ones—to their neighborhoods, there is a palpable sense that some new "neighbors" are more likely to erode community than

[39] Ramsey, interview with author.
[40] Danielle Brown, *East of Flatbush, North of Love: An Ethnography of Home* (New Orleans: My People Tell Stories, 2015), 171.

to participate in it. Writer, activist, and Bedford-Stuyvesant resident Robert Jones Jr., who writes under the pseudonym "Son of Baldwin," commented in 2013 on his Facebook page that he and his neighbors responded to prospective gentrifiers with warmth but also with a challenge to live within, rather than to erode, the community:

> Most people were like "Come on in, but come on in like you want to be here, not like you can't wait to price us out." . . . I am for anyone in my neighborhood who actually wants it to be a neighborhood, who actually wants to build community, and not someone who merely wants to hit it and run (and bleed it of its essence in the meantime).[41]

He posted these comments in response to a contentious discussion sparked by his observations about his neighborhood's new white residents and their preference for living in spite of local community rather than as part of it:

> The white gentrifiers in my neighborhood walk very quickly to and from the local subway station.
>
> And when they do, they never make eye contact with the people whose neighborhood they have invaded, so busy they are drinking their frilly, silly-named coffees, wearing the "hip" jeans we wore ten years ago because we couldn't afford better, and walking big, bulky dogs because, I suppose, they need to have a grip on a chain around somebody's neck.
>
> They don't even say "good morning" or "good evening" to Ms. Barbara, who everybody knows you must greet—that is, if you respect your traditions and you know what's good for you. But how could an outsider recognize the leader of the tribe they have no intention of being a part of? The paved road pays no homage to the dusty ground holding it up.
>
> What to do with a people whose culture is the absence of culture? Afraid of their own shadows, which they mistake us for. Shook.
>
> Love them or leave them alone?[42]

Jones's perspective is echoed by Brown, who observes that white people's sense of entitlement to go anywhere and to have our own values and perspectives not only welcomed but centered—to speak before we listen in both large ways

41 Son of Baldwin [Robert Jones Jr.], public comments on Facebook post [ellipses denote separate comments], main post-dated December 19, 2013, https://www.facebook.com/pg/sonofbaldwinfb/posts/?ref=page_internal, accessed January 29, 2020.
42 Son of Baldwin [Robert Jones Jr.], Facebook post, December 19, 2013, https://www.facebook.com/pg/sonofbaldwinfb/posts/?ref=page_internal, accessed January 29, 2020.

and small—contributes to cultural displacement and erodes community. As Brown explains, "the seeming lack of respect for the culture and tradition of communities is what many long-time residents have been reacting against. And the analogies to [Christopher] Columbus and western pioneers are not without merit; lives and entire cultures have been forever changed, even lost, as a result of the privileging of white bodies over those of darker hues."[43] Brown makes clear that the layers of displacement and cultural erasure that gentrification brings far outweigh any potential economic or infrastructural benefits it might also carry. Going even further, and accessing her perspective as a child of immigrants raised in a predominantly Caribbean neighborhood, Brown argues that the so-called benefits of gentrification are things to which communities of color should already expect access without facing pressure to assimilate to dominant (white) norms:

> You'll be hard pressed to find a person who does not want to have a more economically sound neighborhood that is safe and has good schools, services and amenities. And integration can be a good thing too, depending on how it is implemented. However, integration should not be a solution to better socio-economic conditions for minorities. Economic advancement should not be dependent on how many white faces live in a neighborhood. Better Schools should not be dependent on how many white people live in a neighborhood. In addition, integration should not be a euphemism for "assimilation." It should not require long-standing residents to assimilate to the culture of new residents or vice versa. Integration should be meaningful and beneficial to all parties involved. But true integration cannot take place until the discriminatory practices against black and brown bodies—in housing, banking, the school system, and the justice system—are eradicated.[44]

Jones's and Brown's perspectives resonate with my experience at Jazz 966: the venue welcomes anyone who truly wants to be a part of the community, but it insists on being a community. It will include white people—including those like myself: a millennial of gentrifying age and class—often with open arms and a warm embrace, but it will not center us nor should it. It will continue to articulate the interconnectedness of centering Black music and dance, building and maintaining networks of care and mutual support, resisting community displacement, and fighting for racial justice. It will also proceed without us and persist, thriving in spite of us if need be.

---

43 Brown, *East of Flatbush*, 176–177.
44 Brown, *East of Flatbush*, 177–178.

## "Everything Is Real about This Place"

In September 2019, Jazz 966 held its now annual event, the "Sam Pinn-a-thon," dedicated to the memory of its founder. At this event, pianist Hank Johnson, a relatively frequent performer at Jazz 966, honored Pinn with some reflections that notably echoed Pinn's own 1990s interviews in positioning the midtown Blue Note as a prohibitively expensive, inaccessible counterpart to Jazz 966 and its emphasis on community and inclusion:

> Now, if you know anything about the Blue Note, when you walk in the door you've gotta have some hundred-dollar bills on ya. It's very expensive, they charge you through the nose over there. This Jazz 966 is a blessing. Sam Pinn saw the vision, he wanted to bring jazz into the communities where people don't have those hundred-dollar bills to pay for jazz. Sam Pinn is probably looking down right now blessing every one of you. The way I see it, there's nothing like 966 out there, because here you got the real music, the real people, everything is real about this place.[45]

Johnson's assessment of Jazz 966 and what's "real about this place" recalls Pinn's "entertainment emporium" vision. From the stage to the dance floor to the kitchen serving chicken and fish plates to the announcements for various community events and advocacy projects, Jazz 966 exemplifies the assemblage of praxis Ramsey highlights as central to those nexus points of African American life he terms "community theaters," an explication I will quote here at length:

> The communal rituals in the church and the underdocumented house party culture, the intergenerational exchange of musical habits and appreciation, the importance of dance and the centrality of the celebratory black body, the always-already oral declamation in each tableau, the irreverent attitude toward the boundaries set by musical marketing categories, the same intensive, inventive, and joyful engagement with both mass-mediated texts and live music making, the private performances of class-status and gender, the fusion of northern and southern performance codes, the memories of food, sights, smells, and the ritualized spaces of what the old folks called drylongso, or everyday blackness—all these combine to form living photographs, rich pools of experiences, and a cultural poetics upon which theoretical and analytical principles can be based.[46]

[45] "9-20-19 "SAM PINN-O-THON2," Trivia Answer: "ON THE TRAIL" Ferde Grofé, 1931 The Grand Canyon Suite" posted by "Jazz Corner" on September 21, 2019, https://www.youtube.com/watch?v=Upn9UDtVxk0.

[46] Ramsey, *Race Music*, 4.

Inspired by Ramsey's formulation, I offer two such "living photographs" from my own most recent visits to Jazz 966 in December 2019. These visits were particularly poignant in highlighting the range of ritualized social and spatial practices of, in Ramsey's words, "everyday blackness" that shape community at this Central Brooklyn venue.

On December 15, 2019, a member of the Fort Greene Council began the night on the microphone by advertising books available in the lobby that address issues of domestic violence and addiction. As I sat down alone at one of the few tables not marked "reserved," a woman invited me to come sit at her and her husband's reserved table as several friends who usually share it with them would not be attending and they had extra space. This was a special "Caribbean Night" featuring a jerk chicken plate from the kitchen and the music of the Alston Jack Quintet. Jack is a native of Tobago and a singer and pannist (steel drum player), who led a quintet of musicians from the Caribbean and the West Indies. The Alston Jack Quintet's first set was an eclectic mix of jazz songs including mid-century standards like "Lullaby of Birdland" and Thelonious Monk's "'Round Midnight," "The Girl from Ipanema," ballads such as "Sunday Kind of Love" and "Days of Wine and Roses," as well as the 1960s r&b classics "Walk on By" and "Just My Imagination." Jack sang the ballads and also played solos on steel drum, and his rendition of "'Round Midnight" was particularly striking. When a couple of audience members got up to dance, Jack would encourage more to join them, exclaiming, "this is a party, we don't charge extra to dance!"

The band also played an up-tempo version of "Autumn Leaves"—over 200 bpm by my estimation—to which many people would have tremendous difficulty dancing. While most of the audience did remain seated during such numbers, one older woman consistently got up to dance to the faster jazz songs such as this one, and I felt motivated to join her. Throughout, her movement focused largely on small steps and kicks in various patterns in a manner similar to the dancers I described earlier. Notably, however, during the climax of one particularly intense guitar solo, her movement style changed. The guitarist's solo featured lightning fast runs at the intersection of a Bird-style bebop solo and 1980s guitar hero "shredding," and this woman planted her feet and shifted her expressive corporeal focus to her ribs and shoulders, reflecting the guitar solo's affective emphasis on rapid movement with her own upper body articulations. From my perspective on the dance floor, her movement shift underscored and augmented the sense of catharsis at this intense solo's climax, and in reflecting on it I see a relationship between this adaptive movement choice and Niki Walker's account of dancing by the kitchen during the always crowded Marsalis night years prior: whether within one's body or within the room, be the issue a "tough-to-ride" blazing fast solo or a crowded room with no space for a dance floor: find the place you *can* dance, and make a way out of no way.

The band's second set was the "Caribbean set," featuring an array of calypso and reggae songs. They began the set with Trinidadian artist Lord Creator's scandalously phallic 1964 hit "The Big Bamboo"—complete with a novelty prop to be passed among women in the audience—a request from a woman celebrating her ninety-eighth birthday. The band's rendition of Bob Marley's "Three Little Birds" packed the dance floor, which stayed packed for the remainder of the set. This evening exemplified the contiguous throughline and porous boundary between jazz and other forms of Black popular music, including the diaspora beyond the United States. Jack's musicians moved fluidly between genres and affects—from the romantic to the ribald and from the center of the jazz canon to the heart of popular culture—while maintaining a contiguous and distinctive voice throughout the evening. When I mentioned my experience attending Caribbean night to Mike Howard during our interview the following week, he framed it as an accommodation to help draw in a younger crowd: "we stuck with jazz all those years and jazz is what we're about. Now, you gotta tweak it. The millennials are here, the Caribbean, the reggae (interjection from Carolyn Jennings, also present): put in a little hip hop (Howard's response): Yeah, you gotta do that."[47] While this may be an accommodation in a present context, the "calypso craze" of the 1940s was coterminous with the rise of bebop and of r&b. Thus, for the near-centenarian who requested it, to ask for "The Big Bamboo" immediately following "'Round Midnight" (she made the request during the first set) is a coherent extension of the musical spaces she likely inhabited in her younger years.

I returned the next week, on December 22, for another themed night: a "pre-Kwanzaa celebration" featuring the Nubian Messengers AFE (Ancient Futures Ensemble), "an ensemble of accomplished inter-generational musicians centered in African percussion dedicated to promoting the connection between contemporary forms of music and their African sources." The group's outlook on music stems from a deep dedication to the work of Central Brooklyn native Randy Weston, who also performed multiple times at Jazz 966. As they explain their origin and purpose, "we began with the premise of wanting to fuse the traditional West African percussion of Djembe orchestration with traditional & modern styles of Jazz, R&B, Funk, & Hip Hop, which is representative in the multi-generational make up of our band."[48] Their performance was guided

---

[47] Michael Howard, interview with author (with interjection from Caroline Jenkins, also present).
[48] "Our Story," Facebook post by "Nubian Messengers," March 20, 2019, https://www.facebook.com/nubianmessengers/.

by the principle of #FYAM or "Free your African mind" from Eurocentric domination. They discussed an "African pulse"—deeply informed by the music and philosophy of Weston—that permeates through the music, dance, thought, communities, and lives of African diasporic peoples. The band's repertoire throughout the night ranged from Herbie Hancock's Blue Note Records classic "Cantaloupe Island"—itself a tune with a notable legacy as a hip hop sample—to their own recent original release "Sister Space Shifter," an Afro-futurist neo-soul vocal ballad whose groove is firmly grounded in the ensemble's battery of African percussion. It was far from the most dance-heavy night I've experienced at Jazz 966. The crowd danced intermittently to the band's first set, but a number of people—especially younger people—got up during the band breaks to dance to the DJ'd r&b music. These band breaks did succeed, as Howard had noted, at keeping the dance floor active enough to maintain the spatial conditions of possibility for the dancing that would take place later in the evening.

Interspersed among the band's songs were sections of what were effectively educational lectures—what the band refers to as "edutainment"—regarding Kwanzaa, set to a vamping pattern from the band's percussion section. Two band members explained in detail to the predominantly Black audience the history of Kwanzaa, its role as a non-denominational holiday for African diasporic people, and the symbolism of the Kinara and the rituals surrounding it. In closing, group member Mwata Nubian related the principles of Kwanzaa to Jazz 966, highlighting the venue itself as an example of *umojah* (unity), *kujichagulia* (self-determination), *kuumba* (creativity), and *nía* (purpose). Most emphatically, he underscored the event as an example of *ujamaa*, or co-operative economics, the principle that drove Tanzanian economic policy in the 1960s and that now serves as the guiding principle for Kwanzaa's fourth day. The band underscored the importance of supporting and patronizing community-owned businesses and events, highlighting the necessity of contributing to spaces like Jazz 966, which in turn provide opportunities for jazz musicians and audiences to work and to listen in their neighborhood and also serve as forums for community-based networking. To illustrate this point, the band recommended several Black-owned businesses in the neighborhood that the audience could support in their Kwanzaa gift-giving and asked every audience member who owned their own business or otherwise independently provided a good or service to speak it aloud to the room.

For their final two numbers, the band specifically invited the audience to the dance floor to contribute our own *Kuumba*, our creativity, to the space. Their final tune was the New Orleans second line parade standard "Joe Avery's Blues." Soon after the song began, Sam Pinn's widow Doris got up first and, channeling her late husband's longstanding love of second lining, motivated the mostly seated crowd to get out of our seats and dance. We formed a circular parade around the dance floor, I locked eyes with and caught a knowing glance from drummer Bruce Mack, and we briefly formed a "soul train line," moving two at a time in front of the band. Closing with a second line after an evening spent affirming African diasporic liberation and community-centered economics is a profoundly fitting gesture given dance scholar Rachel Carrico's description of second lining as "a bodily discourse of dissenting mobility that has been deployed by disenfranchised peoples for centuries to maneuver within and against the structural and physical violence of racial capitalism."[49] Moving fluidly from the second line to the soul train line and back also evokes Ramsey's theorization, derived from his own family life, of "Daddy's Second Line," or of the catharsis in Black gatherings accessed through a broader corpus of social and spatial practices that share "the second line impulse" and that serve to "cleanse and renew the spirit of the community."[50]

After spending an evening together listening to a style of music simultaneously global and local—born both from eclectic contributions across the African diaspora and from the life's work of Randy Weston, a Central Brooklyn musician—we answered the call of Kwanzaa's sixth principle. We moved together to a tune central to the musical life of jazz's ostensible "birthplace" of New Orleans, itself a port within a Caribbean diasporic circulatory system, while dancing collectively in a style that moved fluidly between that city's second lining traditions and the spatial re-enactment of a television show that was an iconic vehicle for Black popular culture—music and dance in particular—during the 1970s. The coming together here of community practices exemplified both the "drylongso" of everyday Blackness outlined by Ramsey and the dialectics the Nubian Messengers embody through their music: ancient futures, the local and/as the diaspora. We danced and musicked these dialectics collectively, their torqueing counterbalance holding us in place and propelling us forward. While ever mindful of my status as a guest and an outsider, my lived experience approached the deep listening Becker theorizes in her work: the edges of my roles as music scholar, social jazz

---

[49] Rachel Carrico, "Footwork!: Improvised Dance as Dissenting Mobility in the New Orleans Second Line" (PhD diss., University of California Riverside, 2015), x.

[50] Ramsey, *Race Music*, 16; Michael P. Smith, "Behind the Lines: The Black Mardi Gras Indians and the New Orleans Second Line," *Black Music Research Journal* 14, no. 1 (Spring 1994): 49, as quoted in Ramsey, *Race Music*, 16.

dancer, native New Yorker home to visit my father, and enthusiastic dancing audience member at Jazz 966 simultaneously frayed and fused.[51]

## Conclusion

In any series of chronologically ordered case studies, the final one—especially if it discusses the present day at time of writing—faces an unreasonable burden. It is natural to treat such a case study as an iconic or indicative an-swer to the question of "what's happening right now" and, even more prob-lematically, as some perceived point of arrival in an inevitable march of progress: *"it's all been leading up to this!"* As a counterweight to this narrative gravity, let me pull back the veil that often hides the myriad behind-the-scenes choices that shape a book such as this one: I had originally planned this final chapter as a triptych of smaller case studies that would, in addition to a more truncated discussion of Jazz 966, also include my efforts with the Arizona State University Jazz Repertory Band to reintroduce collaboration with so-cial dancers as a regular practice for big band musicians and my experiences working with blues and jazz dancers and musicians in Hong Kong amid the recent pro-democracy protests there. Both are important subjects, and I will certainly write about them at length in other forums; it simply turned out in the process of writing that there was so much to say about Jazz 966 that it made more sense to craft this piece as a stand-alone chapter than as a "mini" case study. While that choice places an undue burden of representation on this venue, perhaps conscripting it within my broader narrative to serve as *the thing* in jazz right now, I thought it was better to let it have the space I felt it needed and warranted rather than to artificially truncate it in the service of a performatively fragmented ending: *"here are several different things! Behold the world of jazz in all its diversity!"* I detail the nuts and bolts of my writing process here only to underscore that the emphasis on this particular case study comes from the intersection of the happenstance of my own ex-posure to this venue (I will not call it a "discovery" so as to not reproduce the worst indulgences of my white intellectual forebears) and the resonances I felt it held with the broader themes I was exploring during the early stages of researching this book.

---

[51] I allude here to Judith Becker's discussion of cross-cultural notions of "trance events." Becker describes trancing as a particular type of deep listening experience shared at community gatherings. She claims these diverse experiences do share "limited universals" including "emotional arousal, loss of sense of self, cessation of inner language, and an extraordinary ability to withstand fatigue." Judith Becker, *Deep Listeners: Music, Emotion, and Trancing* (Bloomington: Indiana University Press, 2005), 29.

Indeed, as a final case study and in the context of everything else I've written here, Jazz 966 presents two significant narrative dangers. First and foremost, highlighting the age of its participants and the precarious realities of gentrification in Brooklyn drifts perilously close to overtones of a Stearnsian "dying breed" treatment, a discursive gravity I have repeatedly sought to resist without erasing or obscuring important truths about this venue, its neighborhood, and the lived experiences of its participants. Rather than present some morbid fetishization of Black aging and death, I hope I have underscored the importance of intergenerational transfer present in Jazz 966. Indeed, in our interview, Ramsey explicitly framed the significance Jazz 966 and its organizers' persistence to maintain the event specifically in terms of intergenerational transfer and its crucial importance in Black social dance traditions: "What they are trying to hold on to is definitely worth holding on to, but I don't know how you go about that. I remember, in my tradition, the Steppin' tradition in Chicago, it was something that my grandparents did, my parents' generation did, and then we did."[52] Understanding the intergenerational dynamics of Jazz 966 also requires an awareness of the roles and status of elders within Black communities as both tradition bearers and authority figures. Elder, however, is not only a noun in Black spaces; it is also a verb, as "to elder" is, among other things, to take responsibility for transmitting the kinetic orality of Black life: blood memories, survival tactics, rituals of catharsis, and the assemblage of practices that constitute everyday Blackness. Furthermore, even the framework of "intergenerational transfer" is only a partial description of what is important about intergenerational spaces as it instrumentalizes living humans as mere carriers or harbingers of cultural traditions even as their lives are as intrinsically important as anyone else's. To reiterate Charles Carson's caution to us in his work on smooth jazz, jazz scholarship regularly erases the voices of African American audiences, especially the middle-aged and the middle class.[53] That Jazz 966's population skews older is not indicative that its dance practices are dying but rather that they are living as they enacted by older people, who are very much alive, in the present. Broadly, it is important to reframe community spaces for the elderly not as spaces of dying but as spaces of living.

In addition to the problems of gazing upon Black precarity, this case study also continues to center New York City as the hegemonic site of jazz music's production and circulation. There are certainly other instances of post-1990 jazz dance spaces, including ones that still exist, outside of New York City that I could have explored and written about. Still, while Jazz 966 is a

---

[52] Ramsey, interview with author.
[53] Charles D. Carson, "'Bridging the Gap': Creed Taylor, Grover Washington, Jr., and the Crossover Roots of Smooth Jazz," *Black Music Research Journal* 28, no. 1 (Spring 2008): 14–15.

New York City venue, its strongly held identity as a *Brooklyn* venue in specific is significant here. As Travis Jackson notes in his ethnography of the New York City jazz scene, many if not most New York City jazz musicians live in Brooklyn and tend to favor neighborhoods with easy subway access to lower Manhattan, where the bulk of the jazz scene's most lucrative venues are located.[54] One could indeed argue, and many have, that Manhattan functions as a localized hegemon within New York City, absorbing and erasing the distinctiveness of the city's so-called "outer boroughs," which include such ostensibly "un-New-York-like" things as car culture in Queens or conservative politics in Staten Island. Jazz histories, in all their New York–centricity, often still manage to erase the specific importance of Brooklyn as a place for jazz performance and as a borough whose distinctive neighborhoods have given rise to many legendary jazz musicians. As the venue itself arose as a tactical counterweight to Manhattan's vise-grip on New York City's jazz economy, I hope that my choice to feature Jazz 966 and the Central Brooklyn community that sustains it offers at least a compelling variation on the common lick that is the New York-focused jazz story.

As I stated at this book's outset, my goal in this work, rather than to agitate from the margins, is to provoke from the center. As a case study, I hope my discussion of Jazz 966 reads less as a requiem and more as a celebration and a call to action: the venue continues to model principles of community integrity and collaboration that already extend well beyond its walls but that also could, and indeed should, be far more ubiquitous features of jazz's myriad venues. Ultimately, like the venues in which they circulate and have circulated, the possible intersections between jazz music and Black vernacular dance are as limitless as the connections we choose to make and the work we do to forge them. Those that endure depend on community investment, participation, and patronage. Jazz 966, for example, is still going strong, and the Fort Greene Council that stewards it would no doubt welcome your participation—and your contribution—should you wish to check them out the next time you're in Brooklyn on a Friday night. Indeed, I hope that the narratives I've presented here are as generative as they are reflective, inspiring those of us who wish to see jazz music and Black vernacular dance remain in vibrant dialogue with each other to take steps toward collective participation and creative action, always with mindful respect for community elders and the kinetic memory and kinetic orality they hold, as we move into existence those futures we might imagine and to which we might aspire.

---

[54] Travis A. Jackson, *Blowin' the Blues Away: Performance and Meaning on the New York Jazz Scene* (Berkeley: University of California Press, 2012), 67.

# Bibliography

## Newspapers and Periodicals

Atlanta Daily World
Baltimore Afro-American
Brooklyn Paper
Chicago Daily Defender
Chicago Defender
Cleveland Call and Post
Daily Picayune
Dance Magazine
Downbeat
Ebony
Harper's New Monthly Magazine
Hartford Courant
Le Jazz Hot
Los Angeles Sentinel ·
Manchester Guardian
Melody Maker
Metronome
New York Amsterdam News
New York Amsterdam Star-News
New York Daily News
New York Times
New Yorker
Norfolk New Journal and Guide
Our Time Press
Our World
Philadelphia Tribune
Pittsburgh Courier
Soho News
Variety

## Archival Collections

Institute of Jazz Studies, Rutgers University Libraries
Marshall Winslow Stearns Collection, 1935–1966, MC 030
Newport Jazz Festival Records, 1954–1992, MC 038
New York Public Library for the Performing Arts, Jerome Robbins Dance Division
Mura Dehn Notebooks, (S) *MGZMD 408
Mura Dehn Papers on Afro-American Social Dance ca. 1867–1987, (S) *MGZMD 72

## Oral History Interviews Conducted by Christi Jay Wells

Charles, Sylvan. New York, NY. January 2015.
Howard, Michael. Brooklyn, NY. December 2019.
Jenkins, Eddie. Telephone. December 2008.
Manning, Frankie. Telephone. October 2008.
Miller, Norma. Herräng, Sweden. July 2011.
Ramsey, Guthrie. Telephone. March 2020.
Sidbury, Barbara. New York, NY. January 2015.

## Books, Articles, Dissertations, and Essays

Abdoulaev, Alexandre. "Savoy: Reassessing the Role of the 'World's Finest Ballroom' in Music and Culture, 1926–1958." PhD diss., Boston University, 2014.

Ake, David. "Crossing the Street: Rethinking Jazz Education." In *Jazz/Not Jazz: The Music and His Boundaries*, edited by David Ake, Charles Hiroshi Garrett, and Daniel Goldmark, 187–206. Berkeley: University of California Press, 2012.

Ake, David. *Jazz Cultures*. Berkeley: University of California Press, 2002.

Ake, David, Charles Hiroshi Garrett, and Daniel Goldmark, eds. *Jazz/Not Jazz: The Music and Its Boundaries*. Berkeley: University of California Press, 2012.

Amin, Takiyah Nur. "The African Origins of an American Art Form." In *Jazz Dance: A History of the Roots and Branches*, edited by Lindsay Guarino and Wendy Oliver, 35–44. Gainesville: University Press of Florida, 2014.

Armstrong, Grey. "Dance Communities and Time Travel." *Obsidean Tea: A Blackness and Blues Blog*, May 24, 2019. https://obsidiantea.com/2019/05/24/dance-communities-and-time-travel/.

Aslakson, Kenneth. "The 'Quadroon-*Plaçage*' Myth of Antebellum New Orleans: Anglo-American (Mis)Interpretations of a French-Caribbean Phenomenon." *Journal of Social History* 5, no. 3 (2012): 709–734.

Atkins, Cholly, and Jacqui Malone. *Class Act: The Jazz Life of Choreographer Cholly Atkins*. New York: Columbia University Press, 2003.

Backstein, Karen. "Keeping the Spirit Alive: The Jazz Dance Testament of Mura Dehn." In *Representing Jazz*, edited by Krin Gabbard, 229–246. Durham, NC: Duke University Press, 1995.

Bailer, Odysseus. "White People Did Not Save Blues and Jazz Music and the Dance." Document posted to Facebook and OneDrive. May 2019.

Bakan, Jonathon. "Jazz and the 'Popular Front': 'Swing Musicians' and the Left-Wing Movements of the 1930s and 1940s." *Jazz Perspectives* 3, no. 1 (April 2009): 35–56.

Barg, Lisa, and Walter van de Leur. "'Your Music Has Flung the Story of "Hot Harlem" to the Four Corners of the Earth': Race and Narrative in *Black, Brown, and Beige*." *Musical Quarterly* 96 (2013): 426–458.

Basie, Count [William James], with Albert Murray. *Good Morning Blues: The Autobiography of Count Basie*. New York: Da Capo, 2002.

Becker, Judith. *Deep Listeners: Music, Emotion, and Trancing*. Bloomington: Indiana University Press, 2005.

Berliner, Paul. *Thinking in Jazz: The Infinite Art of Improvisation*. Chicago: University of Chicago Press, 1994.

Bhabha, Homi. "Of Mimicry and Man: The Ambivalence of Colonial Discourse." *October* 28 (Spring 1984): 125–133.

Bindas, Kenneth J. *Swing, That Modern Sound*. Jackson: University of Mississippi Press, 2001.

Black, Cheryl. "Looking White, Acting Black: Cast(e)ing Fredi Washington." *Theatre Survey* 45, no. 1 (May 2004): 19–40.

Blumenthal, Bob. *Jazz: An Introduction to the History and Legends Behind American Music*. New York: HarperCollins, 2007.

Brothers, Thomas. *Louis Armstrong's New Orleans*. New York: W. W. Norton, 2006.

Brown, Brandon Keith. "Black Concert Trauma: Why Blacks Don't Go to Orchestra Concerts." https://medium.com/all-the-black-dots/black-concert-trauma-5fa0459e5b3, accessed February 9, 2020.

Brown, Danielle. *East of Flatbush, North of Love: An Ethnography of Home*. New Orleans: My People Tell Stories, 2015.

Brown, Jayna. *Babylon Girls: Black Women Performers and the Shaping of the Modern*. Durham, NC: Duke University Press, 2008.

Burford, Mark. "Mahalia Jackson Meets the Wise Men: Defining Jazz at the Music Inn." *Musical Quarterly* 97, no. 3 (Fall 2014): 429–486.

Burke, Patrick. *Come In and Hear the Truth: Jazz and Race on 52nd Street*. Chicago: University of Chicago Press, 2008.

Cacoullos, Ann. "Feminist Ruptures in Women's Studies and American Studies." *American Studies International* 38, no. 3 (October 2000): 89–99.

Calkins, Susan Lee. "A History of Jazz Studies at the New England Conservatory 1969–2009: The Legacy of Gunther Schuller." DMA diss., Boston University, 2012.

Caponi-Tabery, Gena. *Jump for Joy: Jazz, Basketball, and Black Culture in 1930s America*. Amherst: University of Massachusetts Press, 2008.

Carithers, Kirsten L. Speyer. "The Work of Indeterminacy: Interpretive Labor in Experimental Music." PhD diss., Northwestern University, 2017.

Carrico, Rachel. "Footwork! Improvised Dance as Dissenting Mobility in the New Orleans Second Line." PhD diss., University of California Riverside, 2015.

Carson, Charles D. "'Bridging the Gap': Creed Taylor, Grover Washington, Jr., and the Crossover Roots of Smooth Jazz." *Black Music Research Journal* 28, no. 1 (Spring 2008): 1–15.

Certeau, Michel de. *The Practice of Everyday Life*. Translated by Steven Randall. Berkeley: University of California Press, 1983.

Cheung, Floyd. "'Les Cenelles' and Quadroon Balls' 'Hidden Transcripts' of Resistance and Domination in New Orleans, 1803–1845." *Southern Literary Journal* 29, no. 2 (Spring 1997): 5–16.

Clark, Emily. *The Strange History of the American Quadroon: Free Women of Color in the Revolutionary Atlantic World*. Chapel Hill: University of North Carolina Press, 2013.

Coady, Christopher. *John Lewis and the Challenge of "Real" Black Music*. Ann Arbor: University of Michigan Press, 2016.

Cohen, Patricia. "Jazz Dance as Continuum." In *Jazz Dance: A History of the Roots and Branches*, edited by Lindsay Guarino and Wendy Oliver, 3–7. Gainesville: University Press of Florida, 2014.

Corbett, Saroya. "Katherine Dunham's Mark on Jazz." In *Jazz Dance: A History of the Roots and Branches*, edited by Lindsay Guarino and Wendy Oliver, 89–96. Gainesville: University Press of Florida, 2014.

Crease, Robert P. "Divine Frivolity: Hollywood Representations of the Lindy Hop, 1937–1942." In *Representing Jazz*, edited by Krin Gabbard, 207–228. Durham, NC: Duke University Press, 1995.

Croft, Clare. *Dancers as Diplomats: American Choreography in Cultural Exchange*. New York: Oxford University Press, 2015.

Crutcher, Michael E., Jr. *Tremé: Race and Place in a New Orleans Neighborhood*. Athens: University of Georgia Press, 2010.

Cusick, Suzanne. "On a Lesbian Relationship with Music: A Serious Effort Not to Think Straight." In *Queering the Pitch: The New Gay and Lesbian Musicology*, edited by Philip Brett, Elizabeth Wood, and Gary C. Thomas, 67–83. New York: Routledge, 1994.

Darkenwald, Teal. "Jack Cole and Theatrical Jazz Dance." In *Jazz Dance: A History of Roots and Branches*, edited by Lindsay Guarino and Wendy Oliver, 82–88. Gainesville: University Press of Florida, 2014.

Das, Joanna Dee. *Katherine Dunham: Dance and the African Diaspora*. New York: Oxford University Press, 2017.

Davenport, Lisa E. *Jazz Diplomacy: Promoting America in the Cold War Era*. Jackson: University of Mississippi Press, 2009.

Decker, Todd. *Music Makes Me: Fred Astaire and Jazz*. Berkeley: University of California Press, 2011.

DeFrantz, Thomas F. "African American Dance: A Complex History." In *Dancing Many Drums: Excavations in African American Dance*, edited by Thomas F. DeFrantz, 3–38. Madison: University of Wisconsin Press, 2001.

DeFrantz, Thomas F. "Bone-Breaking, Black Social Dance, and Queer Corporeal Orature." *The Black Scholar* 46, no. 1 (2016): 66–74.

DeFrantz, Thomas F. *Dancing Revelations: Alvin Ailey's Embodiment of African American Culture*. New York: Oxford University Press, 2006.

DeVeaux, Scott. *The Birth of Bebop: A Social and Musical History*. Berkeley: University of California Press, 1997.

DeVeaux, Scott. "Constructing the Jazz Tradition: Jazz Historiography." *Black American Literature Forum* 25, no. 3 (Literature of Jazz Issue, Autumn 1991): 525–560.

DeVeaux, Scott. "The Emergence of the Jazz Concert, 1935–1945." *American Music* 7, no. 1 (1989): 6–29.

Devlin, Paul. "Jazz Autobiography and the Cold War." *Popular Music and Society* 38 (2015): 140–159.

Dinerstein, Joel. *Swinging the Machine: Modernity, Technology, and African American Culture between the World Wars*. Amherst: University of Massachusetts Press, 2003.

Dor, George Worlasi Kwasi. *West African Drumming and Dance in North American Universities*. Jackson: University of Mississippi Press, 2014.

Early, Gerald, and Ingrid Monson. "Why Jazz Still Matters." *Daedalus* 148, no. 2 (Spring 2019): 5–12.

Eidsheim, Nina. "Voice as Action: Toward a Model for Analyzing the Dynamic Construction of a Racialized Voice." *Current Musicology* 93 (Spring 2012): 9–33.

Ellington, Duke [Edward Kennedy]. *Music Is My Mistress*. New York: Da Capo, 1973.

Elswit, Kate. *Watching Weimar Dance*. New York: Oxford University Press, 2014.

Erenberg, Lewis A. *Swinging the Dream: Big Band Jazz and the Rebirth of American Culture*. Chicago: University of Chicago Press, 1998.

Filene, Benjamin. *Romancing the Folk: Public Memory and American Roots Movement*. Chapel Hill: University of North Carolina Press, 2000.

Floyd, Samuel. *The Power of Black Music: Interpreting Its History from Africa to the United States*. New York: Oxford University Press, 1995.

Fosler-Lussier, Danielle. *Music in America's Cold War Diplomacy*. Berkeley: University of California Press, 2015.

Foster, Susan Leigh. *Choreographing Empathy: Kinesthesia in Performance*. New York: Routledge, 2011.

Foster, Susan Leigh. "Choreographing History." In *Choreographing History*, edited by Susan Leigh Foster, 3–24. Bloomington: University of Indiana Press, 1995.

Gabbard, Krin. *Black Magic: White Hollywood and African American Culture*. New Brunswick, NJ: Rutgers University Press, 2004.

Gabbard, Krin, ed. *Jazz among the Discourses*. Durham, NC: Duke University Press, 1995.

Gabbard, Krin, ed., *Representing Jazz*. Durham, NC: Duke University Press, 1995.

Gaunt, Kyra. *The Games Black Girls Play: Learning the Ropes from Double-Dutch to Hip-Hop*. New York: New York University Press, 2006.

Geerlings, Lonneke. "Performances in the Theatre of the Cold War: The American Society of African Culture and the 1961 Lagos Festival." *Journal of Transatlantic Studies* 16, no. 1 (March 2018): 1–19.

Gendron, Bernard. "Moldy Figs and Modernists." In *Jazz Among the Discourses*, edited by Krin Gabbard, 31–56. Durham, NC: Duke University Press: 1995.

Gennari, John. *Blowin' Hot and Cool: Jazz and Its Critics*. Berkeley: University of California Press, 2006.

Gennari, John. "Hipsters, Bluebloods, Rebels, and Hooligans: The Cultural Politics of the Newport Jazz Festival: 1954–1960." In *Uptown Conversation: The New Jazz Studies*, edited by Robert O'Meally, Brent Hayes Edwards, and Farah Jasmine Griffin, 126–149. New York: Columbia University Press, 2004.

Gennari, John. "Jazz Criticism: Its Development and Ideologies." *Black American Literature Forum* 25, no. 3 (Literature of Jazz Issue, Autumn 1991): 449–523.

Gibson, Maya. "Alternate Takes: Billie Holiday at the Intersection of Black Cultural Studies and Historical Musicology." PhD diss., University of Wisconsin-Madison, 2008.

Giddins, Gary. *Faces in the Crowd: Actors, Writers, Musicians, and Filmmakers*. New York: Da Capo, 1996.

Gillespie, Dizzy [John Burks], with Al Fraser. *To Be or Not to Bop*. Garden City, NY: Doubleday, 1979.

Goehr, Lydia. "Political Music and the Politics of Music." *Journal of Aesthetics and Art Criticism* 52, no. 1 (Winter 1994): 99–112.

Goldblatt, Burt. *Newport Jazz Festival: The Illustrated History*. New York: Dial Press, 1977.

Gottschild, Brenda Dixon. "Between Two Eras: 'Norton and Margot' in the Afro-American Entertainment World." In *Dancing Many Drums: Excavations in African American Dance*, edited by Thomas F. DeFrantz, 267–288. Madison: University of Wisconsin Press, 2001.

Gottschild, Brenda Dixon. *The Black Dancing Body: A Geography from Coon to Cool*. New York: Palgrave Macmillan, 2003.

Gottschild, Brenda Dixon. *Waltzing in the Dark: African American Vaudeville and Race Politics in the Swing Era*. New York: Palgrave Macmillan, 1999.

Griffin, Farah Jasmine. *Harlem Nocturne: Women Artists and Progressive Politics During World War II*. New York: Basic Books, 2013.

Guillory, Monique. "Some Enchanted Evening on the Auction Block: The Cultural Legacy of the New Orleans Quadroons." PhD diss., New York University, 1999.

Gushee, Lawrence. "The Nineteenth Century Origins of Jazz." *Black Music Research Journal* 22 (2002): 151–174.

Hagstrom Miller, Karl. *Segregating Sound: Inventing Folk and Pop Music in the Age of Jim Crow*. Durham, NC: Duke University Press, 2010.

Hainilä, Harri. "An Endeavor by Harlem Dancers to Achieve Equality: Recognition of the Harlem-Based African American Jazz Dance between 1921 and 1943." PhD diss., University of Helsinki, 2016.

Hancock, Black Hawk. *American Allegory: Lindy Hop and the Racial Imagination*. Chicago: University of Chicago Press, 2013.

Harker, Brian. "Louis Armstrong, Eccentric Dance, and the Evolution of Jazz on the Eve of Swing." *Journal of the American Musicological Society* 61, no. 1 (Spring 2008): 67–121.

Hazzard-Gordon, Katrina. *Jookin': The Rise of Social Dance Formations in African American Culture*. Philadelphia: Temple University Press, 1992.

Hewitt, Andrew. *Social Choreography: Ideology as Performance in Dance and Everyday Movement*. Durham, NC: Duke University Press, 2005.

hooks, bell. *Black Looks: Race and Representation*. Boston: South End Press, 1992.

Hubbard, Karen. "The Authentic Jazz Dance Legacy of Pepsi Bethel." In *Jazz Dance: Roots and Branches*, edited by Lindsay Guarino and Wendy Oliver, 75–81. Gainesville: University Press of Florida, 2014.

Jackson, Travis A. *Blowin' the Blues Away: Performance and Meaning on the New York Jazz Scene*. Berkeley: University of California Press, 2012.

Jackson, Travis A. "Culture, Commodity, Palimpsest: Locating Jazz in the World." In *Jazz Worlds/World Jazz*, edited by Philip V. Bohlman and Goffredo Plastino, 381–401. Chicago: University of Chicago Press, 2016.

Jones, LeRoi [Amiri Baraka]. *Blues People: Negro Music in White America*. New York: William Morrow, 1963.

Jones, LeRoi [Amiri Baraka]. "Jazz and the White Critic." *Downbeat*, August 15, 1963, 16–17, 34. Reprinted in *Keeping Time: Readings in Jazz History*, edited by Robert Walser, 255–261. New York: Oxford University Press, 1999.

Katz, Mark. "The Case for Hip-Hop Diplomacy." *American Music Review* 46, no. 2 (Spring 2017): 1–5.

Keil, Charles. "Participatory Discrepancies and the Power of Music." *Cultural Anthropology* 2, no. 3 (August 1987): 275–283.

Kennedy, Fenella. "Movement Writes: Four Case Studies in Dance, Discourse, and Shifting Boundaries." PhD diss., Ohio State University, 2019.

Kernodle, Tammy. *Soul on Soul: The Life and Music of Mary Lou Williams*. Boston: Northeastern University Press, 2004.

Klotz, Kelsey. "Racial Ideologies and 1950s Cool Jazz." PhD diss., Washington University in St. Louis, 2016.

Kmen, Henry. *Music in New Orleans: The Formative Years, 1791–1841*. Baton Rouge: Louisiana State University Press, 1966.

Korall, Burt. *Drummin' Men: The Heartbeat of Jazz, The Swing Years*. New York: Oxford University Press, 1990.

Krasner, David. "The Real Thing." In *Beyond Blackface: African Americans and the Creation of American Popular Culture, 1890–1930*, edited by W. Fitzhugh Brundage, 99–123. Chapel Hill: University of North Carolina Press, 2011.

Le Guin, Elisabeth. *Boccherini's Body: An Essay in Carnal Musicology*. Berkeley: University of California Press, 2006.

Lepecki, André. "Choreopolice and Choreopolitics: or, the Task of the Dancer." *TDR: The Drama Review* 57, no. 4 (2013): 13–27.

Lewis, Barbara. "Daddy Blue: Evolution of the Dark Dandy." In *Inside the Minstrel Mask: Readings in 19th-Century Blackface Minstrelsy*, edited by Annemarie Bean, James V. Hatch, and Brooks McNamara, 257–272. Hanover, NH: Wesleyan University Press, 1996.

Lewis, George. "Improvised Music after 1950: Afrological and Eurological Perspectives." *Black Music Research Journal* 22, supplement (2002): 215–246.

Lott, Eric. "Double V, Double Time: Bebop's Politics of Style." In *The Jazz Cadence of American Culture*, edited by Robert G. O'Meally, 457–468. New York: Columbia University Press, 1998.

Lott, Eric. *Love and Theft: Blackface Minstrelsy and the American Working Class*. New York: Oxford University Press, 1993.

Mackenzie-Margulies, Hannah Ziessel. "Where's Leon (or) That Extraordinary Drama: Dancing Jazz, Negotiating Historiography, and Performing Americanism on the Cold War Cultural Tours." BA thesis, Reed College, 2016.

Magee, Jeffrey. *Fletcher Henderson: The Uncrowned King of Swing*. New York: Oxford University Press, 2005.

Malone, Jacqui. *Steppin on the Blues: The Visible Rhythms of African American Dance*. Urbana: University of Illinois Press, 1996.

Manning, Frankie, and Cynthia R. Millman. *Frankie Manning: Ambassador of Lindy Hop*. Philadelphia: Temple University Press, 2007.

Manning, Susan. *Modern Dance, Negro Dance: Race in Motion*. Minneapolis: University of Minnesota Press, 2006.

Martin, Henry, and Keith Waters. *Jazz: The First Hundred Years*. New York: Schirmer and Thomson Learning, 2002.

Miller, Norma, with Evette Jensen. *Swingin' at the Savoy: The Memoir of a Jazz Dancer*. Philadelphia: Temple University Press, 1996.

Miyakawa, Felicia, and Richard Mook. "Avoiding the 'Culture Vulture' Paradigm: Constructing an Ethical Hip-Hop Curriculum." *Journal of Music History Pedagogy* 5, no. 1 (2014): 41–58.

Monaghan, Terry, and Karen Hubbard. "Negotiating Compromise on a Burnished Wood Floor: Social Dancing at the Savoy." In *Ballroom, Boogie, Shimmy Sham, Shake: A Social and Popular Dance Reader*, edited by Julie Malnig, 126–145. Urbana: University of Illinois Press, 2009.

Monson, Ingrid. *Freedom Sounds: Civil Rights Call Out to Jazz and Africa*. New York: Oxford University Press, 2007.

Monson, Ingrid. "Hearing, Seeing, and Perceptual Agency." *Critical Inquiry* 34, no. S2 (2008): S38–S56.

Monson, Ingrid. "The Problem with White Hipness: Race, Gender, and Cultural Conceptions in Jazz Historical Discourse." *Journal of the American Musicological Society* 48, no. 3 (1995): 396–422.

Morris, Gay, and Jens Richard Giersdorf, eds. *Choreographies of 21st Century Wars*. New York: Oxford University Press, 2016.

Morrison, Matthew D. "Sound in the Construction of Race: From Blackface to Blacksound in Nineteenth Century America." PhD diss., Columbia University, 2014.

Moten, Fred. *In the Break: The Aesthetics of the Black Radical Tradition*. Minneapolis: University of Minnesota Press, 2003.

Neal, Mark Anthony. *What the Music Said: Black Popular Music and Black Popular Culture*. New York: Routledge, 1999.

Neville, Art, Aaron Neville, Charles Neville, Cyril Neville, and David Ritz. *The Brothers: An Autobiography*. Cambridge, MA: Da Capo Press, 2000.

O'Meally, Robert G., ed. *The Jazz Cadence of American Culture*. New York: Columbia University Press, 1998.

O'Meally, Robert G., Brent Hayes Edwards, and Farah Jasmine Griffin, eds. *Uptown Conversation: The New Jazz Studies*. New York: Columbia University Press, 2004.

Plastino, Goffredo, and Philip V. Bohlman, eds. *Jazz Worlds/World Jazz*. Chicago: University of Chicago Press, 2016.

Porter, Eric. *What Is This Thing Called Jazz?: African American Musicians as Artists, Critics, and Activists*. Berkeley: University of California Press, 2002.

Pribyl, Ashley. "Sociocultural and Collaborative Antagonism in the Harold Prince–Stephen Sondheim Musicals (1970–1979)." PhD diss., Washington University in St. Louis, 2019.

Prouty, Ken. *Knowing Jazz: Community, Pedagogy, and Canon in the Information Age*. Oxford: University Press of Mississippi, 2012.

Race Card, The [Nick Douglas]. "Know Your Black History: Deconstructing the Quadroon Ball." *Afropunk*, October 27, 2016. https://afropunk.com/2016/10/know-your-black-history-deconstructing-the-quadroon-ball/, accessed October 10, 2020.

Raeburn, Bruce Boyd. *New Orleans Style and the Writing of American Jazz History*. Ann Arbor: University of Michigan Press, 2009.

Ramsey, Guthrie P. Jr. *The Amazing Bud Powell: Black Genius, Jazz History, and the Challenge of Bebop*. Berkeley: University of California Press, 2013.

Ramsey, Guthrie P. Jr. *Race Music: Black Cultures from Bebop to Hip-Hop*. Berkeley: University of California Press, 2003.

Ramsey, Guthrie P. Jr. "Who Hears Here? Black Music, Critical Bias, and the Musicological Skin Trade." *Musical Quarterly* 85, no.1 (Spring 2001): 1–52.

Regis, Helen. "Blackness and the Politics of Memory in the New Orleans Second Line." *American Ethnologist* 28, no. 4 (November 2001): 752–777.

Rodano, Ronald. "Myth Today: The Color of Ken Burns Jazz." *Black Renaissance; New York* 3, no. 3 (Summer 2001): 42–54.

Rosenkrantz, Timme. *Harlem Jazz Adventures: A European Baron's Memoir 1934–1969*, adapted and edited by Fradley Hamilton Gardner. Lanham, MD: Scarecrow Press, 2012. Adapted from *Dus med Jazzen mine Jazzmemoirer: En Bog om Jazz—Og Andet Godtfolk*, 1969.

Rustin, Nicole, and Sherrie Tucker, eds. *Big Ears: Listening for Gender in Jazz Studies*. Durham, NC: Duke University Press, 2008.

Sakakeeny, Matthew. *Roll with It: Brass Bands in the Streets of New Orleans*. Durham, NC: Duke University Press, 2013.

Savigliano, Marta. *Tango and the Political Economy of Passion*. New York: Westview Press, 1995.

Schenbeck, Lawrence. *Racial Uplift and American Music, 1878–1943*. Oxford: University of Mississippi Press, 2012.

Schloss, Joseph. *Foundation: B-Boys, B-Girls, and Hip-Hop Culture in New York*. New York: Oxford University Press: 2009.

Sherwood Magee, Gayle. *Charles Ives Reconsidered*. Urbana: University of Illinois Press, 2008.

Sloan, Nate. "Constructing Cab Calloway: Publicity, Race, and Performance in 1930s Harlem Jazz." *Journal of Musicology* 36, no. 3 (Summer 2019): 370–400.

Smith, Christopher J. *Dancing Revolution: Bodies, Space, and Sound in American Cultural History*. Urbana: University of Illinois Press, 2019.

Spring, Howard. "Changes in Jazz Performance and Arranging in New York, 1929–1932." PhD diss., University of Illinois Urbana-Champaign, 1993.

Stearns, Marshall, and Jean Stearns. *Jazz Dance: The Story of American Vernacular Dance*. New York: Macmillan, 1968.

Stowe, David. *Swing Changes: Big-Band Jazz in New Deal America*. Cambridge, MA: Harvard University Press, 1994.

Teal, Kimberly Hammond. "Beyond the Cotton Club: The Persistence of Duke Ellington's Jungle Style." *Jazz Perspectives* 6, no. 1–2 (2012): 123–149.

Tucker, Sherrie. "Beyond the Brass Ceiling: Dolly Jones Trumpets Modernity in Oscar Micheaux's *Swing!*." *Jazz Perspectives* 3, no. 1 (2009): 3–34.

Tucker, Sherrie. *Dance Floor Democracy: The Social Geography of Memory at the Hollywood Canteen*. Durham, NC: Duke University Press, 2014.

Tucker, Sherrie. "Deconstructing the Jazz Tradition: The 'Subjectless Subject' of New Jazz Studies." In *Jazz/Not Jazz: The Music and Its Boundaries*, edited by David Ake, Charles Hiroshi Garrett, and Daniel Ira Goldmark, 207–221. Berkeley: University of California Press, 2012.

Tucker, Sherrie. "A Feminist Perspective on New Orleans Jazzwomen." New Orleans Jazz National Historical Park, National Park Service, 2004.

Uy, Michael Sy. "The Big Bang of Musical Patronage in the United States: The National Endowment for the Arts, the Rockefeller Foundation, and the Ford Foundation." PhD diss., Harvard University, 2017.

Valis Hill, Constance. "From Bharata Natyam to Bop: Jack Cole's 'Modern Jazz Dance'." *Dance Research Journal* 33, no. 2 (Winter 2001/02): 29–39.

Valis Hill, Constance. *Tap Dancing America: A Cultural History*. New York: Oxford University Press, 2010.

Vogel, Shane. *The Scene of the Harlem Cabaret: Race, Sexuality, Performance*. Chicago: University of Chicago Press, 2009.

Wald, Elijah. *How the Beatles Destroyed Rock 'n' Roll: An Alternative History of American Popular Music*. New York: Oxford University Press, 2009.

Welburn, Ronald Garfield. "American Jazz Criticism, 1914–1940." PhD diss., New York University, 1983.

Wells, Christopher J. "'The Ace of His Race': Paul Whiteman's Early Critical Reception in the Black Press." *Jazz and Culture* 1 (2018): 77–103.

Wells, Christopher J. "'A Dreadful Bit of Silliness': Feminine Frivolity and the Early Reception of Ella Fitzgerald." *Women and Music* 21 (2017): 43–65.

Wells, Christopher J. "'And I Make My Own': Class Performance, Black Urban Identity, and Depression-Era Harlem's Physical Culture." In *The Oxford Handbook of Dance and Ethnicity*, edited by Anthony Shay and Barbara Sellars Young, 17–40. New York: Oxford University Press, 2016. Reproduced here with the permission of Oxford University Press.

Wells, Christopher J. "'Go Harlem!: Chick Webb and His Dancing Audience during the Great Depression." PhD diss., University of North Carolina at Chapel Hill, 2014.

Wells, Christopher J. "Swinging Out in Sweden: African-American Vernacular Dance's Global Revival and Its Scandinavian Roots." In *SDHS 2013 Proceedings: 35th Annual Conference-Dance ACTions*, 391–398. Society of Dance History Scholars, 2013.

Wells, Christopher J. "'*You* Can't Dance to It': Jazz Music and Its Choreographies of Listening." *Daedalus*, 148, no. 2, special issue "Jazz Still Matters," edited by Ingrid Monson and Gerald Early (Spring 2019): 36–51.

Weston, Randy, with Willard Jenkins. *African Rhythms: The Autobiography of Randy Weston*. Durham, NC: Duke University Press, 2010.

Whalan, Mark. "Taking Myself in Hand: Jean Toomer and Physical Culture." *Modernism/Modernity* 10, no. 4 (2003): 597–615.

Whyton, Tony. *Jazz Icons: Heroes, Myths and the Jazz Tradition*. Cambridge: Cambridge University Press, 2010.

Whyton, Tony. "Birth of the School: Discursive Methodologies in Jazz Education." *Music Education Research* 8, no. 1 (2006): 65–81.

Williams, Diana. "Can Quadroon Balls Represent Acquiescence or Resistance." In *Gendered Resistance: Women, Slavery, and the Legacy of Margaret Garner*, edited by Margaret Garner, 115–131. Urbana: University of Illinois Press, 2013.

Williams, Martin. *The Jazz Tradition*. New York: Oxford University Press, 1970.

# Index

For the benefit of digital users, indexed terms that span two pages (e.g., 52–53) may, on occasion, appear on only one of those pages.

Figures are indicated by *f* following the page number